To Moss Nelson

with my best regards

Stephen R Davies

Apr 1998

FIAT JUSTITIA
A HISTORY OF THE
ROYAL AIR FORCE POLICE

Stephen R. Davies

MINERVA PRESS

LONDON

MONTREUX LOS ANGELES SYDNEY

First Published 1997 by
MINERVA PRESS
195 Knightsbridge,
LONDON SW7 1RE

Printed in Great Britain by
Antony Rowe Ltd, Chippenham, Wiltshire

FIAT JUSTITIA

A HISTORY OF THE ROYAL AIR FORCE POLICE

Fiat Justitia
A History of the Royal Air Force Police

*The views expressed in this book are those of the author alone
and do not necessarily represent those of Her Majesty's
Government, The Ministry of Defence or the Royal Air Force.*

Acknowledgements

I would like to express my thanks to the following for their assistance during the compilation of this book:

Air Commodore JL Uprichard CBE RAF
Air Officer Security and Provost Marshal (Royal Air Force),
Chief of Air Force Police, for writing the foreword to my book

Flight Lieutenant Stephen Atkins Provost Branch
RAF Police School

Warrant Officer J Maggs RAF Police
No 32 (The Royal) Flight

Retired Warrant Officer John T Wood
RAF Police February 1954 – May 1988

Retired Warrant Officer Keith I Dobie BEM
RAF Police August 1946 – October 1973

Retired Warrant Officer Albert J Ballard
RAF Police February 1935 – January 1972

Retired Sergeant Drummond F A Window MBE RVM OPR
RAF Police February 1948 – August 1966

Mr Harry Wynne
Researcher of British Colonial & Dockyard Police Forces

The Author

Stephen Davies is married and has been a serving member of the Royal Air Force Police for the past twenty-two years. He was born in Flintshire in August 1955 and is the eldest of three children. After completing his education at Blessed Richard Gwyn School in Flint, he commenced his working life as an assistant supermarket manager and was, for eighteen months, also a member of the North Wales Special Constabulary.

Torn between the burning ambitions of becoming a police officer and travelling the world, he joined the Royal Air Force as a policeman in January 1975 and has to date, completed tours of duty in the United Kingdom and every other continent. In addition, he successfully qualified as a specialist in Royal Air Force Police Special Investigation and Counter Intelligence matters and successfully completed the Home Office Detective Training and Drug Enforcement courses. After qualifying as an RAF instructor, he lectured for three years on management and leadership subjects at the Airmans Command School at RAF Hereford.

Foreword by Air Commodore J L Uprichard CBE RAF Air Officer Security & Provost Marshal (Royal Air Force) Chief of Air Force Police

Following the formation of the Royal Air Force in 1918, the new Service remained dependent upon the Army military police skills until an integral Provost and Police Force could be established. In 1919, the transfer of responsibility for policing RAF stations and units was authorised, and the last Army Officer to hold an appointment at the Air Ministry responsible for police matters was replaced by an RAF Officer the following year. In 1931, the office of Provost Marshal (RAF) and Chief of Air Force Police was approved by King George V and, during the intervening 64 years, nineteen Provost Marshals have held office.

The subsequent growth of the officer corps at home and abroad justified the formation of a specialist branch and, on 1st July, 1947, the Provost Branch was formally constituted by His Majesty, King George VI. In September 1950, the King also approved a badge for the RAF Police which depicts a griffin passant – the heraldic device associated with guardianship, courage and audacity. The motto, *Fiat Justitia*, may be freely translated as 'let justice be done'. Indeed, the RAF Police is the only RAF trade to receive the honour of having its own badge approved by the monarch.

As the nineteenth Provost Marshal, it gives me enormous pride and pleasure to commend this history to you. Stephen Davies has skilfully related world events with milestones in the history of a fine police service and, as befits the RAF Police Service antecedents of the author, the chronological style of his work provides clear but interesting reading. Although a relatively small cadre, the force has excelled in the provision of a professional police and security service to the RAF. Whether the reader is a serving or former RAF Policeman or woman, or anyone with an interest in modern military history, I am sure that all will enjoy this well-researched account of a 'service family' unit of which I am proud to be the latest surrogate father.

Jim Uprichard

Fiat Justitia – A History of The Royal Air Force Police
Synopsis of Each Chapter

Chapter I – The Origins of the Provost

This chapter briefly relates the history of the Provost Marshal from the thirteenth century to the turn of this century. In 1629 King Charles I, issued his Articles of War which described the role of his Provost Marshal. During the Peninsular Wars, the Provost Marshal, serving under the Duke of Wellington, was granted extensive and somewhat harsh powers of punishing soldiers committing acts of indiscipline. In 1855, the Military Mounted Police was formed at Aldershot and Military Foot Police were later formed to enforce military orders and regulations.

Chapter II – Formation of the RAF (1918 – 1939)

Using as a background, the uneasy political situation in Europe between the wars and the struggle to retain the RAF as a viable entity, this chapter describes the formation of the RAF Police, the early training school and the Special Investigation Branch. After years of being controlled by a series of 'caretaker' directors, the first dedicated RAF Provost Marshal was appointed by the Air Ministry in 1931 to organise the development of the branch. In 1936, a Nazi spy was arrested at Harwich and later convicted on the evidence supplied by the RAF Police SIB regarding his clandestine activities in and around RAF stations in Kent and East Anglia.

Chapter III – The War Years (1939 – 1945)

Using wartime events as a background, this chapter describes the rapid growth of the RAF Police and the introduction of their white caps and webbing equipment. During the early part of the war, thirteen geographical District Headquarters were formed within the UK and police dogs were introduced into service, when the branch took over control of the Ministry of Aircraft Production Guard Dog Training School. Prior to D-Day, specially selected and trained RAF Police units were formed which later supported the Allied invasion and subsequent liberation of Europe. Finally, the events concerning the brutal murder, by the Gestapo, of fifty re-captured RAF officers, following their 'great escape' from Stalag Luft 3, is described along with the events which lead to the major investigation carried out by the RAF Police SIB into the circumstances.

Chapter IV – The Post War Years (1945 – 1950)

Using post-war colonial unrest as a background, this chapter describes how before the wartime demobilisation started, the establishment of the branch had reached a record 500 commissioned officers and 20,000 non-commissioned ranks. In the UK the District Headquarters were reduced from thirteen to six and for the first time, commissioned officers acting as Assistant Provost Marshals, were officially appointed into the Provost Branch. In Singapore the first native RAF Police Auxiliary Force was formed and in occupied Germany, following the successful RAF Police investigation, the Nazi defendants, accused of murdering the fifty RAF officers from Stalag Luft 3, were convicted at their war crimes trial. In 1948, the RAF Police Dog Demonstration Team appeared for the first time at the Royal Tournament and instantly won over the hearts and minds of the public. As a result of the largest ever Allied humanitarian airlift and the formation of NATO, the Russians lifted their blockade of West Berlin.

Chapter V – The Cold War (1950 – 1959)

This chapter describes the development of the Cold War and the troubles in Egypt, Kenya and Cyprus. As the RAF Police took over responsibility for security matters within the RAF, the regional policing aspect, under the control of the Provost Marshal, was re-titled as the RAF Provost & Security Service. In addition, RAF Police formations around the world were reorganised into the District Headquarters system. The RAF Police School moved to RAF Netheravon and was retitled as the RAF Police Depot and the RAF Police Museum was established. Air Cmdre de Putron retired after nine years as the Provost Marshal and Lt Col. Baldwin retired as the Chief Training Officer (Dogs). In the UK, six RAF Police Volunteer Reserve Flights were formed and at the start of 1953, RAF Police reinforcements were called upon to assist the civil authorities in dealing with widespread chaos on the east coast following severe weather conditions and flooding. In France RAF Police NCOs were established to join the multinational military police unit providing security at the NATO Headquarters. In Egypt, an RAF Police NCO was killed and his partner was seriously injured during a shoot out with terrorists and at RAF Manston, another RAF Police NCO and two other airmen were shot dead by an American serviceman who went berserk with a rifle. Finally, having taken over responsibility for protecting the RAF nuclear deterrent, RAF Police were established on Christmas Island prior to the British nuclear tests.

Chapter VI – The End of an Empire (1959 – 1968)

As the British Empire started to shrink, the RAF Police Depot moved from Netheravon to RAF Debden and the training syllabus was widened to take on board the newly established Counter-Intelligence, Nuclear Security and Travel Control Security tasks being undertaken world-wide. RAF Police were involved for the first time in recruiting duties while a large number of their colleagues were kept increasingly busy as the Movement for the Campaign for Nuclear Disarmament (CND) increased their protest activity. As National Service in the British Forces ended, the RAF Police 'village constable' system of policing was introduced to make up for the shortfall in the overall establishment. The Annual Working Dog Trials were introduced for all UK Dog Sections and as the Berlin Wall was constructed, Checkpoint Charlie in the British sector of West Berlin was built and manned by both Military and RAF Police. In Cyprus, which had been granted independence, RAF Police were attached to the UN Peace Keeping Force and two British Sovereign Base Areas were formed and a new civilian police force was authorised to police them. However, because of initial manning problems, RAF Police NCOs were attached to the force to run it until sufficient recruits could be engaged and trained to carry out the task. In Aden, the RAF Police were stretched to full capacity as violent terrorist activity increased at an alarming rate and at RAF Changi, RAF Police NCOs acted as Customs and Immigration Officers on behalf of the Singapore government

Chapter VII – Fifty Years and Beyond (1968 – 1985)

The year 1968 marked the Golden Anniversary for both the RAF and its police force and the year also witnessed the formation of the RAF P&SS Support Squadron and the sentencing of Chief Technician Britten to nineteen years imprisonment for espionage. During this period, HRH The Princess Margaret carried out the first Royal Review of the RAF Police at RAF Debden and RAF Police dogs were trained in the detection of dangerous drugs. As the Troubles in Northern Ireland increased, RAF Police NCOs were detached onto the strength of Royal Military Police units, to assist them in policing the province.

Chapter VIII – Thawing of the Cold War (1985 – 1989)

During the four years which witnessed the thawing of the cold war and the collapse of communism and the Warsaw Pact, the RAF Police launched an investigation into the fire which destroyed the Headquarters of RAF Support Command near Huntingdon. RAF Police reinforcements were flown into Gibraltar and Cyprus as the US Air Force launched an attack on Libya and as a consequence of the Police & Criminal Evidence Act 1984, the Service Police Codes of Practice were introduced. The branch was fully vindicated following an independent enquiry into allegations that RAF Police investigators mistreated suspects in the 'Cyprus Spy' investigation, and to assist in combating the ever-increasing problem of drug abuse in the RAF, Drug Intelligence Teams were established. Following the channel ferry *Herald of Free Enterprise* disaster, a number of RAF Police NCOs were attached to the investigation team to assist with the identification of victims. In the Falkland Islands the Joint Service

Police & Security Unit was formed and on the European mainland, the IRA started one of their bloodiest campaigns against British servicemen and their families. Finally, one of the longest RAF Police close protection operations ended when HRH Prince Fiscal of Jordan completed his flying training with the RAF.

Chapter IX – A Time for Change (1989 – 1996)

As the government's defence cuts took effect, Iraq attacked Kuwait and in response the forces of the coalition launched Operation Desert Storm to liberate it. In Florida, RAF Police NCOs provided the security protection for two NATO satellites prior to their launch from the NASA Space Centre. With the formation of the Defence Animal Centre at Melton Mowbray under Army control, independent dog training by the RAF ceased and shortly after the much loved RAF Police Dog Demonstration Team was disbanded. As the civil war in former Yugoslavia developed, RAF Police NCOs were tasked with carrying out Air Transport Security duties at several airheads in the region. In the UK, the RAF P&SS regional headquarters were reorganised and increased from three geographical areas to six. As part of the cost-cutting exercise, the three separate service security organisations were merged to form the MOD Security Directorate and the RAF Provost Marshal left London and re-located at RAF Rudloe Manor with the new title of Air Officer Security & Provost Marshal (RAF) & Chief of Air Force Police. As the RAF Police completed the task of training military and Air Force Police NCOs from Zimbabwe, the news was released that the RAF Police and RAF Regiment would not be amalgamated and that the RAF Police would take over running the guardrooms on RAF stations once again. Finally, the RAF Police School moved once again back to RAF Halton where it originally formed in 1920.

Contents

LIST OF PHOTOGRAPHS & ILLUSTRATIONS

Chapter I
Origins of the Provost

Given that the Royal Air Force provost organisation is relatively recent in origin, the appointment of a provost marshal in England can be traced as far back as the thirteenth century. It was around that period that the king appointed an official, known as the 'Earl Provost Marshal', to enforce peace and order amongst the undisciplined rabble armies, raised by his powerful barons.

Later in 1318, records again show us that a provost marshal exercised his duties with the first expeditionary force led by King Edward III. There is also further evidence of the provost marshal actively carrying out his duties during the campaigns at both Crecy and Agincourt in 1415. Throughout the fifteenth century, deputy provost marshals and their camp police were appointed to various operational field forces with clear instructions to uphold the king's peace and maintain discipline amongst the troops.

Further records, dating from 1549, tell us that Sir Anthony Kingston, who had been duly appointed to act as a provost marshal, was responsible for carrying out several state executions whilst visiting the West Country. In fact, prior to his arrival in the region, he had sent a message to the Mayor of Bodmin asking for a gallows to be erected so he could carry out a number of executions. The mayor, eager no doubt to please, quickly complied with the request. However, when Sir Anthony duly arrived, he used the gallows to execute the unsuspecting mayor, who was known to be a rebel and a traitor. In 1557, the status of the provost marshal was elevated when he was authorised by law to employ the services of two judges, a chaplain, two gaolers and an executioner, to assist him in carrying out his task. However, he had to pay for their services himself from the comfortable sum of one pound a day, which he was paid.

It seems that the first recorded terms of reference for the post of provost marshal were published in the articles of war, issued in 1629 by King Charles I. In them, the articles clearly empowered the provost marshal to hold the first form of court martials, whereby the case of any soldier charged with any wrongful act could be heard and then judged. Thus the responsibilities of the provost marshal were summarised in the articles as follows:

> The provost must have a horse allowed him and some soldiers to attend him and all the rest commanded to obey him and assist him, or else the service will suffer. For he is one man and must correct many and therefore he cannot be beloved. And he must be riding from one garrison to another, to see that the soldiers do not outrage nor scathe about the country.

In 1642, the Earl of Essex, being the commander of the parliamentary army, promulgated his very own 'laws and ordinances of war' and these later became the foundation of all subsequent articles of war. The responsibilities of the provost marshal were extended to other areas of operation. The first included the type of duties which might be carried out today by local authority trading standards officers, and involved checking the proportions, weights and measures of all victuals sold by the merchants within the confines of the camp. The second, and perhaps most important commitment, was described as the "protection of soldiery". For the very first time, it was recognised that the role of the provost marshal and security within the army could not be separated. As such, the directive instructed the provost marshal to:

> Discover the lurking subtleties of spies and by learning the true interpretation of men's words, looks, manners, forms and habits of apparel, to be able to turn the insides of their hearts outwards and to pull out the devil of malicious deceit, though he lie hid in never so dark a corner and truly a better service cannot be done, nor is there any art sooner learnt, if a man will apply his knowledge but seriously thereto.

Although a seemingly complicated brief, today, such activities would be described as intelligence gathering and counter-intelligence duties, activities which are still a most important element of any military force today. Ordinances, which were later published, again changed the role and the powers of the provost marshal. Accordingly he was duly authorised to act as an executioner, in addition to being responsible for the custody and interrogation of prisoners in his charge. Additionally, during the Stuart period, provost marshals were also appointed as peace officers within the capital of London and the surrounding counties.

Following the release of a general order, issued by the Duke of Wellington, in 1811, the provost marshal also became responsible for the custody of prisoners of war. In addition to enforcing good order and discipline amongst the troops, he was also authorised to summarily punish any troops, who in his view had committed a breach of discipline. His assistants were also authorised to exercise summary powers of punishment, whenever an offender was caught in the act of committing an offence and it was required to make an example of him to prevent further indiscipline. However, his assistants did not have the power or authority to inflict capital punishment. During that period and certainly during the peninsular war, Wellington's provost marshals and his assistants were particularly brutal in enforcing their powers over the ill-disciplined soldiers and indeed, floggings were commonplace punishments, usually carried out by the provost marshal's sergeant.

In 1829, revised articles of war abolished the post of Provost Marshal General but expressly provided for the appointment and powers of the senior provost marshal. However, in 1879, his powers of summary punishment were curtailed by parliament under section 74 of the Army Act 1879.

Building work was started at Aldershot, in February 1853, to construct the first permanent home of the British Army. Consequently, a large concentration of labourers, soldiers, their families and their followers assembled in the area and as expected, crime and lawlessness started to increase at an alarming rate. The need for a provost unit to control and police the garrison town was becoming a serious priority. Although there had been attempts in 1813 and 1854 to form a permanent corps of military police, they had been unsuccessful. However, with the situation in Aldershot becoming so serious, the Adjutant General, P A Wetherall, was in June 1855 authorised to form such a force and to do so, sent out the following letter, from his headquarters at Horse Guards to the officers commanding all cavalry regiments:

> The General Commanding in Chief, deeming it necessary to form a Corps of Mounted Police, for the cantonment of Aldershot, and with a view to the internal organisation of a permanent corps, desires me to call for a return of non-commissioned officers and soldiers, not exceeding five in all, as you may consider fit for the duty. They should be not less than five years service, if of ten, the better, of sober habits, intelligent, active and capable of exercising a sound discretion.
>
> They will be organised into one corps, under the direct control of an officer, subject to the immediate orders of the General Officer commanding the cantonment.

In response to his letter, five suitable candidates were selected for the task and in October 1855, Sergeant Major Thomas Trout, accompanied by the other four volunteers, reported for duty at Aldershot to form the new corps of Military Mounted Police. Sergeant Major Trout served with distinction in the newly formed corps over twenty-six years and worked his way up through the ranks to become the first Provost Marshal and Commandant of the Corps of Military Mounted Police. By December 1865, the establishment had been increased to thirty-two personnel. However, in 1877, so successful was the role of the new corps that a decision was made to form further detachments of Military Police within the garrisons towns of Woolwich, Shorncliffe and Portsmouth. Accordingly, to meet the new demands, the establishment was increased yet again to seventy-five personnel.

Between 1885 and 1886, there was a sudden increase of terrorist activity in Ireland, and in order to assist the civilian authorities in dealing with the Troubles, a further establishment increase of seventy-five mounted policemen and one hundred and ninety-seven foot policemen was authorised, and they were despatched soon after, to help restore order in Dublin, Belfast, The Curragh, and Cork. In March 1887, authority was granted for all private soldiers within the corps to be promoted to the rank of acting lance corporal. This decision was taken, mainly as a matter of protecting them from the actions of other soldiers, whilst exercising the duties of their office.

In 1894 the establishment and the professionalism of the corps had rapidly increased and in addition to those serving in Ireland, units of military police were now also deployed on the mainland, at Aldershot, Chatham, Dover, Portsmouth, Colchester, Shorncliffe, Edinburgh, Woolwich, Devonport and Gosport. In addition, there were also units serving overseas in Egypt, at Alexandria and Cairo, and in Malta.

In 1899, Great Britain declared war on the Boers in South Africa, and as a result, troops were mobilised into action and sent to the area by troop ship. As the war escalated, the established strength of both the military mounted and foot police rapidly increased yet again. Consequently, large numbers of both units were detached out to the war zone, where they remained, carrying out their duties, until hostilities ceased in 1902.

On 4th August, 1914, Great Britain declared war with Germany and the Great War in Europe commenced. The establishment of the military police was again increased to meet the new challenges and commitments brought about by conflict on such a large scale. It was with the onset of the Great War that the Royal Flying Corps was formed and brought into operation with the British forces. This was the first time that flying machines had accompanied the British Army into the battlefield and they quickly proved to be a most successful addition, for both intelligence and offensive operations. The Central Flying School was located at Upavon aerodrome while the Headquarters of the Royal Flying Corps was based at Netheravon, both situated on Salisbury Plain.

On 7th July, 1917, a squadron of around twenty German aircraft suddenly appeared over central London, where without warning they launched an indiscriminate attack on the population below, who had come out into the streets to watch them. As the bombs rained down, the full effect of this new type of warfare became terrifyingly apparent as one hundred and three people were killed and three hundred and sixteen were injured in the raid. The attack stunned the nation and for those campaigning for a separate air force, it served only to further their cause. By 29th November that year, as the Air Force Bill received royal assent, there were seventy-three operational airfields in the UK alone, albeit many of a temporary nature.

Chapter II
Formation of the RAF 1918 – 1939

The Royal Air Force was formed during the last part of the Great War, on the 1st April, 1918, by bringing together as one force the former Royal Naval Air Service and the Royal Flying Corps. By late 1919, all personnel serving with the newly formed service were issued with new distinctive uniforms and a newly developed rank structure. Although the RAF became the third fighting service, there was no practical way that it could seek the instant and total independence that it wanted from the Navy and the Army. Although it was not an entirely satisfactory arrangement, it was not a time to make unreasonable demands, after all the country was beginning to recover from the war with Germany and both the Navy and Army made no secret of the fact that they were extremely jealous of the new military air force. As a result, the RAF was forced to rely on the other two sister services for much of the ground support elements needed to keep it in operation. Policing and enforcing discipline within the new force was one such area of support, provided by the Army, through the medium of the military police.

By the time the armistice brought an end to hostilities, the RAF was the largest and best-equipped air force in the entire world. It had a personnel establishment of approximately 27,000 commissioned officers and some 300,000 other ranks, with over 3,000 aircraft and 100 airships, divided up amongst some 188 front line and 187 training squadrons. However, with the end of the war, came demobilisation and accordingly men were rapidly returned to civilian life. By the start of 1920, demobilisation had taken its toll on the RAF, reducing its manpower to 3,280 commissioned officers and some 72,000 other ranks.

Although the newly formed RAF College, at Cranwell, was officially opened on the 5th February, 1920, it was not a comfortable period for the RAF. Certain key figures within the government were calling for the disbandment of the RAF as a separate and vastly expensive service. Of course, both Admiral Sir David Beatty of the Admiralty and Field Marshal Sir Henry Wilson of the War Office stood by, like vultures, offering no support whatsoever to Air Marshal Trenchard, but hoping to increase their own forces from his shattered organisation. Indeed, at one point, even Churchill, the Secretary of War and a firm supporter of the RAF, was beginning to be swayed by the argument. However, after a furious row between Churchill and Trenchard, during which Trenchard threatened to resign, an agreement was reached to retain the RAF, provided it could, of course, prove its effectiveness. Later in the year, the *Trenchard Memorandum*, the White Paper justifying the retention and future organisation of the RAF as an independent third service, was presented before Parliament by Churchill, who successfully obtained the approval required for its survival. Wasting no time, Trenchard started to implement his new policies within the service and accordingly orders and regulations were drawn up and promulgated by the Air Ministry. Trenchard decided that of the twenty-five aircraft squadrons available at the time, nineteen would be deployed overseas in Malta, Egypt, the British Mandate in Iraq and India. His bold decisions started to pay out dividends very quickly, as the RAF started to justify its existence in covering large and troublesome areas of terrain, quickly and effectively, without the use of costly and slow-moving ground troops.

Initially, the policing of the new service, with the exception of Halton and Blandford camps, had been administered by the Army Provost Marshal and the Military Police, resulting from an agreement drawn up between the Air and Army Councils. As for Halton and Blandford, the two former RFC camps, they were policed by personnel from what must have been the very first RAF Police sections to have operated. In 1916, Halton camp, situated near Wendover in Buckinghamshire, had a section of seven RFC policemen, under the command of a sergeant, who had been responsible for the internal policing and security commitments, while the Military Police had retained the responsibility for the external policing arrangements. As such, when the RAF came into existence on the 1st April, 1918, the RFC Police, in effect, became the first units of the RAF Police.

The official RAF uniform of the RAF station police in those early days, comprised of a peaked service dress cap, a high-collar tunic, pantaloons, puttees and boots. In addition, the first RAF policemen to serve at Halton and Blandford were known as 'Unit Police' and were identified as such, by the unit police brassard, worn on the cuff of their right sleeve. They were later known as 'RAF Service Police' and the brassard moved further up the arm, to rest just above the elbow. Additionally, each service policeman was issued with a whistle, which was kept in his left breast pocket and could be quickly removed for use, if required, by pulling on the chain which had been placed through the top buttonhole of the tunic closest to the breast pocket.

As time went by, the RAF steadily took over control of its own policing arrangements and in 1919, Air Ministry Order No 1111, sanctioned the transfer of all policing tasks from the Army and authorised the appointment of a Provost Marshal for the RAF. As a result, the first RAF officer nominated to hold the appointment at the Air Ministry was Wing Commander Brierley, an administrative officer and former Lieutenant Colonel who took over from Major Pryor, an Army officer, seconded to the RAF, to oversee provost matters. While Wing Commander Brierley was not authorised to appoint Assistant Provost Marshals to support him in his task, the order did however, authorise all Air Officers Commanding to appoint, at their discretion, specially selected officers, who could be spared from their primary duties, to act as RAF District Discipline Officers. The duties and limited powers of those selected officers were very clearly defined and monitored and they were only empowered to deal with matters of a purely disciplinary nature, affecting RAF personnel. In respect of all other more serious matters, they were still subordinate to the authority of the area military Assistant Provost Marshals. As such, it seemed that the powers of the first RAF Provost Marshal, in addition to his normal administrative duties, were restricted to studying police reports and advising on their method of disposal.

At the time, a number of RAF stations, both within the country and overseas, were diverting a number of surplus airman from other duties and transferring them into newly formed RAF Service Police sections, under the control of specially selected senior non-commissioned officers (SNCOs). Those first policemen were recruited mainly from the aircrafthand and general duties trade group and although initially trained in basic police and disciplinary matters by the military police at Blandford Camp, in Dorset, the RAF quickly realised the importance of having their own training facility. Consequently, the first RAF Police training school was established soon after at Halton camp, the home of the RAF Apprentice Training, located just outside Wendover. Records show that one of the very first RAF Service Policemen to be formally trained by the Military Police was Mr Charles Guy, who passed out of his basic police training in 1919, with a final examination mark of eighty-three per cent. He subsequently went on to become one of the first RAF Police instructors at Halton where the first organised police courses ran for six weeks. After successfully completing their initial training, newly qualified RAF policemen were returned back to their units, where they found themselves employed controlling entry and traffic into the RAF stations, carrying out regular disciplinary patrols, as well as running the administration of the guardrooms and supervising defaulters and prisoners under sentence.

In line with the mass demobilisation of troops and the massive reductions in the defence budget, the Women's Royal Air Force was officially and sadly disbanded on the 1st April, 1920. Since its formation, exactly two years before that date, some 32,000 women had served with great distinction alongside their male counterparts, earning for themselves the greatest honour and respect.

Although attempts had been made by Major Pryor, in 1919, to have a number of RAF Assistant Provost Marshals appointed to assist him with his task, the proposal was rejected outright by the Army Provost Marshal, who looked upon such appointments as a threat to his own organisation. That rather unsatisfactory situation changed however, in 1920, when the Air Ministry finally realised that Assistant Provost Marshals were urgently required within the new service to support the Provost Marshal. Consequently, official approval was given for the establishment of two such appointments. The first officer to be appointed as an Assistant Provost Marshal in the RAF was announced in the *London Gazette* shortly after, as Flight Lieutenant A E Bishop, whose distinction during the Great War had been honoured by the award of the Military Medal. In addition to the appointment of Flight Lieutenant Bishop, the Air Officer Commanding the British Mandate in Iraq, was also authorised to appoint an officer, at his headquarters, to become the other RAF Assistant Provost Marshal. Shortly after taking up the appointment, Flight Lieutenant Bishop was duly designated as the first officer to command the newly created RAF Police School at Halton Camp, where he was instrumental in setting up the training organisation during the early days. He loved the appointment dearly and remained in post at the school until 1931. Another of the first instructors to be employed at the school, under his command, was Acting Corporal William Kerby, who quickly helped to establish a detailed and professional training programme at the school. He had originally joined the Royal Flying Corps in 1917, as a storeman, before transferring to become another of the very first RAF Station Policemen.

As the dark clouds of the Great War drifted away, calm of sorts had gradually returned to Europe. However, the indignation of the defeated powers, over the terms of the compact imposed upon them by the victorious powers, began to stir uncomfortably and stability was still very fragile indeed. Italy fell victim to the clutches of Fascism and attempts had been made within Germany to mount a revolution. On the 8th March, 1921, British troops formed part of the Allied force, which occupied the Rhineland of Germany, following the German Government's failure to settle various claims for war compensation. In November, a balding, heavy-jowled former editor, by the name of Benito Mussolini, declared himself as the leader of the Italian Fascist Party. A corporal during the Great War, Mussolini vowed to Italy's businessmen that he and his party would free the country from the grip of communism and the problems it had caused.

During that period however, the RAF continued to prove itself to be a most efficient and cost-effective instrument of policing various trouble spots overseas in the Middle East, Egypt and in Northern India. That fact had more than adequately been demonstrated during the brief four-week campaign, the year before, against the uprising lead by the 'Mad Mullah' in British Somaliland. He had been an outlaw with a terrifying record of violence who had, whilst the British authorities had been distracted with the Great War, threatened to take over the region on a permanent basis. He had to be quickly ousted but the Army's estimation that such an operation would take twelve months to complete, using two divisions of ground troops was far too expensive and totally unacceptable. After much debate, the task had been given to the RAF, who quickly established command of the air, over the colony and swiftly brought about a quick end to the troubles using only a small handful of local native ground troops and police. At the end of the operation costing only £77,000, the Mad Mullah had fled the country, his loyal followers dispersed and law and order had quickly been restored once again. As such, that and other successful operations certainly helped Trenchard, in justifying to Churchill his case for further expanding the RAF overseas. Churchill, who had recently taken over as the Secretary of State at the Colonial Office, used that information as the basis for successfully arguing his case to the government that the RAF had the potential to become the most effective way of controlling trouble spots around the empire. As a result of that and the 1921 Cairo conference on the administration of the Middle East, Parliament authorised Trenchard and the RAF to take over control in the Middle East, from the Army, by the end of 1922. Subsequently on the 1 October, Air Vice-Marshal John Salmond, was duly appointed as the General Officer Commanding, all British Forces, within the Middle-Eastern region comprising of Iraq, Transjordan and Palestine.

On 30th October, 1922, in Italy, 30,000 black-shirted members of Mussolini's Fascist Party marched from Naples to Rome, determined to force the government to resign and make way for their leader. Unfortunately, the feeble government was helpless to resist, especially when it became clear that the Fascists would eventually hold the balance of power anyway. As such, King Vittorio Emanuele invited Benito Mussolini to form a government and the rest of Europe silently watched events slowly unfolding before them.

During 1924, the British authorities in Palestine had been extremely occupied dealing with the vast influx of Jewish immigrants, who had entered the country seeking out new lives in what they saw as their promised land. Many of the 14,000 or so involved had left Europe and mainly Poland where radical anti-Semitic attitudes had forced them into unbearable circumstances, causing them to flee for their own safety. As further large numbers tried to enter the country, the British authorities began losing their patience and in addition, the Arab population became totally hostile towards the Jews, causing further internal friction.

Although the RAF had been quick in proving its operational efficiency throughout the Middle East, there was, unfortunately, still a fair amount of high-ranking political, naval and military opposition at

Whitehall, threatening its very existence as a separate service. However, a powerful committee headed by Sir Eric Geddes, a leading economist and railway executive, reported that after studying the cost of running the Armed Forces, that the RAF was indeed an efficient and cost-effective service using its machinery to substitute manpower in times of war. Although winning a certain amount of backing from the right places, Trenchard stood firm in the face of all threats to the RAF, and it was not until 1925 that his fight to retain the RAF as a third service seemed certain.

In Germany on the 18th June, 1925, a then-unknown figure with devastating ambitions published his book, entitled *Mein Kampf* ('My Struggle'). His name was Adolf Hitler, who was a full time agitator and leader of the fascist Nazi Party. He, like his Italian counterpart, Mussolini, had served as a corporal in the Army and had been wounded during the Great War. His vision and ultimate goal was to motivate the German masses to start a revolution and his book, written mainly while he was in prison, following his unsuccessful attempt to start a revolution, blamed Germany's defeat in the Great War and its subsequent political and economic problems on the Jews and the communists.

Following the successful ratification of the Anglo-Iraqi treaty in 1924, the RAF had, by the mid 1920s, taken over their 'policing role' within the region and had firmly established a base at RAF Hinaidi, a very large and self-contained airfield, situated eight miles to the east of Baghdad. The unit housed a large aircraft depot, a hospital, three light bomber squadrons, two squadrons of Vernon troop carriers, a squadron of Snipe aircraft and an armoured car company, together with all the necessary administrative and engineering support required to keep it operating. The whole station and vast perimeter was constantly patrolled by the RAF Police, assisted by units of the Indian Army. However, as the terrain of the station was extremely difficult to patrol by mechanical means and far too large to patrol effectively on foot, an alternative form of transport was required. Though it is not quite clear exactly who suggested using horses, before long, ten rather smart RAF Service policemen formed the first RAF Service Police, Mounted Section and after a very short time in operation, quickly demonstrated their efficiency and also proved to be an extremely cost-effective method of patrolling the airfield. Riding those large Arabian horses, the RAF Service Policemen certainly made an imposing sight.

In Italy on 7th October, 1926, Prime Minister Mussolini, declared his Fascist Party the official party of the state and, in so doing, banned all forms of political opposition from operating within the country. Later in the year, on 25th December, Prince Hirohito became the new Emperor of Japan, following the death of his father, Emperor Yoshihito.

By then the RAF had grown considerably in size, since its formation, both at home and abroad. It had stations located overseas at Aden, Egypt, Palestine, Iraq, Malta, Constantinople and in India and all were supported in some degree or other by RAF Service Police. Although many of the foreign postings sounded grand, some of them were nevertheless considered to be quite tough because of poor living conditions or the local political situation. In addition, postings between units overseas was a commonplace practice, which meant that an airman could be stationed away from home, for periods of between six to twelve years. Despite the rapid growth, the late 1920s saw severe economic restraints on the military budgets of all three services and as such, between 1926 – 1928, there was an almost complete halt to any further expansion of the RAF, both at home and abroad.

During 1929, the Geneva Convention on the treatment of prisoners of war came into force and at home, the RAF Service Police became involved in counter-intelligence work for the very first time when intelligence reports claimed that elements of the British Communist Party were trying to infiltrate themselves into the armed forces. In a determined effort to prevent this from happening in the RAF, the Provost Marshal was tasked to ensure that no such elements were retained or recruited into the service to spread their subversive and dangerous beliefs.

On 1st January, 1930, Air Chief Marshal John Salmond succeeded Trenchard as the Chief of the Air Staff. At the time, the world of aviation was moving along at a fairly rapid pace. There were some remarkable new records being set by aviators, such as Charles Lindbergh, who crossed the Atlantic non-stop, from America to France and Amy Johnson, who completed her solo flight from Britain to Australia. In addition, the passenger airline service had been established between Britain and India and the government was investing in the production of newly designed airships.

During March, British forces were placed on full alert in India as fresh trouble broke out as a result of an organised campaign of civil disobedience against British rule and oppression. The campaign, led by a former Indian lawyer, Mahatma Ghandi quickly gathered widespread sympathy throughout the country, which in turn provoked further trouble over the months which followed and which lead to the arrest of Ghandi by the British authorities.

In September of the same year, Adolf Hitler and the German Nazi Party managed to win 107 seats at the Reichstag, during the German elections. This, in effect, made the Nazi Party under the leadership of Adolf Hitler the second largest political party within Germany. Hitler played on the voters' fears of economic chaos and social disorder, as he made furious and emotional speeches denouncing the Jews and the communists as the cause of all Germany's problems.

By the beginning of 1931, the establishment of the RAF Service Police had become so large that it urgently required a full-time management structure. After a decision at the Air Ministry, an entry placed in the *London Gazette* announced that Squadron Leader F G Stammers OBE, had been appointed as the first dedicated Provost Marshal and Chief of Air Force Police, after the appointment had been approved by His Majesty, King George V. Wing Commander Brierley, the first overseer had retired some years previously and had been succeeded by Wing Commanders Grant-Dalton, Jackson and MacClean, all officers on loan from the Administration and Special Duties Branch. Although the appointment of the Provost Marshal had now been made a permanent position, he still had very little control over many of the RAF Service Police employed on individual stations, who were still directly responsible to their respective station commanders for the varied tasks which they undertook.

Later in the year, Flight Lieutenant C R Richdale took command of the police school at Halton. Additionally, in view of his past experience as a former Detective Inspector with the Kent Constabulary, he was tasked with investigating all serious offences within the country, which involved RAF personnel. By then, the police section at RAF Halton was under the control of Warrant Officer A A Newbury, who, besides carrying out a wide range of policing and administrative duties, found himself responsible for administering corporal punishment with the birch to apprentices at the camp, who had committed service offences and had been sentenced to be punished in that manner.

In the Far East, on 18th September, 1931, Japanese troops which had been sent to Manchuria to guard the South Manchurian Railway complex, launched an attack against the Chinese military garrison at Mukden in a move to annex Manchuria, before occupying the rest of China. The political situation in the region was further damaged in January 1932, when the Japanese forces advanced on and captured Shanghai. The world protested over the military action and as a result, Japan left the League of Nations a month later.

In Germany on the 30th January, 1933, President Paul von Hindenburg, appointed and installed Adolf Hitler as the new German Chancellor. However, soon after taking up office, Hitler started organising his administration as he moved closer and closer to the absolute power he needed to fulfil his ambitions. On 28th February, the German Reichstag was destroyed by the Nazi Party, which set it on fire and blamed the communists, in order to win the forthcoming elections. In March, as the situation in Germany deteriorated, the Nazi's opened their concentration camp at Dachau on the outskirts of Munich. Over the months which followed, the Nazi Party, under the direction of Hitler, carried out a systematic campaign of terror, against the Jews and anyone else who stood in their way. As the political situation became more serious, a pact of non-aggression was agreed and signed in Rome on 15th July, by the governments of Britain, France, Germany and Italy. However, on the 14th October, Germany also left the League of Nations.

On 2nd August, 1934, President Hindenburg died and Adolf Hitler, after a remarkable victory in a referendum, became the new President and Chancellor of Germany, but chose for himself the title, Führer. Shortly after his appointment, he issued orders to rearm Germany contrary to all the restrictions put in place by the Allies at the end of the Great War.

By then, tension in Europe had been steadily increasing, but new heights were reached when the Nazi Government in Berlin made two announcements on 11th March, 1935. The first was the official recognition of the *Luftwaffe*, the German Air Force, under the leadership of Hermann Goering, and the second was the introduction of military conscription. The announcement coincided with the proclamation by the British Government that they were reversing their policy of disarmament and as a result the army was to be expanded along with the navy and the RAF. The government went on to explain that the move was to demonstrate that it did not take lightly to Germany's rearmament programme, which it considered a threat to European peace. Details emerged that in addition to the building of new coastal and anti-aircraft defences, the RAF was to be trebled within the following two years.

In north-west India the RAF were fully occupied in trying to maintain order over the rebellious tribes operating in the area when a severe earthquake struck the region around Quetta (now part of Pakistan) on 31st May, 1935, and with the exception of the aircraft hangars, completely devastated the RAF station which had been located there. The Guardroom at the entrance of the station was totally destroyed when it collapsed like a house made of playing cards, killing those who had been trapped inside. Indeed, the earthquake was so serious, that just on the station alone, 126 RAF personnel and their families were killed and hundreds more were injured. Soon after the disaster, the RAF survivors, although shocked by what had happened, were very quickly mobilised and formed into rescue and first aid parties to assist the casualties trapped and injured on the station. After completing that task, they were then used to assist the civilian authorities in the surrounding area with the massive clear-up operation.

In East Africa on 2nd October, on the orders of Mussolini, Italy used both her ground and air forces during the invasion of Abyssinia. During their ruthless conquest to the capital, Addis Ababa, defenceless villages were ruthlessly bombed and poison gas was used against the unarmed and defenceless civilian population, resulting in many casualties. Emperor Haile Selassie, however, managed to escape the invaders, to the safety of London, shortly before the Italian forces entered the city.

In Spain on 17th July, 1936, following an unsuccessful military coup, civil war quickly broke out between the Republicans and Nationalists, and Adolf Hitler subsequently sent German troops in to assist the Republicans. In addition, his Air Force mercilessly bombed the undefended Spanish town of Guernica, soon after, killing approximately a thousand innocent civilians.

During the latter part of 1936, the RAF Service Police again became involved in counter-intelligence operations when Flight Lieutenant Richdale, Warrant Officer Kerby and Sergeant Clifton provided the evidence required to arrest a German spy, as he re-entered the country for the eighth time in pursuit of his covert mission. The story began earlier in the year when the RAF Service Police had been alerted to the suspicious activities of a German couple who had rented a large house in Broadstairs and were referring to themselves as Doctor Hermann Gortz and his assistant, Fraulein Marianne Emig. Doctor Gortz had let it be known that he was in the country researching a book about two families, one English and the other German, who had been friends but had been separated by the outbreak of the Great War. Under the pretence of researching his book, the couple had travelled quite freely around the Home Counties and East Anglia, where it just so happened that new RAF stations were being built. During their travels, Doctor Gortz and his very attractive assistant were able to gain easy access to a number of those new units and made the acquaintance of a number of officers and airmen who eagerly entertained the couple. However, during one such visit, their presence was noted by a suspicious service policeman, who reported the matter and it was subsequently investigated. It appeared that the couple were interested in all technical details of both the stations and the aircraft which were on, or about to be deployed onto them. In addition, it was known that Doctor Gortz was in possession of sketches which he had made of the then secret RAF site at Manston, in Kent. However, by the time this information was put together, both Doctor Gortz and his assistant had returned to Germany. The investigation continued and further enquiries revealed Doctor Gortz to be an Intelligence Officer with the *Luftwaffe* Reserve. As a result, Special Branch were alerted and when the Doctor tried to re-enter the country at Harwich on the 8th November, he was duly arrested. Unfortunately, his assistant had not accompanied him on that trip for some reason. After interrogation, he was subsequently charged with offences against the Official Secrets Act 1911, tried, convicted and duly sentenced to four years imprisonment. Although the case highlighted the effectiveness of the RAF Service Police in such matters, it also highlighted the poor standards of general security awareness throughout the RAF. Wing Commander Stammers and his

staff, very aware of those problems, started to formulate various ideas
to overcome the difficulty.

In Palestine on the 19th April, 1937, serious civil unrest had
broken out when the Arab population, who were unhappy with the
rapid increase in the level of Jewish immigration, started rioting in the
streets. As a result, all British units were placed on alert and British
troops were swiftly deployed to assist the civil police in restoring law
and order. Military control of Palestine had in September 1935, been
passed back to the Army as their numbers overwhelmed the
establishment of the RAF in the colony. As the troubles continued, a
general state of emergency was declared but the Arabs defiantly
responded by declaring a general strike throughout the country.

During the year, the police school, with premises far too small for
their current use, moved from Halton into new and larger premises at
RAF Uxbridge in Middlesex. The length of the initial police training
course after the move was increased to twelve weeks. The move to
Uxbridge also coincided with the formation of the RAF Service Police
Headquarters, both now being under the command of Flight
Lieutenant Richdale. The new headquarters was responsible for
assisting the Provost Marshal with formulating policy and for training
airmen in police duties. It did not, however, have any real command
responsibility over individual police sections throughout the RAF, but
acted merely as an advisory body. It was, however, staffed by two
civilian clerks and seventeen service policemen, the latter being tasked
with assisting Flight Lieutenant Richdale in his duties and investigating
RAF crime, wherever it occurred, around the country. This, it
seems, was the very beginning of the Special Investigation Branch
within the RAF Police.

By the end of 1937, the RAF and the Service Police organisation
had increased considerably, although there was still no dedicated trade
group for the RAF Police. In addition, the workload of the Provost
Marshal and his limited number of staff had been steadily increasing
as they took on further responsibilities. Flying Officer William
Kerby, the former Halton instructor at the police school, had recently
been commissioned and had been posted onto the staff of the RAF
Service Police Headquarters, under the command of Flight Lieutenant
Richdale.

On 31st December, the RAF station at Hinaidi, in Iraq, closed
down and was subsequently handed over to the Iraqi Government. A

brand new RAF station had been constructed at Habbaniya, some eighty miles away and as such, everything had to be transferred to the new unit. Although it was a two-day journey by horse, the RAF Service Police, Mounted Section, comprising of ten NCOs (some of whom were: J G Blackburn, S Allcock, D McKenzie, Clark and Poole) and their horses, under the command of Sergeant Stanley Moorehen, left Hinaidi, accompanied by only a single support truck which contained their personal equipment, water and rations for the journey. They rode into Baghdad and crossed over the Maud pontoon bridge, which had been erected by the Royal Engineers during the Great War. After leaving the city, they headed west towards the Faluja Plain and followed a tarmac road which gradually dwindled out as they travelled further away from the city. After a very tiring but successful first day, the section made camp for the night at the site of an old Iraqi police post. The following morning after breakfast, they again mounted up and continued their journey across the sandy gravel waste land of the Faluja Plain. The road had by now disappeared and as the desert stretched out endlessly before them, the only sign of civilisation was the line of telegraph poles which marked their route to the town of Faluja. Although the inhabitants of the town were known to be hostile towards the British, the section passed by without incident. After all, it must have been a most unusual and rather impressive sight for the villagers to witness. After crossing the Iron Bridge which spanned the Euphrates, the section made steady progress for the final fifteen miles of their journey into Habbaniya and their new home. As their journey neared its end, Sergeant Moorehen proudly led his impressive-looking section in through the main gates and onto their new station. Their hard two day journey had been a very successful venture for the entire section, earning them additional respect from their colleagues on the station.

By the start of 1938, the political tension within Europe was steadily increasing. Adolf Hitler, acting in response to an 'invitation' from the pro-Nazi Austrian leader, Artur Seyss-Inquart, had moved German troops into Austria on 11th March and then into Czechoslovakia at the beginning of October. While that was taking place, his Italian ally, Mussolini, waited patiently in the wings watching developments. Britain, sensing the increase in tension, reluctantly continued to rearm itself and stated that it was prepared to fight, if Germany attacked either France or Belgium. At the beginning of October, the RAF had 120 operational squadrons deployed at home with a further 29 squadrons deployed abroad in Palestine, Transjordan, India, Aden, Gibraltar, Malta, Iraq, Egypt, Singapore, Sudan and Kenya. Unfortunately, the Munich agreement, for 'Peace in our time', between the British Prime Minister Neville Chamberlain and Adolf Hitler, did nothing to stop Hitler's ambitions for power and his lust for territory within Europe, to expand his empire.

As the political tension mounted within Europe, there was increased talk of war against Germany. Accordingly, gas masks were issued to the general public and the precautions against German air raids were reviewed and reinforced by the building of air-raid shelters in and around London and other major cities. In addition, the Territorial Forces and Auxiliary Air Force had been increased in size and all Naval, military and RAF units, had been placed on a state of readiness, to prepare for the prospect of going to war. As the RAF prepared for war, the establishment of the RAF Service Police expanded to staff the new RAF stations, which had been built up around the country. Accordingly, with that expansion within the branch, Wing Commander Stammers, Flight Lieutenant Richdale and Flying Officer Kerby were all promoted to take on further responsibilities. In addition, a number of specially selected SNCOs from the RAF Service Police were commissioned as Deputy Assistant Provost Marshals (DAPM). The long-standing wish for a separate service police trade group was eventually approved and the new trade was called The Royal Air Force Police. At the time Flight Lieutenants were appointed as DAPMs, Squadron Leaders were appointed as Assistant Provost Marshals (APM), Wing Commanders were appointed as Deputy Provost Marshals (DPM), while Group Captain Stammers held the only appointment as Provost Marshal (PM).

In March, in an effort to increase security, APMs were appointed to the headquarters of Bomber, Fighter, Coastal and Training commands. Once established, they became responsible for all security matters and the supervision of the RAF Police, employed within their respective command formations. Initially, retired officers and officers from the reserve list were selected to fill those posts. Although they were not 'professional' policemen but were taken from all branches of the RAF, each one received elementary training in security and discipline matters before taking up post. As such, they also formed a vital management link between the Provost Marshal, the staff officers at Command Headquarters and the RAF Police serving within their areas. Although each APM was established with an RAF policeman and a civilian clerk to support them in their role, problems were soon encountered in carrying out the task in practical terms. Although the APMs were tasked with controlling the RAF Police employed on stations within their areas, the areas were vast and beyond the reasonable control of just one man and his meagre staff. Eventually, an agreement was reached to overcome the problem by the further establishment of a DAPM at each command. In addition, DAPMs were also posted into each of the 41 Group Headquarters around the country.

On 6th April, the British Government signed a pact of mutual assistance with Poland, while Hitler and Mussolini signed their own military 'Pact of Steel' alliance. Then in a further escalation of political tension, Hitler demanded the port of Danzig from Poland and in response Chamberlain warned him that if force was used to take the port, then Britain would declare war on Germany. By August, events were unfolding with bewildering speed and the threat of war loomed even closer. Conscription was introduced and all personnel on the reserve lists were recalled to active duty. As a result, the RAF, like the other two services, dramatically increased in size. Accordingly, the number of RAF Police entering the service increased and as a result, the instructional staff at the training school at Uxbridge found themselves dealing with a large number of RAF Police recruits. Because of the sudden influx, the initial police course was reduced from twelve weeks to a mere six weeks to cope. Although the trade of RAF Police had been officially approved in March, all the officers employed on provost duties, including the Provost Marshal, had been recruited from the Administration and Special Duties Branch and except for a handful, most had been 'borrowed' for short tours. Although not an ideal state of affairs, it had unfortunately been adapted from the system employed by the Army, who had always considered the role of a policeman to be no profession for a gentleman.

As dawn broke on 1st September, Adolf Hitler launched his 'blitzkrieg' offensive and invaded Poland with a force of six armoured divisions, eight motorised divisions and over a million men. The

Luftwaffe swiftly destroyed both the Polish railway system and the meagre Polish Air Force, leaving the country in chaos. Both Britain and France, who were allied to Poland, protested and gave Hitler an ultimatum that unless he withdrew his forces immediately, a state of war would exist with Germany. Unfortunately, on 3rd September, having heard nothing from Hitler, both Britain and France declared war on Germany. It was estimated that over 60,000 Poles were killed and some 200,000 more were wounded in the German onslaught on their country, with a further 700,000 Poles being taken as prisoners of war. As the situation developed, the Polish Government fled the country and took refuge in Rumania and the RAF, along with both the Navy and the Army prepared for combat in Europe.

Chapter III
The War Years 1939 – 1945

From the RAF Police's point of view, the beginning of the war generated an urgent need to assemble a mobile tactical police squadron, capable of providing the necessary vital support elements for an air force operating under field conditions close to the enemy lines. It was anticipated that such a force would be required to set up and operate out of hastily constructed airfields and as a consequence, fifty RAF Police NCOs were specially selected and trained to undertake that new and somewhat unique role. The new squadron, fully equipped and commanded by an APM and assisted by a number of DAPMs, again specially selected for the task, formed part of the British Expeditionary Force, which landed in France in September 1939. After quickly establishing itself in its new and strange surroundings, the squadron based its headquarters at Rheims, some fifteen miles north of Paris. Having done so, the squadron was fully operational within a very short period of time, carrying out a wide assortment of provost and security tasks which included traffic control and route signing, convoy duties, anti-vice and disciplinary patrols, handling prisoners of war, absentees and deserters, and investigating all manner of criminal and security activities. In addition, they were also responsible for managing a field punishment and detention barracks.

By that time, the establishment of the RAF had increased dramatically and in order to cope with the situation, some seventy-five recruits were accepted each week for basic police training, swelling the establishment of the branch to eleven thousand personnel. In addition, the commitments of the RAF Police were no longer restricted to the confines of RAF stations and units and a regional form of 'county' policing was introduced around the country. However, it was a very large and unmanageable organisation which, shortly after, was restructured once again and based on the thirteen geographical districts already in use by the Civil Defence Authorities. Each of the new district headquarters came under the command of a wing commander, assisted by a number of DAPMs, but in terms of manpower, the reorganisation resulted in an overall saving of some twenty-eight officer posts. While the RAF Police NCOs employed to police those new districts were fully equipped and adequately trained to perform both mobile and foot patrols within their areas of responsibility, the chief constables in those areas maintained and guarded their primary right to deal with, and prosecute any offenders, including RAF personnel. However, notwithstanding that right, the RAF Police quickly established and maintained a very close liaison with the relevant civilian police forces around the country and in turn that provided a very successful and professional working relationship, which prospered throughout the war years and beyond.

By far, the busiest RAF Police District around the country was London, where a multitude of off-duty service personnel congregated to enjoy their brief periods away from their bases. In addition to the many units established within and around the capital, the main RAF aircrew selection centre had been established at St John's Wood, within the confines of the Lord's cricket ground. Understandably, hundreds of young men passed through the centre wanting to enlist and fly, however, at the same time they didn't want to be bothered with the irksome regime of service discipline, which of course had to be strictly enforced. In addition to enforcing purely disciplinary measures, the RAF Police stationed within the capital dealt, on a daily basis, with a wide variety of offences and incidents involving service personnel. To make matters worse, rationing was being introduced which created a steady demand on the black market for all manner of stolen service commodities and fuel. Although dyes had been added to service fuels in an effort to identify it and prevent it from being stolen, it certainly didn't stop large quantities appearing on the black market. Even high-octane aircraft fuel was being stolen and sold off for use in motor cars, often with extremely interesting results. Drunkenness and assaults were commonplace offences and a large number of absentees and deserters were always at large, living rough in and around London. In addition, the RAF Police were also kept very busy conducting numerous investigations into cases of impersonation. It seemed that everyone wanted to be a hero of some kind, either to impress the ladies, or to bolster their credentials when engaged in various criminal activities. It wasn't therefore unusual for young men to dress up in the uniforms of RAF pilots, sporting a wide range of gallantry awards to which they had not been awarded and were not entitled to wear. As almost everyone at the time was wearing a uniform of one type or another, they were fairly easy to obtain, along with all the accessories required to enhance the image.

At that stage of the war, there were two variations of RAF Police operating within the service. Those employed within the newly formed districts were known as 'provost' and were directly responsible, through their own immediate superiors, to the Provost Marshal, while those employed on RAF stations, were known as 'station police' and were accountable to their own respective station commanders and contained their activities to within their unit boundaries. In order to distinguish the two variations, those employed within the districts began to wear their peaked service dress caps, together with a brassard on their right arm, displaying the letters 'RAFP', while those employed on stations wore side hats and wore their brassards on their left arm, displaying the letters RAF SP.

January 1940 recorded the coldest temperatures in Britain for half a century. The River Thames froze over and road and rail communications over much of the country were paralysed by snow drifts and ice. The situation was made all the worse by the censorship of the weather reports, which caught many people totally unprepared for the sudden and extremely severe weather conditions. The situation was made even more dreadful when food rationing started on 8th January, restricting the supply of bacon, ham, sugar, butter and tea. The rationing, vital as it was, further increased the demand on the black market for that type of commodity and accordingly, military stores were stolen to cater for it. On 8th April, German forces launched their invasion into both Denmark and Norway and on 10th May, they quickly invaded Holland and Belgium and started to move into France. As this was unfolding, Winston Churchill succeeded Neville Chamberlain as the Prime Minister and almost immediately started to rally the British population, promising nothing but blood, toil, tears and sweat. Although things looked grim, it appeared that Churchill's appointment marked a positive change in the British public's overall attitude towards the war. Unfortunately, by the end of May, both Holland and Belgium had fallen and the British

Expeditionary Force was being threatened by the German invasion of France. Britain, faced with the possibility of losing its entire army, decided to retreat from France and in doing so, evacuated its troops to the beaches at Dunkirk, where a hastily prepared operation, code named 'Dynamo' managed to rescue some 335,000 British and French troops. However, during the operation, the might of the advancing German forces tried everything within their power to prevent it from taking place.

The outbreak of war with Germany and the swiftness of their onslaught throughout Europe suddenly brought home to the Air Ministry the real threat, from acts of both sabotage and espionage to the British war effort and in particular the RAF. In order to address the problem, a newly formed RAF School of Security was established at RAF Halton during the middle of 1940, in an effort to provide specially trained personnel to counter the threat. In doing so, the school quickly ensured that newly appointed security officers and specially selected RAF Police SNCOs were trained in every aspect of security and counter-intelligence matters prior to being posted into newly formed security sections, set up at airfields, signal units, radar sites and key sea ports. The introduction of those new sections provided a very welcome relief to the hard-pressed army units, who up until that point in time, had been responsible for guarding those installations. Incidentally, as if to reinforce those security precautions, news filtered back to the Provost Marshal, that Doctor Herman Gortz, the German spy who had been brought to trial by the RAF Police and Special Branch in 1936, had been again engaged in the business of espionage while in Ireland. However, since his release from imprisonment, he had proved to be slightly more successful because he was never caught again by the British authorities.

Italy moved into the conflict on 10th June, declaring war on both Britain and France. However, during the following week, France asked the Germans for an armistice, the Germans accepted and France became a divided nation over the issue. The first British territory fell into German hands on 1st July, when German forces swiftly invaded the British Channel Islands and that was followed ten days later by the start of the Battle of Britain. At first the Germans began raiding British coastal ports and shipping within the British Channel. However, as the battle intensified, the German air force turned their attentions to the RAF fighter airfields in an attempt to destroy them and gain superiority in the air prior to launching their invasion. In an effort to bolster the British defence forces and prepare for the German invasion, the Secretary for State for War, Anthony Eden, made an appeal for volunteers to join the newly formed defence force known as the Home Guard. His appeal was extremely successful and by August, over a million recruits had enrolled and the second line of British defence began training to expel the expected German invasion. On 7th September, as the battle for Britain continued, the German air force began their 'blitz' on London and some of the other major cities. Considerable damage was caused on the first night in London alone and some 430 people were killed and another 1,600 were injured. On the 14th November, Coventry Cathedral was destroyed in a German air raid and during the last two days of December, the German air force destroyed most of the square mile within the City of London. While the year ended in misery, flames and destruction, the British people maintained their spirits, displaying incredible heroism and endurance in the face of the German attacks. From the RAF viewpoint, the Battle of Britain had continued in the skies above the country in glorious weather conditions from July until October. However, despite being stretched almost to breaking point, they won their hard fought battle in the end, while the German air force lost well over 2,000 aircraft, the RAF lost fewer than 1,000. It had been a close battle, but the invasion of the British mainland by the German Army had been seriously frustrated. By that stage, the building programme of the newly established airfields all around the country had been increasing with lightning speed and many of those new airfields had properly constructed hard-surface runways and dispersal areas, capable of supporting the heavier aircraft such as the Lancaster bomber. Indeed, nothing which could be used in the war effort was wasted and that included the huge supply of rubble from the bombed-out cities, which was gathered up and used as the hard-core base in the newly constructed runways.

During 1941, the RAF Police Headquarters, which had been at RAF Uxbridge since 1937, moved out and took over splendid new accommodation at Hitchen House at Burnham, situated in Buckinghamshire. In addition to its previous functions, the headquarters also took over the responsibility for selecting new police investigators, as well as assigning them to posts world-wide. As the year drew on, conscription was extended in an effort to build up the armed forces in preparation for the invasion and liberation of the European mainland. Consequently, all men aged between eighteen and fifty-one years of age were called up for military service and of course that reduced the workforce in the factories, which were required to sustain the war effort. To overcome the problem, further appeals went out to recruit women volunteers for all manner of work connected with sustaining the war effort. So successful were the appeals that they were later followed up with the first call up of women, aged between twenty and thirty years of age, for military service. As a consequence, the Women's Auxiliary Air Force was reformed and a decision was made to employ women on security duties. A letter was circulated to all commands asking for suitable applicants to volunteer their services and, as a result, four successful candidates attended training, some time later, at the Security School at RAF Halton. After completing the course they were posted with the rank of acting sergeant to the office of the Provost Marshal at the Air Ministry in London. However, before the year had ended, two of them had remustered into other trades, leaving WAAF Sergeants M D George and E B Moll to continue their task of dealing with security matters, tracing WAAF absentees and dealing with an assortment of WAAF welfare cases. Because such a large number of females were being recruited into the service, it became necessary to provide specially trained female personnel from within the service to police them. As a result, official approval was given for the establishment of WAAF Police and accordingly, an assistant section officer, a flight sergeant, three sergeants and three corporals, were assigned to each of the thirteen RAF Police districts to control the female element. The venture was so successful that the WAAF Police became an authorised trade within the service and by November, direct enlistment was taking place. In addition, Sergeant George was commissioned as the first WAAF provost officer, followed shortly after by her friend and colleague, Sergeant Moll.

The year had seen much activity on the war front, starting in January, when in North Africa, British and Australian forces had captured part of Tobruk from the Italians. Then on the 10th May, Hitler's deputy, Rudolf Hess, suddenly arrived in Scotland after parachuting from his Messerschmitt aircraft. He had wanted to speak to the Duke of Hamilton, whom he had met sometime before the outbreak of war. It seemed, from what he was saying, that the

Germans had wanted to try and make a peace settlement with the British. However, he was promptly arrested and after spending a brief period in RAF custody in Scotland, he was imprisoned for the remainder of the war within the Tower of London. The Germans had suffered another damaging loss on 27th May, when their much prized battleship, *The Bismarck*, was sunk by the British Navy in the North Atlantic Ocean. On 22nd June, undaunted by a number of previous setbacks, the German war machine began its attack on Russia. Then on 7th December, the war took on a new twist when, without warning, the Japanese Air Force attacked the United States Naval base at Pearl Harbour in Hawaii, killing more than 2,000 American servicemen and civilians. After their surprise attack, the Japanese began their ruthless offensive in the Far East, with India as their main prize. Shortly after, both Germany and Japan declared war on the United States of America and as a consequence, America entered the war, both in Europe and in the Far East. On Christmas day, Hong Kong surrendered to the Japanese who had besieged the tiny but strategically important British colony for two weeks.

In February, the Metropolitan Police were called to an air raid shelter in Montagu Place, St Marylebone, where they discovered the body of Miss Evelyn Hamilton, a middle-aged and respectable chemist. She had been strangled. Later that same day, the police attended a flat in nearby Wardour Street in Soho, where Mrs Nita Oatley had been murdered. In addition to having had her throat cut, other horrifying injuries had been inflicted on her. Oatley, also, known as Ward, had been a prostitute and her husband had started divorce proceedings because of her immoral lifestyle. Later that same week, the police were called out to the scene of yet another murder which had taken place in a flat in Gosfield Street near Tottenham Court Road. The victim, Mrs Margaret Lowe, had been strangled and her body had been mutilated. It seemed to the police that all three murders were the work of the same person. Two days later, another victim, Mrs Doris Jouannet, was discovered in her boarding house in Sussex Gardens and she too had been strangled and mutilated. It seemed that another 'Jack the Ripper' serial killer was on the loose and accordingly, every policeman in the capital was put on alert to try and apprehend him before he struck again.

During the course of his enquiries, the officer in charge of the case, Detective Superintendent George Yandell, learned of an earlier incident where an attempt had been made on the life of another local young woman, Mrs Greta Heywood. When she was interviewed, she told of how she had met an airman, who had bought her drinks before taking her into a sidestreet. The airman had then gripped her so forcefully around the throat that she had dropped her torch and put up a fight. During the struggle, she had managed to scream out for help and as he ran off she pulled his gas mask haversack off his shoulder. At that stage, the RAF Police were called into the enquiry to assist in tracing the airman. From the description of the uniform worn by the airman, it was clear that he had been an officer cadet. Enquiries soon established the suspect to be Gordon Fredrick Cummins, a tall, good-looking airman cadet, who had green, staring eyes, which were set wide apart. Further enquiries established that he had been billeted in a block of commandeered flats in St John's Wood, close to where all the murders had taken place. Cummins was subsequently arrested and remanded in custody while further enquiries continued. Another significant witness, Mrs Cathleen Mulcahy, who lived in a flat on Southwick Street, near Sussex Gardens, had also survived an attack from a man who fitted Cummins' description. Cummins, it seemed, had paid her for her company before trying to strangle her. However, she had survived by kicking him in his vital parts and he had run off. Mrs Mulcahy still had the money he had given her and the serial numbers were checked against those issued at the last pay parade which Cummins had attended. They matched, but the evidence was further strengthened when a cigarette lighter owned by Mrs Oatley was discovered in his belongings. In addition, fingerprints belonging to Cummins were found in the flat where Mrs Oatley had been killed. That along with other forensic evidence sealed his fate. However, he refused to admit his guilt or to answer any questions regarding a couple of earlier murders. He was eventually tried and found guilty of the murder of Mrs Oatley and was sentenced to death. He was duly hanged on 25th June, still protesting his innocence.

At the start of the year, the Japanese forces operating within the Far East and the Pacific seemed just as invincible as the Germans were in Europe. As the Japanese advanced swiftly through Malaya, the poorly defended British island base of Singapore surrendered to the Japanese on 15th February, shattering the heart of Britain's presence within the region. The Japanese advance continued and on 10th March, the Burmese capital, Rangoon, also surrendered. In

North Africa on the 27th May, German armoured forces, under the command of General Erwin Rommel, advanced through Libya to dominate the North African desert. It was a blow to the British forces operating in the area. However, over a thousand RAF bombers took part in a night time raid three days later, against the German city of Cologne, inflicting large-scale damage and many casualties. That was followed on 19th August by a daring raid, when British, Canadian, American and Free-French commando units attacked the French port of Dieppe. Unfortunately, the raid did not go to plan and most of the attacking force were either slaughtered or captured by the German defenders. In Russia on 5th September, German troops entered the city of Stalingrad and on 23rd October, the British 8th Army, commanded by General Bernard Law Montgomery, and the German Afrika Korps commanded by Rommel, clashed violently as the Battle of El Alamein began to win back the North African desert from the Germans.

During the early part of the year, an RAF Police sergeant had been detached to the RAF Records Office in Gloucester to establish a Police and Security Liaison Office (PSLO). The move had been brought about after the staff had been inundated with hundreds of personnel enquiries from both the SIB and the civilian police. With the sudden expansion of the service, the overworked staff could not cope with that type of enquiry, which after all was best dealt with by the RAF police. At that time, the Provost Marshal's Department at the Air Ministry had also increased in size to accommodate seven busy departments, each under the command of a Wing Commander and identified simply by the abbreviations PM1 through to PM7. PM1 was responsible for general security matters affecting the RAF, while PM2 looked after organisation, personnel and discipline within the branch. PM3 was responsible for carrying out special enquiries and was manned by a number of former civilian police officers. PM4 looked after WAAF Police related matters. PM5 was responsible for passes, permits and vetting enquiries, while PM6 looked after all special security arrangements connected with operations, inventions, factories and VIPs. Finally, PM7 dealt with matters regarding RAF flying indiscipline over the UK.

On the 13th September, the island of Malta was awarded the George Cross for outstanding valour by King George VI, after its population had bravely held out for several months against the almost constant and heavy bombardment inflicted on the island by the Germans, who had wanted to capture the strategically important Mediterranean base to support their offensives in North Africa.

In November 1942, Flight Lieutenant Hugh Bathurst-Brown, the Adjutant at RAF Staverton, near Gloucester, received a telephone call from Lieutenant Colonel Jimmy Baldwin, an officer on reserve service, who after a brief introduction, asked Bathurst-Brown if he would like the appointment of commanding the newly formed Ministry of Aircraft Production Guard Dog School. Although Bathurst-Brown was not fond of dogs, he had become rather bored with his routine life at Staverton, so he immediately accepted the offer, even though he had no real experience of dealing with dogs to any great degree.

Baldwin had served in the trenches at Picardy in France during the Great War, and had been very impressed by the way the Germans had used their war dogs to good effect, not only in the guarding role but also to locate wounded men and to pull their ammunition supplies around the battlefield. The dogs, which were used by the Germans, were called Deutsche Schaeferhunde, or German Shepherd dogs, and they possessed a keen nose, speed, endurance, aggressiveness and above all, courage. In addition, they seemed able to adapt to all types of weather conditions. The breed was eventually introduced into England in 1920, but was called the 'Alsatian', after the name of the region where they had first been bred. Baldwin had been so impressed by what he had seen that he later discussed the matter with a close friend, Captain Moore Brabazon, who was at the time serving with the Royal Flying Corps. After the war ended, Baldwin left the army and pursued his interest in the dogs and eventually established his own breeding kennels, which he called Picardy Kennels. In addition, he became something of an expert when it came to the Alsatian breed.

Baldwin maintained his links with Moore Brabazon, who, after leaving the Royal Flying Corps, went into politics. However, when war broke out again in 1939, Brabazon was appointed as the Minister of Aircraft Production responsible for thousands of expensive aircraft and a large number of airfields and storage depots around the country. However, with the increasing threat of espionage and sabotage, he was troubled with the problem of providing adequate security cover for his assets. Remembering the conversation he had shared with Jimmy Baldwin years earlier on the subject of dogs, he turned to him for advice and assistance and in the end, Baldwin was able to persuade him that dogs were the most effective and economical method of guarding his interests. After all, dogs had been used to protect and defend armies and their assets going back over many centuries. Convinced that dogs were the only economical way ahead, Brabazon obtained the necessary authority from the government to form the Ministry of Aircraft Production Dog School. As a consequence, Baldwin was offered and accepted the appointment of Dog Advisor and Chief Training Officer, but the actual administration of the school was to be carried out by the RAF.

Some time later, Flight Lieutenant Bathurst-Brown, having received his posting notice from the Air Ministry, reported to Woodfold, the site of the new school, five miles from Staverton. While Woodfold turned out to be a comfortable country manor house set in its own pleasant grounds, the facilities made available to the school turned out to be rather sparse and comprised a garage, which was used as the schools headquarters and administrative centre, and several stables around a courtyard which were used to kennel the dogs. An RAF sergeant was posted in to assist Bathurst-Brown in setting everything up, but it turned out to be several more weeks before any further staff or dogs arrived to join them. Baldwin had hand-picked his staff very carefully and they had consisted of some of the top dog trainers and breeders from around the country. The dogs which were trained at the school had all been donated by the public and had consisted of a wide variety of breeds. As soon as the training programme got under way, student dog handlers arrived from both the RAF and the United States' 9th American Air Force, to undertake their initial six-week training course.

By December 1942, Group Captain Stammers had retired from the RAF. He had been the RAF Provost Marshal for eleven years and during that time had seen the growth of quite a substantial police organisation. Indeed, he had been instrumental in the very formation of the RAF Police, often against determined opposition to some of his plans and ideas. However, when he finally retired, the establishment of the RAF Police was just over one thousand men and women. Upon his departure, he was succeeded in post by Air Commodore Owen Washington de Putron, CB, CBE.

The new Provost Marshal had initially joined the Durham Light Infantry in 1914, before transferring into the Royal Flying Corps three years later. He had served throughout the remainder of the Great War as a pilot and became part of the Royal Air Force when it was formed in 1918. Between the wars, he had spent a short time holding the appointment as a district discipline officer but apart from that, he had very little practical experience of dealing with the RAF Police and their organisation. As such, it seemed that he had his work cut out to effectively fill the gap left by Group Captain Stammers and soon after taking up his appointment, decided that an assistant was required to guide him into his new appointment. The natural choice for the job turned out to be either Wing Commander Richdale or Wing Commander Kerby, but both were serving overseas, the former in South Africa and the latter in the Middle East. After careful consideration, Kerby was chosen, brought back home, promoted to Group Captain and appointed as DPM.

Operation Chastise proved completely successful on 17th May, 1943, when nineteen RAF Lancaster bombers breached the Mohne and Eder dams, in the manufacturing region of the Ruhr. As a result, some 134,000,000 tons of water from the Mohnesee had swept away power stations, factories and villages as the torrent had roared down through the Ruhr valley. The situation in the region had been even more chaotic as some 202,000,000 tons of water, forming a thirty foot tidal wave, had rushed out of the Edersee and into the town of Kassel, killing many people and destroying everything in its path. From a security point of view, the operation had also been a success; during the trials, the training and the build up to the raids, the RAF Police, supervised by provost officers from within PM6, had established and maintained a round the clock security blanket over the secret mission, both at bases in Lincolnshire and at RAF Manston in Kent.

In July, two provost officers, Group Captain L G Brown and Squadron Leader F A Instone, were posted onto the strength of the Headquarters of the 2nd Tactical Air Force at Bracknell, with the responsibility for organising and training a number of specially selected RAF Police personnel for the invasion of Northern Europe. Although a difficult task, Wing Commander Brown was no stranger in preparing for such an invasion, having served with the original Advanced Striking Force in France until their withdrawal in 1940. In November, the RAF Police school moved out of RAF Uxbridge, because of overcrowding and a requirement by the army, for additional accommodation. As a consequence, the school took up residence as a lodger unit at RAF Weeton near Blackpool. At the time, training had reached its peak as 1,200 recruits had undertaken their basic RAF police training and initial driving courses.

Earlier in the year, the Commander of the British North African Air Force, impressed with the work he had seen carried out by the RAF Police, requested the establishment of suitably equipped RAF Police units within his own command. As a result, a number of new mobile police units were quickly assembled, based on the one set up to accompany the British Expeditionary Force into France, and sent out to the region. In addition to supporting the provost units in the Middle East which had been previously established, the new formation also provided provost and security support elements to the RAF throughout the North African campaign. By then, the number of RAF Police being employed on RAF stations had steadily increased and to ensure that they were being properly used, an RAF Police Inspectorate was formed, made up of teams comprising of a Flight Lieutenant, a Warrant Officer and five Flight Sergeants. Each team was well experienced in all aspects of police operations and resource management, and their main function was to ensure that manpower was being allocated in the most economical way. To do that, they visited every RAF unit in the country, setting up and standardising the operating procedures used by the RAF Police. Surpluses in manpower were commonplace and were duly skimmed off from the station establishments to form the RAF Police squadrons required to support the Allied Tactical Air Force being prepared for the invasion of Europe. In addition, over that period, the RAF Police districts were once again reorganised and reduced from thirteen to eight districts. The new areas covered approximately the same geographical areas being used by the eight civilian police districts on the British mainland. The exception, Northern Ireland, was not part of the United Kingdom's civilian police organisation and all RAF Police resources in the province were detached from No 1, RAF Police District and controlled from London. Each of the newly formed districts, with the exception of Nos 1 and 5, continued to be commanded by a Wing Commander, with the exceptions being commanded by Group Captains. By the end of 1943, having successfully completed its task, the inspectorate was disestablished and its staff were returned to normal duties.

As the year progressed, the war, at last had started to turn in favour of the Allies. They had entered Tunis on 7th May, having ended the North-African campaign in a blaze of victory. Then on 10th July, they began their invasion of Sicily, which was followed fifteen days later by the downfall of Mussolini. The airfields at Catania and Palermo were quickly secured by the RAF Regiment and soon after were in operational use by the Allied Air Forces. The Allied advance pressed on, supported by units of RAF Police, until on 1st September, they crossed the Straits of Messina and landed on mainland Italy at Reggio, Bari and Foggia. As a result, Italy was quickly removed from the war and on 8th September, the new Italian Government swiftly announced Italy's unconditional surrender and during the same month, Portugal allowed the Allies to establish a military base on the Azores. By 6th November, the war on the eastern front was also causing major problems for the German high command as the Russians began their counter-attack and pushed forward towards the west and retook the city of Kiev, repelling the cold and confused German Army along the way. In Iran on 29th November, Churchill, Stalin and Roosevelt attended a summit in Tehran to discuss, amongst other things, the final plans for the Allied invasion into France. It was the very first time that Stalin had ventured outside the USSR since the revolution in 1917.

In the vicious war being waged in the Far East, the first Japanese forces, under the command of General Kimura, crossed the Chindwin River and the border from Burma into India during March 1944. However, British and Indian troops, supported by the RAF, advanced to engage them at Imphal and Kohima and during the subsequent bitter battle, some 65,000 Japanese troops were killed. The Allied victory marked the start of their counter-attack to push the Japanese out of Burma.

During 1944, the RAF decided to change the design of their personal identification cards as a result of a number of rather embarrassing experiences during the early stages of the war. During the disastrous events leading up to the withdrawal of the Allies from Dunkirk, a number of English-speaking German agents, dressed in captured uniforms, had successfully joined various British and French units and made their way back to the coast. The stories they told about having lost their personal identification documents during the battle seemed plausible and they had been accepted at face value.

Unfortunately, at the time, there were no master records maintained of identity cards to verify their stories and as such, their true identities could not be easily validated. As a result of the unsatisfactory system, the Provost Marshal urgently called for a new and reliable scheme to be introduced as quickly as possible. As you can imagine, with so many personnel in the service at that time and with the war in full swing, it was quite a mammoth task to take on. However, after careful consideration, it was decided that the RAF Police would be given the responsibility for carrying out the commitment. As such, from that date onwards, all the new cards, known as the RAF form 1250(R), which were produced were authenticated and backed up by duplicates held in an index, set up within PM5. During the same period, a criminal records office was also established by the RAF Police and soon proved to be a most useful source of information, not only to the RAF investigators but to the civilian police as well.

Since the beginning of the war, a considerable amount of manpower had been taken up by the RAF, in providing physical security to protect its stations, aircraft and equipment from the threat of sabotage, espionage and theft. Not only was the practice expensive but it also diverted a large number of essential personnel from other more important tasks connected with the war effort. As a result, a number of solutions had been discussed at the Provost Marshal's Office in an effort to alleviate the problem. As a result, the use of properly trained Alsatian dogs and handlers was suggested by Squadron Leader F A Instone, an APM employed within PM6. The Provost Marshal was impressed with the suggestion and shortly after visited the Ministry of Aircraft Production Guard Dog School, at Woodfold, where after a briefing from Colonel Baldwin, he witnessed an impressive demonstration from the dogs and their handlers. Air Commodore de Putron returned to the Air Ministry extremely impressed by what he had seen and after a considerable battle within the Air Ministry, approval was granted from the Chief of Air Staff himself, making the Dog School part of the RAF Police organisation. It was a successful venture and at Woodfold on the 24th March, the first batch of RAF Police NCOs commenced their training as dog handlers.

At that point in the war, given the operational aerial activity over Europe, a considerable number of captured Allied airmen found themselves detained by the German authorities in prisoner of war camps, located deep inside Germany and Poland. Whilst security at the camps was strict, it didn't prevent a large number of inmates escaping from the camps and getting back into the war effort. After all, it was every British serviceman's duty to try and escape if he could. In February, in response to a number of embarrassing large scale escapes, Field Marshal Wilhelm Keitel, Chief of the German High Command, issued an order, personally approved by Hitler himself, stating that re-captured POWs would be dealt with by the Gestapo from that point on.

Of all the escapes which took place during the war, one such attempt has since been made famous by the film, *The Great Escape*. However, the real event, on which the film was based, happened in March 1944 at the prisoner of war camp known simply as 'Stalag Luft 3', situated near Sagan in Silesia (Poland) and some hundred miles south-east of Berlin. After months of work, three tunnels had been constructed at the camp and were given the codenames 'Tom, Dick and Harry'. Unfortunately, Tom had been discovered by the Germans and had been blown up. However, Dick and Harry continued to remain undetected; after all, it was extremely unusual for more than one tunnel to be constructed at a time. While Dick became the store for the equipment used to build Harry, Harry itself, became a very elaborate 400 foot tunnel, constructed to a very high standard of workmanship. It had been properly shored up throughout, had a railway track complete with carts, its very own ventilation system and even the mains electricity had been diverted from the camp's main supply. When completed, the tunnel had lead out beyond the perimeter fence and into the cover and safety of the woods beyond.

Although the senior British officer, Group Captain Massey, had been warned by the Camp Commandant, Colonel Lindeiner-Wildeu, against planning any large-scale escapes, Harry was put into use during the moonless night of 24th and 25th March. Although seventy-nine prisoners, in possession of forged papers and extremely good disguises, managed to escape, the alarm unfortunately was quickly raised. Because of the large scale search which had been mounted for the escaped airmen, only three made it successfully back to England. The remainder were quickly captured but instead of being returned to Stalag Luft 3, they were, in line with the latest directive from Kietel, handed over to the Gestapo for interrogation. On 26th March, at a meeting attended by Keitel, Herman Goring and Heinrich Himmler,

Hitler directed that over half of the recaptured RAF officers had to be shot, as a warning to others planning similar escapes. Consequently the following day, Himmler ordered his assistants, Ernst Kaltenbrunner and Artur Nebe to organise the execution of fifty of the recaptured officers. As a result, over the weeks which followed, fifty officers of different nationalities, who were serving with the RAF, were murdered, cremated and their ashes returned in urns to Stalag Luft 3. When news of the murders reached London, the then Foreign Secretary, Anthony Eden, pledged to hunt down all of those involved in the conspiracy.

Throughout April and May, with the build up of troops for the almost imminent Allied invasion of Europe, the RAF Police were, in addition to their normal duties, kept extremely busy with escorting convoys, route signing and controlling traffic in the southern assembly areas. By the third week of May, the huge invasion force was confined within their camps and in order to preserve the total secrecy of the operation, all communication with the 'outside world' was strictly prohibited. As such, the RAF Police, along with their Allied counterparts, were employed on maintaining the security of those assembly areas.

On 4th June, Rome fell to the Allied forces, virtually unopposed. Then two days later, just after midnight, Operation Overlord was finally put into action. The Allied invasion to liberate France and the rest of northern Europe had started and the invasion force quickly made for the beaches in Normandy. The Americans were tasked with landing on the beaches, code named 'Utah' and 'Omaha', while the British and Canadian forces were assigned to 'Gold', 'Juno' and 'Sword' beaches. At dawn, the largest invasion force ever assembled lay off the coast of France in some 7,000 ships of assorted designs. Once again, the invasion force was accompanied by units of RAF Police, who were there to provide support, not only for the 2nd Tactical Air Force, but also for the 1st Canadian and 21st Army Groups.

Prior to the invasion taking place, Squadron Leader S Mumford, a provost officer holding the appointment as Officer Commanding Provost & Security Unit, 83 Group, 2nd Tactical Air Force, compiled the following operation order, on the 5th June, 1944, whilst travelling to France on board craft USS LST 175.

83 GROUP 2ND TACTICAL AIR FORCE PROVOST AND SECURITY UNIT ORDERS FOR PROVOST & SECURITY 'E' ECHELON D-DAY LANDINGS

OPERATIONS ON LANDING

General Position

'A' Echelon Provost & Security Forces together with Canadian Air Force Police reinforcements will land on the first tide of 6th June, 1944. 'E' Echelon will land on the day following D-Day. Vehicles will pass individually as best they can over King Beach through the appropriate Assembly Area. Vehicles of 'E' Echelon will assemble on the Assembly Area and proceed thence as one convoy to the camp site, map reference T 882808.

At the time 'E' Echelon lands, A, B, C and D Echelons will already have landed. B Echelon, Sgt Baxter + 4 will be operating on the extreme left RAF Assembly Area No 4. A Echelon, Flt Lt Barrett-Lennard, Sgt Hallam + 4 will be operating in RAF Assembly Area No 3 to the right of No 4 Assembly Area. Sgt Kelly + 4 will be ready to join up with the Main HQ 83 Group for special duties. C Echelon, Sgt Gifford + 4 will be operating in No 2 RAF Assembly Area, to the right of No 3 Assembly Area and D Echelon, Sgt Conrad + 4 will be operating No 1 RAF Assembly Area on the extreme right flank.

As soon as the Unit camp is established the four RAF Assembly Areas will be operated from Unit Headquarters, and A, B, C & D Echelons will cease to operate as separate units. A diagram of the above is roughly as follows;

HQ 83 Group	HQ P&S		

| RAF Assem Area No 4 | RAF Assem Area No 3 | RAF Assem Area No 2 | RAF Assem Area No 1 |

///

English Channel

Pitching Camp

Comprising (a) parking of vehicles, (b) unloading vehicles, (c) siting camp, (d) digging slit trenches invisible from the air, (e) erecting cookhouse and orderly room, three tents for officers, offices cum living, Provost, Security and SIB, Traffic and Guard Tents, detailing guards, (g) organising fitters and MTMs into repair and service operation, (h) establishing source of supply of water, rations, POL, stores, medical services etc.

Pitching camp to be carried out by all personnel under their Senior NCOs under the supervision of Sqn Ldr Rawlins and Sgt Major Jerome, with the exception of Flt Sgt Thomas and the traffic NCOs with jeeps and m/cs that are required immediately for Traffic Duties.

It is the responsibility of vehicle drivers to ensure that vehicles do not bunch together, except on shaded roads, and that when stationary their vehicles are camouflaged.

It is the responsibility of each man to make himself as useful as possible as inconspicuously as possible. Senior NCOs are also responsible to see that their men are not hanging about with nothing to do.

It is vital that all ranks conserve supplies of water, food and POL until plentiful sources of supply are established.

On arrival at battle station Flt Sgt Thomas will dispatch a m/c or jeep to Group HQ to report our arrival, giving details of any casualties to personnel or vehicles.

As soon as camp routine is established Sgt Major Jerome will inform all NCO i/c sections of the personnel he requires daily for camp duties.

Traffic Control Duties.

Traffic Control duties should have already commenced with A, B, C, & D Echelons. Flt Sgt Thomas at the time of arrival, should be *au fait* with the general landing programme. He will contact Flt Lt Barrett-Lennard to ascertain what has already happened and what traffic control programme has already been laid on. Flt Lt Barrett-Lennard will then proceed to hand over all traffic operational work to Flt Sgt Thomas. Flt Lt Barrett-Lennard will then proceed to establish continual contact with Sqn Ldr Hargreaves of Sea Movements, who will also establish contact with Army Provost Group and Army Movements to keep *au fait* with any changes with Traffic Control circuit and with heavy Army movements. Flt Lt Barrett-Lennard will advise Flt Sgt Thomas immediately with all developments of this kind.

Pending the arrival of Flt Lt MacKenzie, Flt Sgt Thomas will be i/c operational Traffic Control. As far as possible he will –

(a) have routes of all units to their battle station checked over before arrival of Units to ensure they can proceed

(b) Sign routes for convoys of 25 vehicles or more

(c) Establish points manned by pointsmen in pairs in strategic places from RAF Traffic point of view

(d) Keep a short record or log and make a full weekly report of such assistance rendered and

(e) Keep all traffic personnel as fully informed as possible concerning the –

   (i) Whereabouts of Group Units.
   (ii) The Traffic services, and
   (iii) the locations of important services, food, water, POL, medical, repair shops, etc.

Traffic Police when on duty will, if riding m/cs, wear m/c boots and pantaloons. Socks are not to be worn above boot tops. Battledress and short gaiters will be worn by drivers of jeeps and 15 cwts. Steel crash helmets will be worn at all times on m/cs. Where long periods of static point duty are involved, and conditions are quiet, side caps may be worn at the discretion of NCO i/c Traffic Sections. As far as possible, during the early stages, pointsmen will work in pairs. On isolated points they will be particularly cautious if approached by civilians. It is the individual pointsman's responsibility to ensure that appropriate cover is available at their posts. During enemy activity they must remain at their post so long as their services are required by passing traffic. If there is no traffic they may take cover and emerge immediately that approaching traffic requires their presence at their posts.

It is the duty of all Traffic personnel at all times to make themselves as well informed as possible concerning (a) the location of Group Units and useful services, such as medical, POL, DID, etc., (b) the traffic circuit, and (c) the locality in which they are working. Further, any information coming to the knowledge of one policeman, such as mines exploding and destroying a certain bridge, or repairs completed to a damaged bridge, or the clearance of a particular minefield, must be circulated immediately to Flt Sgt Thomas, so that the information may be circulated to all personnel. Further, before proceeding on duty, all Traffic Police will consult the notice board outside the Traffic Office so that they are in possession of the latest information. Such information is referred to by the Army as Road Intelligence. Only in this way can the Traffic Section fulfil properly the vital function it has to perform.

All Traffic personnel must appreciate that any written information of this kind would be of immense value to the enemy if captured. As such, as much as possible must therefore be committed to memory. Any written matter must be disposed of or destroyed prior to being captured by the enemy.

It must be remembered that a 24-hour Traffic Control Service must be provided. In normal times, three 8 hour shifts daily will be worked, but in times of strain it may be necessary to have an 8 hours on and 8 hours off period.

It is also the duty of Traffic Police to check individuals RAF, Military, Naval and Marine for deserters and stragglers.

SECURITY AND SIB

Security and SIB personnel will first give assistance in erecting the camp site and setting up the Security & SIB Office. Work will fall into the following sections:

(a) Liaison with Army Security, Civil Affairs and GISO and obtain what possible concerning local suspects, political parties and security objectives in RAF areas. Also name of reliable local inhabitants of RAF areas. If possible to define definite operational area of RAF security.

(b) Positive action to round up suspects and search security objectives referred to in para (a).

(c) To man Emergency Landing Strip (ELS) as soon as operational with one Security NCO and one Provost NCO to check identities of pilots and passengers landing. This would be the preliminary of proper control as laid down in AEAF directive.

(d) Contact reliable inhabitants, local officials and RAF units to make presence known with a view to ascertaining if there are any security matters worrying persons concerned.

(e) Vetting of civilian labour used to assist the RAF.

(f) Ascertaining where airmen are coming into most contact with civilians and commencing routine observations.

(g) Investigate all incidents of a security nature reported or coming to notice, including espionage, sabotage, spreading of rumours, suspicious behaviour etc.

All investigations under the heading (g) to be carried out by SIB, who will undertake also any investigations relating to crime etc. Pending the arrival of Flt Lt Buchan, Flt Sgt Davison will be NCO i/c Security and Flt Sgt Bradley NCO i/c SIB.

PROVOST

Pending the arrival of Flt Off Sohier, Sgt Major Jerome will be i/c Provost for the Unit. It is not known definitely at what stage heavy provost commitments will arise, but it must be ready to provide the following services almost from the moment of landing:

(a) Collecting stragglers, deserters and prisoners of war from units and traffic posts.

(b) Patrols in Caen and Bayeux as soon as RAF units are up that far, say D + 2, also in the more important villages.

(c) To accompany one Security NCO for duty at the first ELS to check pilots landing there.

(d) To take up duty at the artificial port being constructed by, say D + 4.

Provost personnel in normal times must pay particular attention to their own appearance to offset the tendency there may be for RAF and RCAF personnel to allow their own appearance and bearing to fall much below the standard in Britain. This definitely happened in both Africa and Italy until RAF Police arrived.

Dress will be battledress and gaiters with brassards and steel helmets or side hats at the discretion of the NCO i/c.

In addition to the above duties, the following special duties will be performed:

TRAFFIC POLICE

One NCO detailed as outrider to AOC on m/c to carry his priority flag.

PROVOST

Cpls Shears, Farmer, Mugan, Pincombe, Creed, Alston special duties. Cpl Collins DR motorcyclist.

GENERAL

RAF Police will co-operate at all times with Military, Naval, and Marine Police. Authority of Service Police under Sect. U, subsection 2 of the 21st Army Group Standing Orders are as follows:

(a) Military, Naval, Marine and RAF Police of all forces of the Supreme Allied Command are authorised and empowered to maintain order, enforce authority and make arrests amongst the forces and in the area of this command, without regard to the nationality or service to which such personnel may belong.

(b) Where practicable, arrests will be effected by police of the same nationality as the offender. Any offender arrested will be delivered promptly to the proper authorities (Army, Navy, Marine, RAF) of the Allied Force to which he belongs, for trial or other appropriate action.

ARRESTS

Service personnel. When service personnel are arrested by RAF they will be disposed of as follows;

(a) Air Force personnel - handed over to their unit.

(b) Army or Navy - handed over to the nearest Military or Royal Marine Policeman.

(c) Personnel of Allied Armies - handed over to the nearest police of appropriate nationality.

Civilians. Detailed instructions will be issued at a later date for the disposal of civilians arrested by RAF Police which will depend upon the degree of efficiency of the indigenous police and other factors as yet unknown.

Civilians employed by the RAF are subject to Air Force Law as airmen under the Air Force Act.

It may well be that certain civilians will be denounced by other civilians to RAF policemen as spies or collaborators. In these circumstances, RAF will have to exercise their discretion as to whether the denunciation is genuine or the result of a personal grudge. Whenever possible, suspected civilians should be handed over to Security staff for interrogation.

Some doubt exists as to the legal status of merchant seamen, until further orders, merchant seamen committing offences will be handed over to the nearest RM Police.

RELATIONS WITH THE CIVIL POLICE

The introduction of Provost to the indigenous police will be effected in the first instance through the appropriate CA Public Safety Officer. Thereafter, Provost may deal direct with indigenous police.
CA Public Safety Officer is not under the command of Provost but in cases involving Air Force considerations the instructions of Provost for the control of the civil population will prevail.

TRAFFIC CONTROL

Police will enforce the traffic regulations and will report any persons contravening them regardless of rank.

In the event of a breakdown which causes a road block, the first RAF policeman on the scene will ensure that the nearest recovery section (REME) is informed by the most expeditious means.

Road obstructions caused by broken-down vehicles must be removed instantaneously without regard to damage being caused to the vehicle concerned.

When a recovery vehicle has to be summoned, RAF Police will ensure that it has free passage both to and from the scene of the obstruction.

No vehicles, with the exception of the following, will be permitted to double bank:

(a) Cars flying a commander's flag

(b) Jeeps

(c) Motorcycles

(d) Ambulances

The only vehicles allowed to travel in a direction contrary to a one-way circuit are motor cycles driven by –

(a) Despatch riders on most urgent duties wearing armbands on both arms.

(b) RAF Police. Even in these cases RAF Police on traffic control duty will have an overriding authority to prevent the passage of any vehicles contrary to the one-way route.

MAINTENANCE OF ORDER

RAF Police are responsible for the maintenance of good order outside unit areas.

They will enforce any orders or regulations made by the AOC or any subordinate commanders.

They will adopt an impartial and impersonal attitude to all personnel, whether they are sailors, soldiers, airmen or personnel of any Allied Army.

Looting and pilfering will be suppressed. Under no circumstances should any man be allowed to get away with an offence of this nature because the circumstances are not convenient for affecting an arrest.

RAF Police will endeavour to exercise an intelligent discretion in dealing with minor offences. As a general rule an airman should not be arrested in the early stages of an operation if it can be avoided. Pettiness will be avoided.

ABSENTEES AND DESERTERS

Absentees and deserters of any service will be arrested and dealt with as laid down in Arrests above.

The certificate required under Sec. 163 of the Air Force Act will be completed for soldiers in exactly the same way as for airmen but a decision on this matter will be given in due course where sailors are concerned.

RAF Police must be alert to detect personnel attempting to desert to the UK by means of returning craft. RAF Police will have to be extremely vigilant to prevent this offence which is likely to be attempted frequently.

STRAGGLERS

Air Force stragglers will be questioned by RAF Police who will ascertain whether they are –

(a) Genuinely lost and are trying to return to their unit

(b) Attempting to desert

(c) Shell-shocked and not capable of self-preservation

In the case of (a) and (c), every possible assistance will be given. In the case of (b) the offender will be arrested.

Stragglers of other services or nationality will be handed in to the appropriate police.

CURFEW

A curfew will be imposed. This will be enforced by RAF Police. Detailed instructions will be issued in due course.

BROTHELS AND PROSTITUTION

Detailed instructions for the control of brothels and prostitutes will be issued in due course.

DEFENCE REGULATIONS

The Defence Regulations will apply in a theatre of war overseas in so far as they lay down offences, but any authority which may be derived from these regulations at home (such as the right to demand the production of identity cards) is not effective outside the UK.

GENERAL

No smoking will be permitted on duty.

RAF Police as a whole will at all times maintain a smart, airman-like and clean appearance.

RAF Police will remain at their posts during air raids or bombardments unless specifically relieved by a superior officer or NCO. Advantage may be taken of any adjacent cover.

In the event of an RAF Policeman receiving a direct order from a superior officer or NCO who is not a member of the RAF Police, he will request the officer or NCO to write the order in the policeman's notebook and sign it. The policeman will then render a report.

RAF Police will work harmoniously with police of other services or allies and with the Field Security personnel of the Army Intelligence Corps.

While it isn't actually known for sure, it seems highly probable that the first RAF Police NCO who stepped ashore in Normandy onto Gold Beach, (Between Arromanches and Vers-sur-Mer) on that first day, was either Flight Sergeant Frost or Corporal Appleton. Whoever it was, they landed with a party of assault troops at 10.30 later that morning. They were accompanied on to the beaches by other RAF Police NCOs, some of whom were identified as being Sergeant Horseman and Corporals Hyde, Foad, Eardlye, Peacock and Deighton, all part of No 83 Group RAF Police, under the command of Squadron Leader Mumford, who was the first RAF provost officer ashore. In addition, other units of the RAF Police belonging to 84 Group, under the command of Flight Lieutenant H Baker and 2 Group, commanded by Flight Lieutenant G Swanswick, also landed on the beaches of Normandy later that day to support the invasion.

Once ashore, the RAF Police were initially tasked with moving troops and equipment off the beaches of Normandy and escorting RAF units to their pre-arranged formation points. Later, when the Mulberry harbour was constructed, members of the RAF Police, working closely with the military police, supervised the disembarking troops and their equipment. They also assumed responsibility for the security of stores, munitions and other key points ashore. As and when other ports along the coast were secured, personnel from those RAF police units were used to form Dock Units. As such, RAF Police personnel were deployed at Dieppe and Calais, and thereon after, at the ports at Antwerp, Hamburg and Cuxhaven. To assist them with their task, the traffic sections were equipped with 1300cc Harley Davidson motorcycles and American-issued jeeps. While the jeeps performed well the motorcycles unfortunately didn't because they were too heavy for the rough terrain and war-damaged roads. Escorting RAF unit convoys to liberated airfields was probably their greatest task, having simply been given map references, then instructed to deliver the convoy as quickly and safely as possible. While most of the convoys were delivered safely, there were odd occasions when convoys were stopped and turned back because the airfields hadn't at that time been liberated and secured. In all, the

RAF Police escorted over fifty operational flying units, some twice, to the first nine liberated airfields, within three weeks of landing on French soil. Escorting convoys also had its dangers and some motorcyclists were killed and some were seriously injured as they drove into piano wire, which the Germans had stretched across roads at head height. To overcome the problem, jeeps fitted with cutting devices were subsequently used to lead the convoys.

Later in the month, the Germans started another deadly offensive against Britain, by launching the deadly V1 rocket, mainly at London and the southern counties. After a month of severe resistance in Northern France, the airfield at Carpiquet, just outside Caen, was eventually taken from the Germans and secured for use by the RAF. As the Allied forces continued to establish their positions further inland, the RAF Police fulfilled their usual wide variety of commitments, in conjunction with the Military Police and their American and Canadian counterparts. Vital re-supply routes between the docks and the forward positions were secured, airfields were defended and town patrols were established and maintained. In addition, a large number of Nazi collaborators and Prisoners of War were detained and displaced persons were processed and handed over to the Red Cross. The Allied offensive continued both from the west and the east and by the 15th August, Operation Dragoon, the second Allied invasion force landed on the south coast of France. In the north, the 'Maple Leaf Route' in support of the Canadian Army was fully operational and RAF Police units were escorting essential re-supply convoys from Lille to wherever the front line started and on their return journeys, they provided escorts for enemy prisoners of war. Within a month, the American armoured divisions had started their invasion of Germany and the end of the war in Europe loomed closer.

At the height of the German bombing campaign in Britain, certain key figures at the Air Ministry had asked if it was possible to train dogs to detect the presence of human victims buried under rubble and debris. The question was put to Colonel Baldwin who thought it possible. Consequently, a number of dogs were taken from the Police School to Birmingham, where they took part in such an exercise to find a number of men who had been 'buried' under about four feet of debris. The exercise was highly successful and the dogs located all the victims very effectively. As a result of their success, the dogs were sent to London to help the hard-pressed ARP in locating victims buried during the bombing raids. Colonel Baldwin, impressed by his success, accompanied the dogs, one of whom was Air Dog Gundo, under the control of his handler, Alec Thompson, to London and on their first night in the capital, they were summoned to assist in searching for the victims of a rocket attack, but the conditions at the site were appalling. The quiet ruins in Birmingham, where the trials had been so successful, were a far cry from the chaos and devastation of London at the height of the German V1 rocket attacks. Water and gas mains had burst and earth had been showered up into the air and thrown everywhere. The smell was foul and the overall conditions were about as bad as they could ever be. It seemed hopeless amongst all the chaos and the confusion but Colonel Baldwin and his team went ahead with searching an area which had been declared free of victims. After about fifteen minutes, a handler reported that his dog had made a positive indication. The spot was marked and the dog was taken away. A second dog was brought into the area and it too indicated on the same spot. The search continued and a further two indications were given by the dogs and three bodies were subsequently recovered by the rescue parties. After that occasion, the dogs were regularly used to good effect and over five hundred buried victims were successfully located in the first four months of their use.

In Germany on 20th July, an unsuccessful attempt was made to assassinate Adolf Hitler, by detonating a bomb inside his Rastenburg headquarters during a conference. Although four of his staff officers were killed, Hitler, it seemed, was extremely lucky and received only minor injuries. One of the many men who were later implicated in the plot to kill him was Artur Nebe, one of the key organisers in the Stalag Luft 3 murders. Another important figure also implicated was Field Marshal Erwin Rommel. As a result of their involvement in the conspiracy they were both executed by the Gestapo. In Algiers during the same month, the RAF Police were engaged in something of an unusual search. A plague, known as the 'Black Death' had broken out in the region and lice living on the bodies of rats were thought to have been the source of the problem. In an effort to contain the problem and confirm their theory, the medical authorities required a number of dead rats for examination. As a result, a request for RAF Police assistance was made to Group Captain Richdale, the local Provost Marshal, and soon after, a team was quickly assembled, which successfully carried out a search through the streets of Algiers and recovered a number of suitable specimens.

By the beginning of September 1944, the British forces operating in the Far East had commenced their advance into central Burma, where they continued to oust the Japanese. During the same period, the RAF were operational on the Greek mainland and although the Germans had been ousted, the political situation there became rather complex and deteriorated very quickly. It was due mainly to the confrontation between the communists and anti-communist organisations, and after a while the situation became even more serious when, in December, the communist organisation ELAS, began attacking British Forces stationed in the country. At the time, there was also fierce fighting going on in Athens and at Kifissia, where the RAF had their headquarters and No 44, RAF Police Flight, commanded by Squadron Leader S N Kettle, were stationed. The communist uprising had devastated much of Athens and was beginning to threaten the safety of the RAF Police, both inside and outside the city. As the situation became worse, the RAF Police stationed at Tatoi airfield were ordered to evacuate the base and recover into Kifissia. However, on the 19th December, one of the RAF Police NCOs taking part in the evacuation, Corporal V A Payne, was captured by ELAS. In a subsequent incident report he told of being held for the first day in a house at Kifissia, along with some other prisoners. After that, he and the others had been marched about eight miles to the north of Tatoi, where they had been detained for a few hours in another larger house. It was while he was there that he was searched and relieved of his greatcoat, gloves and his money. After a brief rest, they were again marched a further fifteen miles to the village of Avalon, where they had spent the night. The following day, they were marched yet again another fifteen miles, before spending the night in a church in some unknown village. Their routine of forced marches between various villages continued until 25th January, 1945, when they were suddenly released and handed over to the Red Cross. However, by then Number 44 Flight had also been forced to evacuate their headquarters in order to preserve their own safety.

In December, an Air Ministry order was released regarding the armband or brassard worn by the RAF Police. Originally, the station police had worn an armband with the letters 'RAF SP' on it to signify RAF Service Police. However, the order informed all police NCOs to remove the letter 'S' from the brassard and place the remaining letter 'P' against the letters 'RAF' to form 'RAFP', until newly designed brassards could be issued.

By late 1944, the RAF were keen to recruit additional but suitable candidates to become provost officers. To assist in attracting the right calibre of person, the Provost Marshal released the following information about his branch and the duties undertaken by his officers. It started by explaining the general functions of the Provost Marshal's branch:

> The functions of the Provost Marshal's branch may be roughly classified under three broad headings; the safeguarding of security, the prevention, detection and investigation of crime and the maintenance of discipline. The duties of provost officers, wherever they are, embrace all three responsibilities, as it rarely occurs that an officer is doing a job which concerns one of them and disregards the other two. For some reason, men who imagine that they would willingly serve as security officers, express a marked disinclination to do so as provost officers, though some of them, perhaps feeling themselves attracted by the romantic traditions of detective fiction, would not be averse from trying their hand at criminal investigations. There is no doubt that owing to persistent misconceptions concerning the nature of provost duties, many men fight shy of undertaking them.

> Security work, at one time of the first importance, is now officially recognised to be relatively subsidiary in the United Kingdom. Overseas, of course, and particularly in the actual theatres of war, it continues to take on a high priority. In this country. Now, except for the routine enforcement of security regulations and orders, security work must be considered more as a mere incidental of the provost officer's work. The activities of enemy agents, never dangerously widespread even in the war's early days, are now much reduced, and reports and statistics show that a considerable success has crowned past campaigns to achieve 'security mindedness' amongst RAF personnel. Cloak and dagger

spies are not likely to come our way nowadays, although a certain amount of injudicious talk, frequently by aircrew, discussing in public places matters they should keep to themselves, has to be kept in check.

Crime is prevented merely by the fact that the Provost Marshal's branch is known to exist and to do its job well. Its detection and investigation is a rather more specialist matter, requiring more than ordinary intelligence, common sense, patience, persistence, determination and tact, apart from sufficient knowledge of service and civil law to enable the investigating officer to combine efficient work with the necessary degree of self-protection. Although successful investigations are being conducted daily by officers who had no civilian experience of such work, there is however, a section of the branch called the Special Investigation Branch, which undertakes particularly difficult or delicate cases. Most of the SIB officers have had long experience of the work in civilian life, and have brought many long and painstaking investigations in the RAF to a successful conclusion. In 1943 alone, 1,894 enquiries were conducted by the SIB, ranging from the case of a leading aircraftsman who promoted himself to sergeant and arranged himself a compassionate posting by means of a number of forged documents, to cases of sabotage and murder.

Amongst the crew of an aircraft, in order to make for its efficient operation, discipline must be maintained, albeit somewhat informally. How much more essential, and difficult, is it to maintain discipline amongst more than a million men, in order to make for the efficient operation of the service which they comprise? Discipline has been defined, perhaps a little roughly, as 'doing what you know is right when there is nobody looking'. In other words, discipline has to be taught, rather than hammered into people. If a man doesn't know what's right, then he can't do it. If on the other hand, he knows what's right and doesn't do it, then he can expect to be hauled over the coals, not for the satisfaction of a sadistic policeman, as many seem to think, but for the maintenance of the efficiency of the RAF. The provost officer is not a social cannibal, seeking whom he may devour, he is merely the instrument whereby the rules drawn up by intelligent men for the sensible government of the service, are put into practice. The methods he adopts to do this work are, within reason, his own. However, if he chooses to adopt the bullying and terrorising tactics associated with the 'Red caps' of World War I, methods which have fastened the hard dying stigma upon all police work in the uniformed services, he will probably find himself out of the branch considerably faster than he came into it. The Provost Marshal is firmly opposed to such methods.

The Office of the Provost Marshal, at the Air Ministry, has seven departments or sections through which the work of the branch's hundreds of officers and thousands of NCOs are controlled. The work of the officers lies mostly outside RAF stations, they are not posted into stations but to districts or areas. The UK is divided into eight districts, each under the command of a Deputy Provost Marshal, usually holding the rank of wing commander, but two districts are commanded by group captains. In turn, these districts are divided into areas, under the command of Assistant Provost Marshals of squadron leader rank. Each is assisted by two or three Deputy Assistant Provost Marshals of flight lieutenant rank. These officers, with their detachments of NCOs are responsible for carrying out the aforementioned duties within their own geographical boundaries, and particularly for maintaining a friendly liaison with the commanding officers of the RAF stations within those boundaries by frequent visits, tendering of advice and assistance and being generally helpful over security, criminal and disciplinary matters. Station commanders are encouraged not only to accept such assistance when proffered but to seek it whenever necessary.

So much for the UK. Overseas, provost officers are doing their duty in all theatres of the war, Cairo, Egypt, Palestine, Syria, Iraq, Persia, South Africa, East Africa and Madagascar, Aden, Malta, Italy, Corsica, Sicily, Gibraltar,

Iceland, the Azores, the Bahamas, India, Ceylon, Burma and of course, in France, Holland and Belgium. Shortly their work will begin within Germany itself. The work of the branch in these overseas commands is greatly directed towards policing the native populations and safeguarding the life and property of RAF personnel, as well as towards the protection of government property of which many thousands of pounds worth are recovered monthly by the efforts of provost officers and NCOs.

More necessary to the provost officer than any previous knowledge or experience of police work are his personal qualities. He must be of good appearance and of good address, so that in meeting senior officers of all three services, or civilians holding high office, he will impress instantly as being dependable and efficient. He must be plentifully endowed with tact, must be firm where firmness is called for, must put duty before self, must be capable of making decisions quickly, though never rashly, and will be considerably assisted in his work if he has the sense of humour necessary to enable him to retain a sense of proportion. It should be clearly understood that previous police experience or legal knowledge, though undoubtedly helpful, are not indispensable pre-requisites for an officer coming newly to the branch. The necessary elements of knowledge will be taught him in a six-week course at the RAF Police School, the rest depends on his qualities as a man and his readiness to profit by experience.

Although it is not yet known exactly what the post-war size, shape or organisation of the Provost Marshal's branch will be, it is at any rate clear that its size will be considerably greater than it was before the war, and that its officers will continue to operate not only in the UK, but in all parts of the world. It also seems certain that with the end of the fighting in Europe, a formidable job of police work will remain to be done in Germany, and that officers of the branch will make a considerable contribution to the successful discharging of this task.

No provost officer holds a lower rank than that of flight lieutenant and there are good opportunities for promotion, which is based on seniority and ability,

Finally, the duties of a provost officer consist not only in suppressing the unruly elements which, through selfishness and ignorance, would impair the efficiency of the service as a whole, but guiding and assisting and protecting the law-abiding, vast majority. It is the natural failing of most people to wish to do what they please, some have the sense to know that this is not possible, others have to have its impossibility demonstrated. It is members of this second category who dislike policemen, and a provost officer will feel that he can endure the scorn of the few with equanimity in the knowledge that the execution of his valuable duties secures him the approval of the many.

Although that release of information described a somewhat exciting and challenging position as a provost officer, they were at the time, still mainly being recruited from within the Special Duties and Administration Branch.

By the beginning of January 1945, the establishment of the WAAF Police had reached its peak and in his annual report for 1944, the Provost Marshal commented favourably about the WAAF Police, by saying that they had coped well with the pressure of work during the past year. There were 55 officers and 260 airwomen employed at home and a further officer and 38 airwomen employed in the Middle East. Although they had been established to prevent and detect crime and enforce discipline within the WAAF, they had demonstrated their professionalism further by offering guidance and welfare services to troubled airwomen. The Provost Marshal went on to say that they had indeed served a most useful purpose within the service. So much so, that the Home Office had sponsored, with the blessings of many Chief Constables, the forming of the Women's Auxiliary Police Corps.

By late January, the last German resistance had been broken in Western Europe and the Allied air forces were operating out of some 200 airfields in France and Belgium alone. On the Eastern front, the Russians were also on the move west from the Baltic in the north down to the Danube in the south. Warsaw had been liberated and that was followed shortly after by Budapest. In February, Stalin, Churchill and Roosevelt met once again at Yalta in the Crimea and during the meeting, Stalin was given a free hand in Eastern Europe, in return for his assistance against the Japanese, who were still fighting in the Far East. On 5th March, the first Russian troops liberated Sagan and with it, the Stalag Luft 3, prisoner of war camp. Further west, Allied troops had crossed the Rhine on 26th March and had started their final assault into Germany. Unfortunately, President Roosevelt didn't survive to see the end of the war because he died suddenly on 12th April and was immediately succeeded in post by Harry S Truman. Later in the month, horrified British troops liberated the concentration camp at Belsen and the world quickly learned of the horrific activities inflicted by the Nazis, which had been kept hidden for so long. The full magnitude of what had taken place was further highlighted to the world when American troops also liberated the concentration camps at Buchenwald and Dachau.

As the Allied advance continued, American and Russian troops met up on 24th April, at Torgau, on the River Elbe, which effectively divided Germany into two zones. As Allied troops entered Berlin, on 30th April, Adolf Hitler and Eva Braun committed suicide in his underground bunker. In Italy, Mussolini, the former Italian dictator, his girlfriend and his deputy had been shot dead two days earlier by their fellow countrymen. By the 8th May, 1945, the war with Germany was officially over, bringing an end to hostilities in Europe. Two days later, Wing Commander H R Baker, the Officer Commanding, No 84 Group RAF Police, published his daily routine orders, in which he relayed a message dated, 5th May, 1945, from Field Marshal Montgomery to the Chief of Air Staff, it read:

> At this historic moment, I feel I would like to express to you, the head of the RAF, the deep sense of gratitude that we soldiers owe to you and your splendid force. The mighty weapon of air power has enabled us firstly to win a great victory with fewer casualties than would otherwise be the case, and we are all deeply conscious of these facts. The brave and brilliant work of your gallant pilots and crews and the devotion to duty of the ground staffs has aroused our profound admiration. I would be grateful if you would

convey the gratitude of myself and all those serving under me to all your commanders and all ranks throughout the RAF, and perhaps you would include a special word of greeting and good wishes from myself personally to every officer and man in the RAF.

Although there was much celebration with the victory in Europe, the savage war against the Japanese still continued out in the Far East, where British and Commonwealth troops, along with their allies, were fighting hard, gruelling battles in their attempts to force the Japanese out of Asia. In mid-July, Stalin, Churchill and Truman met in Potsdam, just outside Berlin, where they estimated that the invasion of Japan would result in the loss of over a million and a half Allied troops. However, on the 6th August, in an effort to reduce those predicted Allied losses, the Americans dropped their first atomic bomb on the Japanese city of Hiroshima, killing 80,000 people and completely destroying the city. A second atomic bomb destroyed the city of Nagasaki three days later, killing a further 40,000 people. Although the new weapon brought about mass destruction on a scale never before witnessed, it did bring about the sudden and unconditional surrender of Japan on 14th August, thereby ending the war in the Far East. At the time of the Japanese surrender, a considerable invasion force made up of British, Empire and Commonwealth troops had been assembled along the east coast of India in preparation for Operation Zipper, the offensive to recover Malaya and Singapore. During six years of conflict, the Second World War had claimed the lives of some fifty million people.

As the British started to recover territory in the Far East after the Japanese surrender, the full horror of life as a prisoner of war in the hands of the Japanese became apparent. Changi Prison in Singapore alone was found to contain some 6,000 British and Commonwealth prisoners of war, who had been badly treated and detained under abominable, inhuman conditions. Over the following weeks and months, thousands of starved and emaciated inmates spoke of the terrible ordeals which had been inflicted upon them by their Japanese captors. Adding to the catalogue of horror, more Japanese atrocities were uncovered as further territory was recovered and more prisoners of war and internment camps were liberated in Burma, Indo-China, Siam, Malaya, Sumatra and Java.

By the end of the War, there were some 540 operational airfields scattered around the UK, supported by many more non-flying units and headquarters formations. The size of the RAF Police had reached its peak, with an establishment of 524 commissioned officers and 20,700 non-commissioned officers, making it one of the largest police forces in the country. During the conflict, RAF Police units had been provided to support operations in India, the Far East, the Middle East, West Africa, North Africa, South Africa and throughout Europe. The organisation had certainly proved its value during the war years, having dealt with 687 investigations into acts of sabotage, espionage and subversion, submitted some 15,360 charges in respect of larceny, fraud and forgery, as well as having detained thousands of service absentees and deserters. In addition, considerable assistance had been given to other law enforcement agencies in pursuit of their enquiries and during routine patrols, some 375,281 service personnel had been reported for minor disciplinary and dress transgressions.

Although the war had ended, severe rationing was still restricting the sale and issue of petrol, clothing and food. As such, the RAF Police were certainly kept busy policing a large number of 'de-mob happy' airmen, who, with an eye to getting rich quick, were making off with a wide variety of military equipment and stores and essential commodities, amongst other things. Indeed, with the ending of hostilities, many troops serving in Europe had been released from the forces quite quickly. Unfortunately that wasn't the case elsewhere around the world. Many had only joined up for war service and soon got disgruntled and impatient with the delays in releasing them back into civilian life and the overall problem wasn't helped by the lack of information on the matter. In Iceland there was an RAF Airfield Construction Squadron, situated close to the military camp at Baldur, made up of conscripted civil engineers and artisans who had never really considered themselves to be military men, having joined up to help their country out during the war. However, with the war over, they were eager to return to their former professions, where they felt they could be of more use in rebuilding the damage caused by the years of conflict. Their feelings and frustration at the delay in being repatriated became clear one morning during the usual parade when they refused to dismiss and stood their ground. A senior RAF officer was summoned to the parade square, along with the small detachment of RAF Police from the nearby Daniel Boone Camp. The RAF officer again ordered the men to march off and again they refused to do as they were ordered. The incident was getting serious and bordered on mutiny. The RAF officer then read them the relevant sections from the Air Force Act, which dealt with disobeying orders and mutiny but they remained undeterred. Eventually, they were all persuaded to assemble inside their canteen, where their grievances were all recorded. Normality was eventually resumed, with promises that their grievances would be brought to the attention of higher authorities. That was duly carried out and those overdue for discharge were quickly repatriated. While that action was in hand, the RAF Police were tasked to investigate and identify the ringleaders. However, the investigation was called off soon after when it became clear that it would be impossible and impracticable to prosecute all those involved.

On the other side of the world, similar morale problems were quickly developing with conscripted RAF personnel who were serving in the Far and Middle East. The problem had first started in India at RAF Mauripur where the men, frustrated by the delay in repatriating them home to England, simply went on strike and refused to work. The Indian Army was called in by senior officers and normality was restored after four days of tension. However, signal traffic regarding the incident was widely circulated to other RAF stations within India, Ceylon, Singapore, Burma and the Middle East and over the months which followed, RAF personnel serving there who were just as frustrated with living conditions and the delay in sending them home took similar action and refused to parade. At RAF Drigh Road in India, over a thousand men signed their names to a petition which they sent to the British Prime Minister, asking him to explain the delay in bringing them home. The overall situation was made worse by the fact that there were very few regular commissioned and non-commissioned officers serving in the region with any real military experience and as sixty stations went on strike and the situation threatened to get out of hand, Air Chief Marshal Sir Keith Park, AOC SE Asia, urgently signalled London for instructions. In response, the RAF Police SIB were tasked by the Air Ministry to investigate the mutiny and identify and prosecute the ringleaders. As the investigation quickly got under way, four airmen, considered to be the main ringleaders were identified, arrested and subsequently charged with inciting a mutiny. Norris Cymbalist was arrested at RAF

Kallang in Singapore and, after his trial, was initially sentenced to ten years imprisonment which was later reduced to five years. The charges, however, against Arthur Attwood who was arrested at RAF Drigh Road in India and James Stone and Nicholas Noble, who had been arrested at RAF Cawnpore, also in India, were later withdrawn. Although it had been a very serious situation, the authorities called off the investigation and the repatriation programme, Operation Python was given priority.

On 20th November, the Allies, having rounded up most of the Nazi hierarchy, began to organise their war crimes trial at Nuremberg in Germany. It was time for the world to learn the full catalogue of the horrors inflicted by the Nazi regime during their evil period in power. A United Nations War Crimes Commission had been formed two years earlier after seventeen nations had agreed to investigate and punish all those believed to be responsible for committing war crimes. As part of the elaborate investigation process, the RAF Police SIB were tasked by the Judge Advocate General's Office to investigate the murders of the fifty RAF officers from Stalag Luft 3. The file, containing statements recorded from the survivors and other inmates at the camp was forwarded to the Headquarters of the RAF Provost Marshal, at Princess Gate, Kensington. In due course, Wing Commander Wilfred Bowes, who was the head of the SIB, summoned Flight Lieutenant Francis P McKenna into his office and fully briefed him on the matter. After reading through the detailed statements, McKenna flew out to Germany, together with Flight Sergeant H J Williams, to commence enquiries. Both men were experienced former police officers prior to joining the RAF. McKenna was thirty-eight years old and had been a detective sergeant with the Blackpool Borough Police, while Williams had served with the Police at Portsmouth. Shortly after their arrival in Germany, they set up their office at the RAF Police Headquarters situated at Buckeburg, thirty miles west of Hanover and close to Minden. As the enquiry swiftly produced effective results, the size of the investigation team was increased to cope with the immense quantity of evidence. In December, Wing Commander Bowes was posted and took up his new appointment as head of the SIB, British Air Force of Occupation (BAFO) in Germany. During the same month, McKenna was promoted to the rank of Squadron Leader and Williams to the rank of Warrant Officer. By that stage, the team had been increased in size and was made up of twelve RAF Police SIB NCOs, supported by a further twelve interpreters.

As 1945 came to a close, the RAF Police underwent yet another significant change which involved the authorisation to wear white webbing equipment and the now familiar white tops to their service caps. Since the Great War, the Military Police had been instantly identified by their distinctive red cap covers and white webbing equipment, whilst the RAF Police wore only their identifying brassards. In an effort to overcome that unsatisfactory situation, two provost officers, Group Captain McLaren and Wing Commander Brown, began putting their case forward to the Provost Marshal for a change. It seemed that they were keen on the idea because whilst serving in Brussels, they had authorised RAF Police NCOs under their command to wear white bands around their caps to identify them as RAF Policemen. That had apparently been brought about when the Air Officer Administration at 2TAF, Air Vice-Marshal T Elmhirst, had complained that he was unable to identify the RAF Police in his unit because they looked like all the other RAF trades. After careful consideration of the proposals put to him by McLaren and Brown, the Provost Marshal, along with the Ministry, gave their approval for the change in dress. As a consequence, an order was released which authorised RAF Policemen on duty to start wearing the new accoutrements over their battledress uniforms. Unfortunately, there was a considerable hold up, because that mode of uniform wasn't widely issued at the time. Apparently, only aircrew and other personnel serving in Europe with 2TAF were kitted out with battledress uniforms. However, the new style was gradually adopted over a period of a year or so. Even so, it seems that one of the first RAF Police Flights in the UK to be completely kitted out in the new style was located at RAF Locking, near Weston-super-Mare. With the issue of that new equipment, a new nickname for the RAF Police NCO appeared on the scene, when they became known for the first time as 'snowdrops', because of their white-topped caps.

The scroll depicting the 'Articles of War' issued by King Charles I in 1629.

Group Captain F. G. Stammers OBE, the first dedicated RAF Provost Marshal.

Air Commodore O. W. De Putron CB CBE, the second RAF Provost Marshal.

Lieutenant Colonel J. Y. Baldwin, Chief Training Officer (Dogs) with a course of trainees – circa 1944.

Lieutenant Colonel J. Y. Baldwin, Chief Training Officer (Dogs) and kennel-maids with some of the German Shepherd puppies produced during the experimental breeding phase – circa 1944.

An RAF Police unit specially selected and trained to support the Allied invasion of Europe, is inspected shortly before D-Day – 1944.

Corporal Bob Farebrother RAF Police, attached to 84 Group Tactical Air Force, somewhere on the European mainland shortly after D-Day – 1944.

Squadron Leader F. McKenna OBE, the RAF SIB officer in operational control of the investigation into the murder, by Gestapo, of fifty RAF officers who were recaptured following their great escape from Stalag Luft III – 1944.

The front cover of the RAF Police journal, *The Provost Parade,* which was issued – May 1947.

RAF Police Auxiliary cap badge and shoulder insignia.

Crest of the Royal Air Force Police with the motto *Fiat Justitia* which was authorised by the king in 1950.

'The RAF Police mount an ambush'.

RAF Police admire the haircut.

RAF Police confronted by a smart airman.

Cartoons drawn in 1953 for the *Provost Parade,* by Flight Lieutenant 'Dusty' Miller, an Armament officer stationed at RAF Waddington.

The RAF Police, assisted by the Royal Military Police and an impressive looking camel-mounted guard, escort the Commander in Chief at RAF Khormasker in Aden – circa 1950.

Air Commodore W. I. G. Kerby CBE, the first RAF Provost Marshal to have ever served in every rank in the RAF Police on his way up to the top position – 1956.

Chapter IV
Post-War Years

With the exception of the continuing conflict in Java and the resumption of the civil war in China, the war was over and 1946 saw the RAF not only widely dispersed around the UK, but also overseas in Germany, Gibraltar, Malta, Aden, Egypt, Palestine, Iraq, Cyprus, Kenya, Rhodesia, Libya, Singapore, Malaya, India, Burma, Hong Kong and the Cocos Islands. In order to support that massive global presence, the RAF Police continued to provide their full range of police and security services to their various local commanders. However, like most other trades and branches within the service, the RAF Police were also being subjected to the large-scale post-war re-organisation and demobilisation process being carried out. As a result, the world-wide structure of RAF Police assets was totally re-organised into four separate Wing Headquarters formations, controlled by the Provost Marshal from his department in London. As a consequence, the UK became the Headquarters of No 1 RAF Police Wing, under the command of Group Captain A A Newbury, while the RAF Police stationed in Germany, as part of the BAFO, became the Headquarters of No 2 RAF Police Wing, under the command of Group Captain L G Brown. The Headquarters of No 3 RAF Police Wing, commanded by Group Captain T E H Grove, was located at RAF Ismailia in Egypt and looked after the interests of the RAF Police deployed throughout the Middle East and finally, the Headquarters of No 4 RAF Police Wing, under the command of Group Captain T R Champion, was located in temporary accommodation in the former Sea View Hotel at Katong in Singapore and looked after the interests of the RAF Police deployed throughout the Far East. In line with the restructuring and demobilisation, the overall establishment of the RAF Police by the beginning of January had fallen to around 13,000 personnel.

In the UK, No 1 RAF Police Wing comprised of six reorganised District Headquarters, under the command of a Wing Commander APM. No 1 District was located in Edinburgh, No 2 District was located in Newcastle, No 3 District was located at Upper Parliament Street, Nottingham (it later moved to RAF Syerston), No 4 District was located at Duxford, No 5 District was located in London and finally, No 6 District was located in Bristol. In addition, each of the newly established district headquarters was responsible for looking after the interests of all the stations within their respective areas, as well as providing assistance and professional advice to the unit commanders and their RAF Police Flights.

In January, the Englishman, William Joyce, better known by his broadcasting title 'Lord Haw Haw', who had worked hand in hand with the Germans by broadcasting their propaganda to Great Britain during the war was hanged for treason. Later that month, fifty-one nations came together at the very first meeting of the United Nations General Assembly. In line with the post-war reorganisation, The RAF Police School moved from RAF Weeton in Lancashire to a temporary base at RAF Great Sampford, near Braintree in Essex, and was joined there a little later on by the Headquarters of No 1 Wing RAF Police. In addition, the Ministry of Aircraft Production's Guard Dog School, which had, by then, been fully taken over by the RAF Police and re-titled as the RAF Police Dog Training School, also moved from its cramped accommodation at Woodfold to larger premises at Staverton. Although Colonel Baldwin remained as the Chief Training Officer, the school was commanded for the first time by an RAF provost officer, Flight Lieutenant R D Cooper. Enquiries into the Stalag Luft 3 murders continued quite successfully and a special filing cabinet had been assigned at their headquarters to hold the case investigation files, one for each murdered officer. In addition, arrangements were made through British diplomatic sources for Wing Commander Bowes and a new member to the investigation team, Flight Lieutenant A R Lyon, to pursue their enquiries inside the territories of Czechoslovakia and Poland.

Overseas, the British colonies were unsettled and political tensions began to rise as anti-British demonstrations started to gather pace in both India and Egypt. In addition, the situation in occupied Germany was very poor. The German people were totally demoralised and bewildered, and there were vast numbers of displaced refugees roaming about trying to trace lost relatives, friends, and in many cases, their lives. To make matters worse, a great many of the towns and cities were lying in ruins, and their utilities were all but non-existent. Essential commodities were in short supply and many people were on the point of serious malnutrition. The economy had collapsed and as such, black market trading and corruption were rife and all other types of crime had increased because there was no system of law and order in place to control it. To overcome the situation, the Allied military powers quickly formed a governing body in an effort to bring about some form of stability within the country. Consequently, the Allied military police organisations serving in Germany at the time, became the only trustworthy law-enforcement agencies capable of dealing with the situation surrounding them. As a result, they found themselves working alongside each other and dealing, on a daily basis, with every aspect of serious crime. In order to assist with the training of the RAF Police NCOs, who had been hastily posted into the region, a second RAF Police training school was formed at Buckeburg.

On 18th June, in an effort to overcome post-war manpower shortages within the branch, the first thirty locally recruited RAF Police Auxiliaries reported for duty with the Far East Air Force in Singapore. After successfully completing their training programme at RAF Changi, they were employed on a wide variety of duties throughout the region, assisting their British counterparts to carry out many of their commitments. In comparison, they fulfilled a similar role as that exercised by the 'special constabulary' within the UK. Indeed, they had their own rank structure which started with constable, followed by corporal and then sergeant in the lower ranks and sub-inspector, inspector and assistant superintendent in the officer ranks. Although they wore similar uniform to that of their regular RAF Police counterparts, including the brassard, they were honoured with the privilege of wearing their own distinctive cap badge, while unfortunately, members of the regular branch had to be content with wearing the general issue RAF cap badge. As the system developed, the formation of the Auxiliaries became so successful in the Far East, that the idea of developing a similar unit in the Middle East was seriously considered.

Palestine was administered as a colony by the British, who had gained control of the territory after the defeat and disbanding of the Ottoman Empire at the end of the First World War. In 1917, the

British agreed to establish Palestine as the homeland of the Jewish people, without affecting the rights of the non-Jewish and mainly Arab communities already living in the country. When the plan was originally proposed, the British authorities assumed that only a limited number of Jewish people would be attracted to the prospect of settling in the new state. Unfortunately, the Arab population didn't look upon the formation of a separate Jewish state too favourably, having been promised the territory for themselves, after assisting the British to rid the region of the Turks during the Great War. Even so, the plan went ahead and in 1939, in complete ignorance of the impact that the war in Europe would have on the Jewish population, an announcement released by the British authorities stated that 75,000 Jewish people would be allowed to emigrate to Palestine over the following five years. However, with the end of the hostilities in Europe, many thousands of displaced European Jews attempted to make their way into Palestine to find their promised homeland. The sudden influx caused considerable hostility amongst the Arabs, hostility which the British authorities tried desperately to subdue. The operation to land the Jewish immigrants illegally into Palestine had been well organised and in an effort to prevent it, the Royal Navy and RAF were tasked to identify and stop all ships suspected of carrying them. As a result of the RAF involvement, Jewish terrorist organisations started their violent campaign against the RAF stationed within Palestine.

Consequently, during the first few months of 1946, those terrorist organisations mounted a number of highly organised, and in many cases, successful raids on RAF units, inflicting serious damage and in a number of incidents, casualties. In a large number of cases, they also managed to steal a large quantity of weapons, ammunition and uniforms, which they put to good use. A radar unit on Mount Carmel was attacked and destroyed on the 20th February, and during a highly organised raid six days later, a total of twenty-three aircraft were totally destroyed when three separate airfields were attacked simultaneously. Although the facilities had been guarded, because of demobilisation the RAF presence in the region was seriously undermanned and in no way prepared for such organised terrorist action. In an effort to combat the threat of further terrorist activity from that point on, the RAF Regiment and the RAF Police were deployed to implement both security and defensive countermeasures at all RAF units.

Whilst the increased security measures reduced the number of attacks launched against RAF units, the terrorist action continued throughout the country with many of the bridges connecting Palestine to its neighbours being blown up and destroyed. There were many reported cases of sniping against the British forces and on one Sunday afternoon, a black Mercedes car containing two Jewish men and two Jewish women approached the main gate at RAF Ramleh and reported to the RAF Police on duty that they had been shot at whilst passing through the local Arab village. As both men had received flesh wounds to their heads, they were treated by the RAF medical team before being released. As a result of the continued terrorist operations, countermeasures were mounted by the authorities and some of the terrorists were captured, tried and in a number of cases, sentenced to death. However, in an effort to prevent the executions from taking place, the terrorists started taking Army and RAF hostages. Again the authorities responded by mounting large-scale searches during which over 2,000 suspects were taken into custody and a large amount of weapons and munitions were impounded. During one incident, a number of RAF vehicles were stolen and subsequently used by the terrorists in a raid to steal ammunition and equipment. However, one of the vehicles was discovered abandoned a few days later. The official military paperwork, authorising the use of the vehicle, was still inside and upon checking it, the police were surprised to see that the daily record of movements for the day of the raid had been duly completed by someone. Subsequent enquiries established that the author of the incriminating entry was indeed a terrorist, who had formerly been employed by the British forces as a civilian driver.

In Tel Aviv, on 19th June, Flight Lieutenant T A E Russell, a provost officer serving with the RAF Police District Headquarters, situated in the requisitioned Kate Dans Hotel, left his office, intending to go for lunch at the nearby officers' club. However, as he approached the club in the former Yarkon Hotel, he was alerted by a street vendor, to the presence of two armed men outside the building. He suspected that a crime was taking place and, although unarmed, went over to investigate. However, the civilians who had seen him approaching produced a gun and ushered him into the dining room of the club. Once inside the room, he saw another four, heavily armed civilians holding a large number of guests and staff at gunpoint. The men, he thought, were obviously terrorists but before he could contemplate the scene further, orders were shouted out in Yiddish and four British Army officers were hustled outside and forced into two waiting taxis.

As the taxis sped off, he thought the raid was over and carefully made his way over to a nearby side door to summon assistance. However, as he stepped into the corridor he came face to face with a Sten gun being held by another terrorist. He was ordered out of the building and two other armed men forced him into a third taxi, where his RAF cap was replaced by a panama hat. The taxi containing the three terrorists and their driver quickly sped away from the club and whilst having his wrists and ankles bound, he was informed that he was being taken hostage. After only a few minutes, the taxi stopped in a side street next to a truck and he was bundled out of the car and forced to join another bound and gagged British Army officer, inside a crate on the back of the truck. After the lid had been secured, the truck started up and drove off to some unknown destination. After a while it stopped again and the crate was rather roughly unloaded. When it was opened, they found themselves inside a cellar where they were detained. After the kidnappers had left the cellar, Flight Lieutenant Russell introduced himself and established his fellow hostage to be Captain Rae of the REME. Later that evening, one of the kidnappers, wearing a Ku Klux Klan style hood to disguise himself, told the officers that they were being held pending the confirmation or commutation of the death sentence which had been passed on two Jewish terrorists the previous week. It was obvious to the two officers that the General Officer Commanding Palestine would not back down from any such demands and that as a result, they would probably be killed by the terrorists.

They remained imprisoned inside the cellar for four days and each evening the masked man returned and brought them food and water. During the evening of 23rd June, the masked man arrived again and ordered the guards to remove the ankle chains from the prisoners and they were bundled out of the cellar, blindfolded and pushed into a waiting car. The two officers feared for the worst and mentally prepared themselves for the inevitable. After only a short journey the car stopped, their wrist restraints and blindfolds were removed and they were informed that they had been held captive by the Irgun Zvai Leumi faction. They were each given a one pound note, pushed out of the car and told to walk one hundred steps without looking back. As the car drove off, the two officers looked around and realised that they were close to the officers club in Tel Aviv, from where they had been originally taken hostage.

Although the other hostages were released a few days later, the hostility towards the British presence in Palestine continued and on 22nd July, the terrorist group Irgun Zvai Leumi, headed by Menachem Begin, blew up the King David Hotel, in the centre of Jerusalem, which was being used to house the local British administrative and Military Headquarters complex. The bomb had been delivered to the basement earlier that day, hidden in a number of milk churns. Shortly after midday, the bomb exploded and the blast completely demolished the east wing of the hotel and killed seventeen British personnel and seventy-four civilians, comprising of both Jews and Arabs. In addition, many more were injured. At that time, Corporal R S Edmunds, RAF Police, had been delivering some classified documents to an office on the sixth floor but as the explosion ripped through the building, all the floors within the hotel collapsed. Consequently, Corporal Edmunds fell through to the ground floor along with a considerable amount of debris, and although he survived, he was nevertheless seriously injured and bled badly. However, despite his own personal injuries, he managed to escort two service girls out to safety before losing consciousness for a while. When he did come round again, his first thought was for the important documents which he had been delivering. He managed to recover them and handed them over to a colleague before being taken to hospital for treatment. For his courage and dedication to duty, he was later awarded the British Empire Medal.

The Americans exploded their first peacetime atomic bomb, on the 1st July, during a test on the deserted Bikini Atoll in the Pacific. In Libya, later the same month, three renovated former Italian airfields at El Adem, near Tobruk, Castel Benito (later renamed RAF Idris) near Tripoli and Benina situated near Benghazi, were officially taken over by the RAF as operational airfields.

In Egypt, diplomatic relations with the British were seriously beginning to break down as anti-British demonstrations continued throughout the country. After lengthy political negotiations, Britain agreed to withdraw her military forces from around Alexandria, Cairo and the Nile Delta and relocate them in the narrow strip of land bordering onto the Suez Canal. Concerned with the morale of his men, the Provost Marshal conducted a tour of inspection in the region and was pleased to see for himself that, generally, all was well with his troops. In addition, he was particularly impressed with the use of the two-way radio communications system, which had been installed for use between the RAF Police Headquarters at Ismailia and the patrolling RAF Police vehicles. Being a relatively new innovation, pioneered by the Command Provost Marshal, Group Captain T E H Grove DSO GM, the radios greatly increased the overall efficiency of the RAF Police in the region, as well as providing a similar service to that of the UK 999 system. Military personnel requiring emergency police assistance only had to telephone 'Moascar 519' the control room and a radio car was despatched to assist them soon after. The system was so effective that the 'ever listening' ears of the Police radio system helped to patrol an area stretching from Port Said in the north to the southern RAF Police detachment at El Hamra. Additionally, it had been particularly helpful in co-ordinating the successful search for the body of an airman, who had been murdered and buried somewhere out in the desert. The airman, AC Walker, a Mechanical Transport driver, from No 107 Maintenance Unit, RAF Kasareet, had disappeared one day after dropping off some locally employed Egyptian labourers who had been tasked with spraying an area with DDT, to prevent the spread of malaria. When he failed to collect the labourers at the end of the day, the authorities suspected that he had gone absent without leave and details of him and the vehicle he was driving were circulated to the various service police agencies in the region. As the investigation into his disappearance continued, evidence emerged which suggested that he and his vehicle might have been abducted. As a result, an area in the desert where a witness had last seen his vehicle was searched by a team from No 6 RAF Police Flight SIB comprising of Flight Lieutenant W H Gerrard, Flight Lieutenant J E Churcher, Warrant Officer A J Ballard and Sergeant E Dawson. After following vehicle tracks off the road for approximately two miles into the desert, the team saw a human hand and arm sticking out of the shallow grave where the body of an airman had been buried. A search of the surrounding area was carried out and a side hat and a pay book belonging to the missing airman were discovered, however, the search failed to locate his vehicle. During a subsequent 'on site' *post mortem*, it was established that the body was in fact that of AC Walker who had been killed after being shot in the head by a .38 bullet. His murderer, a Sudanese national, was later arrested in Khartoum by the RAF SIB, after being found in possession of a cigarette case and a tie pin belonging to Walker, which had been given to him by his girlfriend. The assassin was taken back to Egypt and after being found guilty of the murder by an Egyptian Army Court Martial, was sentenced to twenty-five years imprisonment.

In India, during the period between August and November, the uneasiness which had been brewing up in Calcutta for a number of months between the Muslim and Hindu population suddenly flared up and was followed by widespread sectarian violence and rioting throughout the city. The civil unrest had originally started with strikes and demonstrations, but as the situation had quickly deteriorated, mobs of heavily armed rioters, mainly from the appalling slum areas, ran amok in the city, killing and assaulting innocent bystanders who were unfortunate enough to be caught in their path. The number of seriously injured victims began to rise very quickly and the British Military Hospital in the city was used to cope with the chaos. In addition, a large number of private and commercial properties were systematically ransacked, looted and destroyed by the mob. Although the trouble was between the Muslim and Hindu population and not actually aimed towards the British or European population, property belonging to them, together with service and military assets, was nevertheless attacked and during one incident, a military vehicle was caught up in the trouble and was set on fire. Unfortunately, the driver was trapped inside and was burned to death. No 46, RAF Police Flight, stationed in the city, under the command of Squadron Leader D R Halsey-Jones, was fully mobilised and worked very closely with the Military Police and the civilian authorities in an effort to contain and end the violence. At the height of the trouble, in addition to patrolling the city and detaining looters, the RAF Police were also used to provide escorts for the many Red Cross convoys used to evacuate some 30,000 refugees away from the city to places of safety. Although the troubles quickly spread to other regions, it was estimated that some 7,000 people had been killed during the first three days of the rioting which quickly spread throughout Northern India.

In October, the RAF Police School and the Headquarters moved again to a more permanent base at RAF Staverton, where it joined the Dog Training School. The entire station was under the command of

Group Captain Newbury, who as station commander became the first provost officer to hold such an appointment. Although all the elements of the RAF Police formation were for the first time together, the new unit soon experienced severe difficulties in providing adequate accommodation for everyone serving there. As a result, a satellite unit was opened up shortly before Christmas at an old balloon-repair station at Pucklechurch, situated in a rather desolate spot between Yate and Bristol. The new site was to be home for the National Service RAF Police trainees during their initial six-week police training, while Staverton continued with the main bulk of the training programme. The unit was surrounded by open and rather bleak-looking countryside at that time of year and consisted of basic accommodation huts and a large building which was later turned into the Navy, Army and Air Force Institute (NAAFI). The task of preparing the unit for operational use was soon under way with four courses of trainees, supervised by a flight sergeant, three sergeants and fifteen corporal instructors, having the place fully established and ready for habitation and training within four days. Once everything had been completed, 'A' Squadron, under the command of Flight Lieutenant J L Schooling, was chosen to start their initial police training there.

Shortly after moving to Staverton, the Police School, under the direction of Squadron Leader J Coulson, a former Metropolitan Police detective, started to re-organise its training objectives and as a result, a new advanced police training course was developed. However, life at both Staverton and Pucklechurch was not an entirely comfortable one for the trainees, especially during the winter. The trainees were accommodated in wooden Nissen huts which, despite having a pot-bellied stove, described as central heating, were rather cold and draughty places to live. In addition, the newly issued white webbing equipment was largely unpopular amongst the trainees, because the roughly cast brasses had to be smoothed down and highly polished and the webbing itself had to be meticulously cleaned and whitened, ready for the daily inspections. It is interesting to note that during that period, the school had formed their very own and rather impressive looking RAF Police Band under the control of band master Warrant Officer Banks. Another member of the band during that period was Acting Corporal D A Window who was the bass drummer and the top tune played at the time was entitled *Sussex by the Sea*.

By early 1947 the Arabs in Palestine, fearing that the British were going to give in to Jewish demands, started mounting their own terrorist campaign. Accordingly, the overall situation in Palestine became so serious that a decision was taken to evacuate all service families and non-essential British personnel from the country for their own safety. Unfortunately, at the time, there was a considerable local workforce of both Jews and Arabs at every military unit, which supplied the terrorists with an abundant amount of valuable intelligence, to assist them in mounting their operations against the British. As the year went by, a decision was made at Whitehall to leave Palestine and in October, as a result of that decision, all remaining RAF personnel were evacuated to RAF Ramat David, near Haifa, ready for their final withdrawal from the country.

Up until early 1947, every commissioned provost officer serving within the RAF Police had been on loan from the Administrative and Special Duties Branch but with the expansion of the RAF Police organisation, authority was granted on 1st January, 1947, for the establishment of a specialised Provost Branch. As a result, from that date onwards, all serving provost officers were transferred into the newly formed branch.

As the year progressed, things at RAF Staverton were beginning to shape up. During one of the Station Commander's regular meetings in January, a suggestion was proposed that the station should start its own magazine. There had been a similar *Provost Bulletin* news sheet in existence during the war, but it had petered out as hostilities ended. However, the idea of a new magazine was duly approved by Group Captain Newbury, who was keen to have the first edition published as quickly as possible. As a result, he sanctioned a competition within the station to find a suitable name for the new publication and it was subsequently won by Flight Sergeant G Pidgeon, a clerk employed at the school, who won a pound, by coming up with the name '*Provost Parade*. Pilot Officer G Waddington was detailed as the editor and after accumulating enough material, a local printer, Albert E Smith of 87 Stroud Road, Gloucester was engaged to print the magazine, which was duly published in May. The first issue was sold for one shilling and contained forty pages of stories, sporting reports and a few cartoon drawings. The front cover displayed the photograph of an RAF Police Alsatian dog, which had been specially taken for the purpose by Colonel Baldwin. The foreword was written by Group Captain Newbury, who wrote:

> It is with pleasure that I welcome this, the first issue of Staverton's own magazine, a new feature of the station's life and activities which will, I most earnestly hope, be eagerly accepted as a permanent and popular feature.
>
> I feel that not only is it a new facet in our social affairs, it will indeed develop into a record of our station life, which most of us will find of interest not only now, but in years to come, because it is about us all, at work and at play, about our welfare and our entertainment, an expression of our tastes and an exchange of our views.
>
> In welcoming its appearance, as I feel all of you will, we are subject to the critical eye for which the serviceman is famous. This Headquarters has a consistently high standard to maintain in everything it does, and our magazine will, I am confident, prove to be no exception to the rule. With the publication of this first edition, those amongst you who have helped in its production will be able to look upon the finished article with a certain degree of satisfaction, in the midst of the evolution of your plans for subsequent issues of *Provost Parade*.
>
> I wish the venture every possible success, and hope that this new mirror of the station's activities will eventually weld together our many units beyond Staverton into a friendly, co-operative whole, and become an institution of which all our personnel, present and future, will be proud.
>
> As a final word, I would like to point out that so far, the interest created has been rather disappointing. This is, I know, only a temporary setback, and I have every confidence in the publicity provided by the first issue arousing in every one of you a personal interest as great as my own in the continued successful publication of *Provost Parade*.

Unfortunately, the magazine failed to be quite as popular as it was hoped. It was, after all, quite an ambitious venture which quickly ran into financial problems and after the publication of the very first issue, the editorial balance sheet showed a deficit of thirty pounds. As a result, later editions were reduced from the initial forty pages to a mere single typewritten newsletter, which sold for a penny. *Provost Parade*, it seemed, was doomed before it had really started.

On 1st July, after submitting an immense amount of evidence, the trial of the first eighteen defendants, accused of murdering the fifty RAF officers from Stalag Luft 3, finally started in Nuremburg. However, the investigation team, which now comprised five commissioned officers, one Warrant Officer, thirteen NCOs and twelve interpreters, was still deeply involved in gathering the vital evidence needed to implicate many others involved in the murders. It was a huge and difficult investigation being carried out in countries which had been devastated by the war. Indeed, many of those involved had disappeared or had changed their identities to avoid detection by the Allies. However, despite all of those difficulties, the investigation team continued to make very good progress.

During that period, the RAF introduced a newly designed identity card (RAF F1250), to replace the F1250(R), which had been issued to RAF personnel in 1944. The new card, designed by Mr A J Creedy, an ex-Naval officer and head of the Air Ministry department known as PM5, was compact, strong and for the first time, displayed a photograph of the person to whom it had been issued. In addition, a corresponding form, containing all the holder's details and a duplicate photograph, was filed at PM5 for reference. The new identity card was recognised throughout the empire as an official document and, as such, the holder did not require a passport to travel on duty.

On 15th August, as the sectarian violence continued to rage, India was finally granted her independence from Great Britain and the independent Muslim state of Pakistan was also formed on former Indian territory. Although the RAF had maintained a presence in the region since 1918, the event meant the subsequent withdrawal of all British forces stationed within the country. That unfortunately included the large RAF Police contingent, under the command of Group Captain G A Perkins, the Command Provost Marshal, assisted by Wing Commander J S Mason, who had provided provost and security support to the local commanders stationed around the vast country. With the close down and withdrawal, Group Captain Perkins transferred with his headquarters from Kandy in Ceylon to Singapore, leaving Wing Commander Mason to assume the responsibilities of Command Provost Marshal in Delhi. Many were sad to leave India, which had offered them not only a very comfortable life style over the years but a busy and interesting insight into professional police work under very difficult circumstances. Indeed, one notable RAF Police investigation carried out in India just prior to independence involved a somewhat persuasive RAF Wing Commander, who became friendly with a rather wealthy rajah who a had an eye for further investment. So when the time was right the Wing Commander persuaded the rajah that he was authorised to sell off the mineral rights to a large area of land in the Shan states. When the rajah showed interest in the venture, worth a small fortune, the Wing Commander produced a contract, authorised by the signature of the Viceroy of India, Lord Louis Mountbatten, but the rajah became suspicious and reported the proposal. As a result, the RAF Police took on the investigation and quickly established the contract and the signature to be a forgery. Consequently, the Wing Commander was successfully convicted by a court martial. He was subsequently discharged from the service and in addition, was sentenced to a long term of imprisonment for his efforts.

Since its creation the year before, the *Provost Parade* had been struggling to stay alive. It had been reduced to a single page news sheet, being produced and circulated each month. It seemed that it was on the verge of collapsing unless something was urgently done to save it. Consequently, a determined effort was made to publish it once again in its original magazine format and that was done by enlisting the help of a young journalist by the name of Keith McDowall, who at the time, was undergoing his national service at Staverton as an RAF Police NCO. He took over from Geoffrey Waddington as the editor and with the assistance of a commercial artist and another national service policeman, Robin Clarke, and Colonel Baldwin, they managed to revive the magazine. In fact, so successful were their efforts that the magazine went on from being merely a station magazine to becoming the official RAF Police journal with a world-wide circulation. Later, as an extra service, readers of the journal could have each year's supply of the magazine professionally bound and covered for a mere six shillings.

On 14th May, amid continuing terrorist violence, Israel was proclaimed as an independent Jewish state and the RAF finally withdrew from the territory a month later, leaving RAF Ramat David to its fate. Between the period 1946 - 1948, some 65,307 illegal

Jewish immigrants had either been turned away from, or, interned within Palestine. RAF casualties during the final operation between October 1947 and their withdrawal were light compared to those suffered by the Army. Even so, fifteen personnel were killed, seven were injured and one was missing, believed killed.

In early June, the Three Counties Agricultural Show was held on the Staverton airfield, and attended by a huge audience. One of the biggest and most popular attractions of the day turned out to be the parade of some forty smartly turned out RAF Police dog handlers and their dogs, lead by Flight Lieutenant Cooper, the officer in charge of the RAF Police Dog School. In addition, the parade was accompanied by suitable music for the occasion, supplied courtesy of the RAF Police Band. It turned out to be a splendid day for everyone and marked the start of things to come for RAF Police Dog participation in major public events.

As the year progressed, the RAF quickly settled into their cramped accommodation in the hastily constructed units along the Egyptian Suez Canal Zone. On 26th June, at RAF Ismailia, Flight Sergeant L H McNeil, RAF Police, was on duty as the senior NCO in charge of the shift at the Headquarters of No 3 RAF Police Wing. During the course of the day, he received a request to collect some equipment from the military airfield at Fayid, some twenty miles away to the south. The driver detailed for the task reported sick so Flight Sergeant McNeil volunteered to do the run himself. As a result, he left Ismailia in a jeep, just after lunch but when he failed to arrive at his destination by early evening, his unit became concerned and a full search was organised to locate him.

The search continued for two days, until finally, his body was discovered, lying face down in the sand, not far from Fayid. There was no trace of his jeep, which had been stolen and he had died from gunshot wounds to his chest and stomach. He was later buried with full military honours at the military cemetery in Fayid. His killers, three Arabs, were arrested a few months later after committing an armed robbery and during the subsequent interrogation, they also confessed to his murder. After being convicted, they all received long prison sentences.

In occupied Germany, the relationship between the eastern and western alliance was beginning to show signs of tension. The USSR had been making a number of unreasonable demands and the West was in no mood to submit to them. As the overall situation deteriorated in June, Russia further increased her pressure on the west by throwing a cordon around West Berlin and cutting it off from the outside world. Obviously, that action prevented anything entering or leaving the city but the western Allies didn't want to storm and relieve the city in fear of starting another war. So, in an effort to break the Berlin Blockade, the western Allies mounted Operation Planefare, and the Berlin airlift started. During the operation, all the RAF units in Germany were used as staging posts for the mountain of food and medical supplies required to support the city's population under siege.

Back in the UK, the RAF Police School and the Headquarters had hardly settled down at RAF Staverton, when in June, they were on the move once again, leaving the Dog Training School to remain at Staverton. On that occasion however, the move was only up the road to RAF Pershore in the Vale of Evesham. Pershore however, proved to be an even less popular base than Staverton had been. Again, there was poor accommodation and the station was extremely isolated, making visits off camp very expensive. However, everyone quickly settled in to the new accommodation and in August, the Secretary for Air, Mr Arthur Henderson, flew into the unit to carry out a formal inspection. When he left later the same day, he was suitably impressed by what he had seen. In November, the RAF Police basic training course was again re-structured and extended from six to nine weeks and designed so as not to differentiate between the training undertaken by regular or national servicemen. In addition, RAF Police recruits, after the successful completion of their basic training were sent out onto RAF stations where they received six months practical experience before being recalled for assessment and a decision as to whether they should continue to be employed on station police duties, or be selected for provost duties.

The war had been over for three years and most of the men who had been conscripted for war duty had returned to their pre-war lives and occupations. However, young men were still being called up by the forces to complete their obligatory two years national service. Some of those conscripts found the life offered by the forces quite challenging and in some cases, re-engaged for regular service. Others, whilst not enjoying it, simply did their duty as quickly and as smoothly as time would allow before returning to their normal lives. Others however, totally resented being called up and continually found themselves getting into various degrees of trouble and as a result often came to the notice of the service authorities or indeed the RAF Police. Invariably, that class of national serviceman was openly hostile towards the RAF Police for enforcing the strict rules of service discipline and upholding what they deemed to be extremely oppressive and petty laws and regulations.

In September, the RAF Police, SIB, were called in to investigate the cause of three suspicious fires which had occurred at an RAF station in East Anglia. The first fire had occurred on a Saturday evening in a small office within the Station Headquarters, where a number of secret documents were secured. Unfortunately, the fire completely gutted the office and of course, the documents were also destroyed. While the cause of the fire was about to be investigated by a unit board of enquiry, a second fire broke out the following evening in a hangar containing a mosquito aircraft, fitted with the latest radar equipment. As a result, the aircraft was destroyed and the hangar was extensively damaged, despite the efforts of the fire fighters. For some strange reason, even after the second incident, arson was not suspected until a third fire was discovered the following morning in the Navigation Section. Fortunately, on that occasion, the damage was only slight but it was enough for the Station Commander to seek the immediate assistance of his local SIB unit.

During the early stages of the investigation, it became clear that the fires had in fact been started deliberately. Traces of an accelerant were found at the scene of all three incidents and the motive seemed to be sabotage. All personnel serving at the station were interviewed and as a result, the investigators learned of an another airman, who for some strange reason kept a bottle of petrol and a bottle of dope in his locker. Further enquiries revealed that the suspect had an unusual interest in fires and a fixation for lighting matches and throwing them about while they were still alight. It also appeared that the suspect had told another airman about the fire in the Navigation Section, some forty-five minutes before it had actually been discovered.

As a consequence, the suspect was duly arrested and during a search of his kit, the containers of petrol and dope were discovered and impounded, along with his diary, which described in detail how he had started the fires. During a subsequent interview, the man admitted starting the fires, simply because his call-up for national service in the RAF had interrupted his studies. As such, he hated the

RAF and wanted to be discharged from the service. His scheme actually worked because he was eventually discharged, but only after serving two years hard labour in the military prison.

On 11th October, the second trial, involving a number of defendants implicated in the murder of the fifty RAF officers from Stalag Luft 3, took place. By that stage, many of the major war criminals had been dealt with by the authorities and although the murder investigation continued to trace a number of other people involved in the incident, it seemed unlikely, at that stage, that the Allies would hold any further war crime trials.

During December, the last remaining members of the RAF, including the RAF Police, finally left India. However, Flight Lieutenant R C Forrester, a DAPM, remained in the region as a provost liaison officer and was subsequently attached to the Royal Pakistani Air Force in Karachi. He was joined by another RAF Policeman, Sergeant D Hullah, who had been sent from New Dehli to assist him with the task of training personnel from the newly formed Royal Pakistani Air Force Police, at their training school near Karachi. The training programme was based largely on the one being used by the RAF Police and proved to be very successful. As a consequence of their hard work and dedication, three officers and sixty airmen successfully completed their very first course. The venture turned out to be so successful that the Pakistani Government asked for the contract of assistance to continue and as a result, Flight Lieutenant Forrester's secondment to the Royal Pakistani Air Force was extended. In India however, the civil disorder and violence continued and it was estimated that some 600,000 people had been killed throughout the country and many thousands more injured since independence had been granted.

In 1948, in an effort to promote all-round efficiency within the branch, the Provost Marshal introduced an annual competition between all RAF Police Flights stationed within Europe. He envisaged that the competition would create a spirit of enthusiasm and rivalry, as each flight sought to become the overall winners of the competition. A suitable reward, which became known as the 'de Putron Trophy' was commissioned by the Provost Marshal and later presented to the winners during a formal ceremony to mark the occasion. The winning flight became the one achieving the maximum marks for overall operational efficiency, which included smartness, professionalism, drill, administration, personal kit and the state of both working and living accommodation used by the flight concerned.

In gratitude for their assistance during the war, the British Government had made a pledge to the people of America to return, when requested, the bodies of every single American serviceman who had been killed in action during the conflict. Given the number of American casualties sustained during the war, it was quite an undertaking, which was finally completed in January 1949. During the occasion, five NCOs from No 128 RAF Police Flight, stationed at Hooton Park in Cheshire, undertook the special task of supervising the loading of the last three hundred coffins, as they were loaded aboard the USS *Atenas* at Liverpool Docks, to begin their final journey home to their waiting relatives. While it was a sad and emotional experience for the NCOs concerned, they maintained their high levels of professionalism, together with an air of dignity and respect throughout the task.

In the New Year's Honours of 1948, Squadron Leader F P McKenna, one of the men responsible for bringing to justice those involved in the Stalag Luft 3 murders, was appointed the OBE by His Majesty King George VI, in gratitude for his outstanding work during the complicated and heart-rending investigation. Shortly after his award, Squadron Leader McKenna left the RAF and resumed his career with the Blackpool Borough Police in order to qualify for his civilian police pension. During the early part of the year, no doubt inspired by the large number of former RAF Police personnel, who had already served during the branch's brief but colourful existence, the Ex-RAF Provost Association was formed by a number of former provost officers in Edinburgh.

The Berlin blockade and the deterioration of relations with the Soviet Union had spurred the United States of America, Great Britain, France and other countries within western Europe to create a counter balance to the threat from the Soviet aggression. As a result of their combined political and military efforts, twelve nations signed the North Atlantic Treaty on the 4th April, and in so doing, formed the western alliance which became known as the North Atlantic Treaty Organisation (NATO). Eight days later, the Berlin Blockade, which had been in force for 322 days, was called off by the Russians. However, the airlift continued after that date in an effort to build up the stock of supplies in the western sector of the city. While the efforts of the aircrews involved in the operation were later highly praised, they could not have carried out the task without the support and efforts of all the personnel working on the ground, which of course, included the RAF Police. Throughout the entire operation, approximately one hundred members of the RAF Police, from No 2 RAF Police Wing (Germany), had been employed on security and airport control duties at all the RAF bases within Germany, including RAF Gatow, one of the Berlin airfields used in the airlift. At that one airfield alone, the task was immense, with an aircraft landing and taking off every three minutes, twenty-four hours a day, every day. The aircraft landing at Gatow and the other airfields in West Berlin, brought in the urgently needed supplies to sustain the population, while the outgoing aircraft took manufactured goods and people out of the city. Throughout the entire period, various tasks were undertaken by the RAF Police at those airfields and involved guarding the huge quantity of relief supplies, preventing them from being stolen and sold on the 'black market', which was thriving within the western half of the city. In addition, they were responsible for controlling passengers boarding the aircraft and ensuring that they carried no stowaways. Obviously, with the increased volume of vehicles entering, leaving and operating within the units, they were also heavily involved in traffic control and control of entry duties.

Unfortunately, over that period, all the hard work and the gallant efforts of the aircrew involved in the airlift was overshadowed by a handful of renegades, who were only interested in making a profit out of the situation. Their damaging activities were disclosed during a discussion between the station commander at RAF Gatow and his Commander-in-Chief, when facts emerged that suggested that some of the RAF aircrew had been bringing into Berlin private supplies of food and cosmetics, which they were exchanging for cameras, fur coats and jewellery. The Commander-in-Chief had been so alarmed by what he heard that he ordered the RAF Police to investigate and put a stop to the practice as quickly as possible. As a result, all subsequent inbound and outbound aircraft were searched for such contraband within the strict turnaround period allotted to the aircraft.

Although instructional courses had been held at the RAF Police School for a number of years, teaching RAF Police NCOs the necessary skills of driving motor vehicles, motorcycle training courses had been discontinued after the war. However, during May they were once again introduced into the training programme, with members of Initial Qualifying Police Course 495 being the first students to successfully complete the full training.

In the Far East, a state of emergency was declared in Malaya on 18th June, following a number of serious terrorist attacks against Police stations and European-owned rubber plantations throughout the country. Up until that point, the guerrilla attacks had resulted in the murder of a number of European police officers and plantation managers and the destruction of a considerable number of plantations. Although security measures within the country had been tightened, the Chinese communist 'bandits' of the MPABA (Malay Peoples Anti-British Army), backed up with logistical support from the Min Yuen, had mobilised in the jungles and had threatened to carry out further attacks in an effort to destabilise the country by disrupting the economy. As the situation developed and the country became more unstable RAF units were moved from the mainland and on to the island of Singapore in an effort to improve their security situation.

By now, the training of all RAF Police dogs and their handlers was firmly under the control of the branch, with Colonel Baldwin still in charge of all operational training. His original intention had been to train and use only the German Shepherd breed for the task but problems arose when the supply of suitable public donations failed to maintain the requirements of the service. In an effort to overcome the problem, a breeding programme was started but that too proved to be problematic. The programme was not cost-effective because the dogs had to be looked after for about fifteen months until they were old enough to be trained. Even at that point, many dogs were rejected because they didn't have the right qualities in responding to the training programme. As a result, the experimental breeding programme was abandoned and other suitable breeds, offered by the public, were tried out by the service. The overall situation, however, took a turn for the best when, in June, at the Olympia stadium in London, the newly formed RAF Police Dog Demonstration Team, using their German Shepherds, appeared for the very first time at the Royal Tournament. The commentary throughout their performance was delivered by Group Captain Richdale, who described the RAF Police German Shepherds as "£2,500 worth of high-explosive dog". The public loved them and as such, they were an instant success, proving to be a first-rate publicity boost for the branch. Both *The*

Daily Telegraph and *The Manchester Guardian* newspapers reported that "The RAF Police Dog Demonstration Team, under the command of Flight Lieutenant Cooper, stole the whole show." After their first and highly successful public appearance, there were no further problems in obtaining suitable gift dogs from the general public who, it seemed was only too willing to donate German Shepherds to the RAF Police.

On the outskirts of Bristol, during the early hours of 3rd September, a newly developed passenger aircraft, called the Brabazon, was, for the first time, towed out from a large hangar at RAF Filton. The new aircraft, which was equal in length to six double-decker London buses, drew a considerable amount of interest from the general public, who had lined the perimeter fences of the unit, in the hope of catching a glimpse of it. In fact, so great was their interest and their numbers, that most of No 6 RAF Police District were tasked to assist the station police in preserving the security of the unit. Although the aircraft was only conducting engine tests and was soon safely back inside the hangar, a large number of the public remained at the perimeter fences all day just in case the aircraft was brought out again. However, the real event took place the following day, when the aircraft took off on its short but successful maiden flight. The crowds were out in abundance, accompanied by a considerable number of reporters and cameramen from the media. Once again, the RAF Police were kept extremely busy in maintaining the security of the unit and preventing the more enthusiastic spectators from running amok in their keenness to get closer to the runway and of course the aircraft.

During the same period, the RAF Police Dog Training School received an urgent request for assistance from the Gloucestershire Constabulary. It seemed that a dangerous prisoner, convicted of armed robbery, had escaped from Leyhill Prison. The urgency to recapture him increased when the police received a report that three people, living on a lonely farm in the area, had been brutally attacked and robbed by a man answering the prisoner's description. In response to the request, five dogs and their handlers, under the control of Colonel Baldwin, were sent to assist in searching the area where the prisoner was believed to be hiding. Shortly after the search commenced, the dogs gave a positive indication that someone was hiding in a field of kale. As the dog teams went into the field to check it, a man, answering the description of the prisoner broke cover and tried to run off. He was challenged, and when he refused to stop, a dog was released and the man was apprehended and swiftly arrested. The search for, and capture of the convict had been witnessed by Mr A H Carter, the Assistant Chief Constable of the force, who it seemed was most impressed by the professionalism of the dog teams involved and of course, the speed with which the man had been recaptured.

On the 1st October, Peking announced the ending of the civil war between the Nationalist and Communist factions. The Nationalists had suffered their final defeat at Mukden in Manchuria, when 300,000 Nationalist troops had surrendered to the Communists. During the official celebrations, their first communist chairman, Mao Tse-tung, declared to the world the formation of the People's Republic of China. A sigh of relief came to the British community in Hong Kong, who had been watching the Chinese civil war as it unfolded, wondering whether China would invade the colony. The declaration from Mao Tse-tung might have eased the minds of those living in Hong Kong, but it did little to stem the flood of the Nationalist Chinese refugees, who daily crossed the border into the safety of Hong Kong. No 3 RAF Police District Headquarters, commanded by Squadron Leader D R Halsey-Jones was at the time situated at Kai Tak airport in Kowloon. His men employed at the airport's Travel Control Section continued to be kept extremely busy helping to process the influx of refugees as well as maintaining their normal patrols throughout the crowded, bustling colony.

In occupied Germany, a team of eighteen RAF Police NCOs, from their headquarters at Buckeburg, were formed into a flight in order to provide escorts and protection for the British High Commissioner for Germany, General Sir Brian Robertson, the former military governor. The team comprising of a flight sergeant, a sergeant, eleven corporals and five dog handlers had all been specially selected, trained and equipped to carry out a wide range of duties connected with the task. In addition to guarding his official residence and escorting him around Germany, the team was responsible for escorting and protecting his official visitors. Up until that point, the list of VIPs provided with that service had included the Right Honourable Ernest Bevan, the Foreign Secretary, Viscount Montgomery, Lord Henderson and Lord Tedder, as well as the French and American Governors. In addition to wearing their normal RAF Police accoutrements, members of the elite team were also authorised to wear the British Army on the Rhine (BAOR) shield emblem on the right arm of their tunics, just above their badges of rank.

Members of the RAF Police had been serving with the RAF on the tiny island of Malta since before the start of the second world war and had remained on the Island during the German siege and bombardment which had almost reduced the entire island to rubble. After hostilities ended, they were kept busy carrying out their routine patrols of the island as well as providing the necessary security support for the small number of units based there. The Headquarters of No 14, Flight RAF Police, under the control of No 3 Wing Ismailia, was located in the capital of Valetta, while the main base at RAF Luqa was situated approximately four miles outside the capital. In addition to being used by the RAF, the airfield at Luqa was also used by the Maltese authorities as their main civil airport and as such, was used by a number of commercial airlines. The airfield had been completely destroyed during the war by German bombing raids, but as soon as the war had ended it was quickly repaired and once again became operational. RAF Safi, a much smaller unit, was situated a few miles from Luqa and was home to No 137 and 397 Maintenance Units, while RAF Siggiewi supported the RAF signals unit.

In Southern Rhodesia, No 9 RAF Police District Headquarters, under the command of Flight Lieutenant A Bullen, was situated at RAF Kumalo. Southern Rhodesia, though providing little in the way of operational history, was interesting from the organisational point of view. Its brief history dated back to 1940, when the nucleus of the Rhodesian Air Training Group had been formed. Initially, Sergeant W Pender had been the sole RAF Police representative there and became responsible for establishing and maintaining a number of provost and security commitments within the group. After a period, he was joined by other RAF Police personnel, who then went on to form the basis of an RAF Police Flight. In May 1940, having had time to assess the RAF Police at work, the Southern Rhodesian Government decided to form their own Military Police Force and Sergeant Pender was asked to assist in setting it up. It was a challenging task, but from the nucleus of just four NCOs, all former members of the British South Africa Police Force, he succeeded in building up a force consisting of a Colonel who held the appointment of Provost Marshal, eight Assistant Provost Marshals and 140 Provost

NCOs. At the completion of the task, the newly formed Military Police Force took over responsibility for policing outside the RAF stations, leaving the RAF Police to police inside their own units. Sergeant Pender was subsequently commissioned whilst in Rhodesia, and as a Flight Lieutenant, assumed the duties of RAF Assistant Provost Marshal. The district title 'No 9' unfortunately didn't relate to any particular formation or wing at that time. It seemed that during the war it had simply been designated as No 9 District by the then Headquarters of the Middle East Air Force (MEAF), and during subsequent post-war reorganisations had been overlooked. Although it was a relatively small unit in relation to other district headquarters around the world, it nevertheless had an impressive area of responsibility at the height of its existence, which included all of Rhodesia and the Union of South Africa. In addition to the staff employed at the headquarters, RAF Police were also stationed at RAF Heany, RAF Bulawayo and RAF Thornhill. In keeping with the best traditions of the service, an excellent relationship was maintained with their civilian counterparts in the British South Africa Police and their colleagues in the Military Police. That excellent working relationship was clearly demonstrated earlier in the year when two RAF Police NCOs on patrol stopped to check a seemingly abandoned taxi on a road, sixteen miles outside the capital, Salisbury. After finding the keys in a ditch close by, the NCOs discovered the body of a man in the boot. The civilian police were alerted and a short time later, a European was arrested ninety miles away trying to flee the country. He was subsequently charged with murdering the taxi driver.

With the coming of 1950, Doctor Klaus Fuchs, a German born physicist, was sentenced to fourteen years imprisonment by Lord Justice Goddard at the Old Bailey after being found guilty of giving away nuclear secrets to the Russians between 1943 and 1946. Prior to being employed at the Harwell Atomic Energy Research Establishment, he had helped the Americans to develop their atomic bomb.

In response to a request from the Commissioner of Police for the Federation of Malaya, for RAF Police assistance, two RAF Police dog handlers, Corporals Stapleton and Thackray, were sent out to Malaya to the Federation Police Training School in Kuala Lumpur, where they successfully organised and assisted in the training of a number of civil police dogs. The training programme was a very successful venture and the dogs were subsequently used to effect, in numerous police operations against bandits in the difficult jungle territories.

In Korea on 25th June, North Korean troops crossed the 38th parallel and invaded South Korea in support of their government's claim of sovereignty over all the territory in the Korean peninsular. As a result, the matter was brought before the United Nation's Security Council, who deemed the invasion to be unlawful. As a consequence, the United States of America, Great Britain and a number of other British Commonwealth countries assembled troops and went to war once again, in the defence of South Korea.

On 7th July, their Majesties the King and Queen, together with Princess Margaret and the Duchess of Kent, attended the opening day of the first post war RAF Display, which was held over two days at RAF Farnborough and attended by some 80,000 members of the public. During the highly successful show, some 5,400 members of the RAF were on duty at the unit, with 400 of them being RAF Police personnel carrying out a wide spectrum of police and security commitments in support of the event. In addition, the RAF Police Dog Demonstration Team also appeared during the display to entertain the crowds.

In Egypt later that month, Flight Lieutenant E R Rawlings, a DAPM serving with No 3 RAF Police Wing at Ismailia, was asked by the War Graves Commission to assist with the search for the lost grave of a Canadian pilot. Apparently, the pilot, Flight Sergeant A M Rowe, had been killed in August 1942 when his plane had been shot down near the El Ballah airfield, somewhere between Port Said and Ismailia. The pilot had been buried close to the crash site soon after by tribesmen, but the location of the grave could not be found. Although an unusual request, Flight Lieutenant Rawlings readily accepted it and enlisted the help of Sergeant G Illachevitch RAF Police and a local bedouin, Sheikh Selim, to guide the search team into the desert. Eventually, with the help of their guide, the team finally located the crash site and soon after, the grave was located and the remains of the pilot's body were recovered and taken back to Ismailia, where he was finally laid to rest in the Military War Cemetery. Identification of the body had been easily established because the pilot's leather wallet, containing his driving licence, was found with the body.

By that stage, the RAF Police both at home and overseas were carrying out security vetting enquiries in relation to civilians seeking employment at RAF units. Normally, the procedures were fairly straightforward. However, in Hong Kong, having special regard to the political situation over the border in China, they were beginning to experience a number of problems. A large influx of refugees had crossed into Hong Kong from China and many came looking for work with the British forces and in the Royal Naval Dockyard. Identification of the Chinese population was, at the best of times, extremely difficult to validate. Their Chinese names were strange to Western eyes, very difficult to anglicise and to complicate the problem further, many of them changed their names frequently. A large number of instances emerged which revealed that personnel who had been dismissed from employment with one of the service organisations had easily obtained employment with another, which had been totally unaware that they were undesirable. In an effort to overcome the problem, a decision was reached by the three services to form a joint security vetting system within the colony.

Subsequently, with the agreement of the three heads of service security, an organisation was formed in September, under the chairmanship of Superintendent R J Wigginton of the Royal Naval Dockyard Police. The new formation, entitled The Inter-Services Identification Bureau (ISIB) was accommodated in new headquarters within the Royal Naval Dockyard, and was staffed by members of the three services. Accordingly, a number of RAF Police NCOs were assigned to the organisation and one of the first was Corporal P Thornton. In an effort to overcome the problems of positively identifying an individual employee, they were photographed and their fingerprints were recorded on a specially designed form, which was then classified and filed in the ISIB master index. Within a short space of time, the system appeared to be a very effective way of vetting civilian employees and preventing undesirable persons from gaining employment within the three services. In addition, it proved to be a most useful source of information to the Hong Kong civilian police, who maintained a close liaison with the ISIB and the service police in the colony.

The majority of service personnel who arrived on the island of Singapore, located at the southern tip of the Malay Peninsula, did so by the troopships which took approximately twenty-eight days to complete the journey from the United Kingdom. The city itself was, as it is today, a teeming mass of activity and home to a million people, with twenty per cent of the population of Chinese origin. The other eighty per cent was made up of Malaysians, Indians, Pakistanis, Eurasians, and Europeans.

On 11th December, a large crowd had gathered around the Supreme Court Building in Singapore where a controversial case was being heard regarding the proposed marriage of Maria Hertogh, a half-caste Catholic to a Malaysian of the Muslim faith. The case had attracted such wide attention that the civilian police riot squads had been placed on standby to deal with any expected outbreaks of trouble. However, even as the crowd gathered at the court, the majority of the population of Singapore went about their normal routine, not realising that before the day would be through, the city would be the scene of bloody and brutal rioting by a large percentage of the Muslim population.

As far as the RAF Police stationed within the city were concerned, it was just a normal day and from their city centre district headquarters in Waterloo Street, the routine daily commitments were being carried out. However, during the early afternoon, staff at the headquarters received a telephone call from a warrant officer, at Changi, saying that an RAF despatch rider had been attacked and abducted by an angry mob on Beach Road. A number of patrols were despatched to investigate, but as the trouble developed, and the situation became serious, all RAF Police personnel were recalled, armed and placed on duty. At first the RAF Police, like their military counterparts, were not really aware of what was happening. However, as detailed reports came into the headquarters, it soon became clear that the rioters were mainly Muslim and that they were in control of large sections of the city. Unfortunately, many European and Eurasian residents and visitors who happened to be in their way were brutally attacked and many were killed.

Reports flooded in of RAF and government vehicles being attacked and their occupants, irrespective of sex, being assaulted and robbed. Police roadblocks were set up on the roads leading into the troubled areas and all non-service Europeans and Eurasians were directed to clear routes out of the area or to the safety of nearby police stations. Military vehicles were stopped and marshalled into convoys, which were then escorted to safety by RAF Police, RAF Regiment and

Military Police patrols. However, it soon became clear that a large number of military vehicles had fallen victim to the rioters.

Married service families living in the affected areas were in danger of being attacked and a urgent operation began to identify and evacuate them as quickly as possible. Many servicemen and their families sought refuge in the Police Headquarters building and as more and more military vehicles converged there, police escorts were quickly arranged to take them back to the safety of military units outside the city. By then, other families had sought refuge in the Union Jack Services Club. However, the rioters converged on it and it was only the speedy reaction of the RAF and Military Police which prevented bloodshed. As the rioters were kept at bay with Sten guns, the families were quickly evacuated to safety.

At midday on 12th December, the situation was still out of control and many local civilian police officers had begun to mutiny, leaving their senior British officers unable to cope. An RAF Police patrol, on duty at the Union Jack Club, received a report that three Europeans were being attacked by a mob nearby. The patrol responded and using their vehicle, charged at the mob, who thankfully released their prisoners. However, the mob remained defiant and refused to disperse. Suddenly, shots were heard and the patrol came under fire. The patrol returned fire, shooting over the heads of the crowd who quickly ran off. Although that was the first incident which called for the RAF Police to open fire, it was by no means the last. A few hours later, another RAF Police patrol was forced to fire warning shots when rioters threatened to hold up a convoy which they were escorting. As the second day of the rioting continued, the mob tried to get close to the Police Headquarters, but were prevented from doing so by the combined efforts of both the RAF and the Military Police manning the roadblocks around the area.

After seventy-two hours of rioting, the police finally regained control of the city and the full cost of the situation was assessed. Nineteen people had been killed, including two RAF personnel. Over two hundred people had been injured, many of them seriously and some eighty-three vehicles had been damaged or destroyed. Considerable damage had been inflicted on buildings all over the city and a curfew was quickly imposed. Luckily, the RAF Police did not sustain any casualties and none of their vehicles were seriously damaged. In recognition of his valuable services during the rioting,

Corporal A T D Gilmer, an unarmed RAF Police NCO, who continued to carry out his duties despite the fact that he was in grave danger, was subsequently awarded the King's Commendation for Brave Conduct.

In December, His Majesty King George VI graciously approved a badge for the RAF Police. The idea of a badge had first been discussed in September 1943 when a request was circulated to units asking for the submission of suitable designs. Unfortunately, nothing suitable was produced and the idea was suspended. However, in early 1949, negotiations were resumed and in June of that year a competition was launched in the *Provost Parade*, asking for readers of the magazine to design and submit a suitable badge. Cash prizes were also offered for the best designs and although the response was good, nothing really suitable was accepted by the College of Heralds. As a consequence, Group Captain Newbury decided that the design for any suitable badge, had to be based on fact and not fancy. He therefore investigated the symbols of Nemesis, the goddess of vengeance and bringer of swift and terrible retribution to those doing wrong. Of the four attributes of Nemesis, the griffin emerged as the most attractive and appropriate for the badge because it was the symbol of guardianship. The motto, or any reasonable suggestion for one, seemed as difficult to design as the badge. However, after much thought, the motto *Fiat Justitia*, meaning 'let justice be done' was chosen. Although Group Captain Newbury was the driving force behind the design, the first prize in the competition was shared between Wing Commander P Henniker-Heaton and Flight Lieutenant G McMahon, who together came up with a design acceptable to the College of Heralds.

Since the end of the war, many former British colonies and territories had gained their independence. Accordingly, as responsibilities for the administration of those countries was handed over to their native officials, many of the British colonial police officers found themselves unemployed. As a result, many, no doubt attracted by the life that the RAF offered, sought out commissions and new careers with the RAF Provost Branch. Amongst some of those who joined the branch under those conditions were Flying Officers J Biggie, H St Chair-Stacey, R Truscott and finally, E Walsh, who were all former officers serving in the Indian Police. In fact, Flying

Officer Walsh had actually been a former Inspector General in the force for a number of years.

By the end of the year, the intensive investigation into the Stalag Luft 3 murders had all but drawn to a conclusion. In all, some seventy-two defendants had been identified by the team as being involved in the affair and twenty-six had been personally tracked down and arrested by the RAF Police. Of those identified, six remained at large, three were acquitted at their subsequent trials, five had the charges against them dropped, ten were believed to have been killed during the war, eleven committed suicide, seventeen received varying prison sentences and twenty-one were sentenced to death and duly executed by the Allies. The complex investigation into the murders had been the only major war crime entrusted to a single service police organisation of the British forces. However, the RAF Police team involved had proved themselves to be part of a very competent and professional organisation throughout the lengthy and at times, frustrating enquiry. Many miles around Europe had been covered in the search for the truth and some hundred thousand interviews had taken place, during which written statements had been recorded in several different languages.

Chapter V
The Cold War Era

Unfortunately, around this period, the political tension both within Europe and around the world was beginning to increase once again and the relationship between the Americans and the Russians was rapidly deteriorating. The Russian leader, Stalin, was steadily absorbing all the countries of Eastern Europe into the Soviet Union and the Russians were particularly active in recruiting new allies elsewhere around the world in addition to spreading their communist politics. The Russians were also rapidly building up their military strength again and were eager to develop a nuclear capability all of their own. Consequently, that tended to fuel American suspicions of Russian expansion and likewise the Russians were very wary of the Americans. As such, military espionage was high on the agenda of their secret intelligence agencies and the recruitment of spies dramatically increased in order to obtain the information they required to stay one step ahead. As the Russians began to pose a threat, the West prepared to respond to any hostility, if it came their way. In addition, relations between the East and West had deteriorated considerably since the Berlin airlift and the formation of NATO. Given all the political, economical and military circumstances, the arrival of the 1950s heralded the start of the period known as the Cold War between the NATO and the Soviet Bloc alliances.

In an effort to counter the obvious threat from Soviet Bloc espionage, the RAF reviewed its own security policy and procedures again. Unfortunately, the security procedures adopted by the service up to that period had covered only physical aspects of security, such as control of entry onto RAF units, patrols, the issue of passes and permits and the security of keys. Although classified material and information had been given the appropriate protection, there was clearly an urgent need to expand the security blanket to other important areas of operation. The Army for instance, had its own separate Intelligence Corps, which looked after security matters in preference to the Military Police. However, after much discussion on the subject, it was decided that security matters in the RAF would remain the responsibility of the RAF Police and as a result of that decision, the regional aspect of RAF Policing, under the control of the Provost Marshal, was re-titled to reflect the new commitment and became known as the RAF Provost and Security Service (RAF P&SS). Consequently, with the expansion of the new organisation, the headquarters moved to Acton in West London and took over the second floor of the large government building in Bromyard Avenue. At the same time, the Provost Marshal and his staff also moved into the building, having vacated cramped accommodation inside central London. From there, the immense task of setting up the RAF security system began and it became the responsibility of the RAF Police to safeguard all RAF personnel, materials and information from the threat of espionage, subversion, terrorism and sabotage.

During February 1951, the RAF Police Dog Training School moved from RAF Staverton and joined the RAF Driving School at RAF Netheravon, on the edge of the Salisbury Plain. At the same time, plans were also made to move No 1 RAF Police Wing and the training school to the same unit later that year. Netheravon was one of the most historic RAF stations, having been one of the first permanent airfields built for the Royal Flying Corps during the Great War. However, during the second world war, it had also taken on an active role when it was used to train glider pilots and to plan Operation Market Garden, the ill-fated Allied airborne landings at Arnhem.

It was around that period, that a number of RAF Volunteer Reserve Police Flights were formed around the country and in turn, they proved to be very popular, especially amongst former serving RAF Police personnel. There were six of them in all, No 261 Flight located in Cambridge, No 262 Flight at Pucklechurch in Bristol, No 263 Flight at Fazackerly in Liverpool, No 264 Flight at Alvaston in Derby, No 265 Flight at Stanmore Park and finally, No 266 Flight was located at Bishopbriggs, just outside Glasgow. Candidates were required to sign on for an initial period of five years, during which they were expected to carry out fifteen days compulsory training each year. However, to make life easier, the training could be carried out at a number of specified RAF units around the country and former members of the RAF Police who applied, retained their former ranks on being successfully accepted. For many, it was an excellent way to retain their connections with the service in which they had served and of course renew old friendships.

In Iraq on the 4th April, in the early hours of the morning, Corporal H T Raybone, a twenty year old RAF Police dog handler, attached to No 3 RAF Police District, was on patrol at RAF Habbaniya, when his dog suddenly indicated something suspicious ahead of them. He started to investigate and discovered four bandits, two of whom, were armed with rifles, standing not far from his position. He challenged them all but they started to run away, so he immediately released his dog, which was unfortunately shot as it fearlessly attacked one of the villains. Despite the fact that his dog lay dead, Corporal Raybone, who was himself armed, continued to pursue the four men and in the process, one of them turned and aimed a rifle at him. In response, Corporal Raybone shot the man dead but the other three continued with their escape. The bandits were armed and out to steal whatever they could and would have done so, had the RAF Police not been on patrol that night. In recognition of his prompt and courageous action that morning, Corporal Raybone was subsequently awarded a commendation for bravery from the Commander in Chief, MEAF.

At RAF Pershore on 26th April, before an assembled parade, Air Vice-Marshal A C Sanderson CB, CBE, DFC, formally and proudly presented the newly authorised RAF Police badge to Air Commodore de Putron. In his speech before the presentation, the Air Vice Marshal spoke warmly about the branch as he said:

> It is appropriate, I think, before presenting this badge, to look back and see how our Royal Air Force Police first came into being. You will remember how on 1st April 1918, just thirty-three years ago, the Royal Flying Corps and the Royal Naval Air Service merged to form the Royal Air Force. At the same time, the Army Provost Marshal of Great Britain was made responsible for the policing of this new force. He appointed Major Pryor to act as Provost Marshal of the Royal Air Force.

In 1919, Major Pryor was demobilised and Lieutenant Colonel Brierley, who later became a Wing Commander, took over the provost duties in addition to his normal personnel staff duties at the Air Ministry, and for some years, the duties of discipline and Provost Marshal were combined.

By 1920, an RAF Police School had been opened at Halton with intakes of fifteen trainees, undergoing six week courses. It was commanded by Flight Lieutenant Bishop who had been appointed Assistant Provost Marshal and the instructors were loaned temporarily from the Military Police School, until such time as RAF Police instructors could be trained to supersede them.

By 1931, Squadron Leader Stammers, who was struggling with the dual role, found that because of the expansion of the Royal Air Force, it was necessary for him to concentrate all his energies on the full time duty of Provost Marshal. By 1934, the global establishment of the RAF Service Police at home was 254 and 160 overseas.

In the spring of 1939, provost officers were recruited for the first time and were posted for duty at Command and Group Headquarters, whilst by the summer, the RAF Police strength had increased to 1,470 men all told.

When war was declared, the RAF Police were ready and in fact, a small party under the command of Squadron Leader Richdale, now the Command Provost Marshal, Middle East, was already serving with the Advanced Air Striking Force in France. Naturally, with the rapid expansion, there were mounting demands for Service Police and although the school had by this time moved to Uxbridge and had increased its intake considerably, we were not able to meet all our requirements and were in fact some 1,500 men deficient.

It is interesting here to mention that the WAAF Police were formed in 1940 and gradually grew in numbers as the war progressed. When Group Captain Stammers' eleven year tour as Provost Marshal came to an end in 1942 and he was replaced by Air Commodore Owen de Putron, the RAF Provost Police had already been formed and were active in Iraq and the Middle East in addition to the United Kingdom.

As the war increased in size, so RAF Police were needed in almost all theatres.

The Special Investigation Branch which had been formed in 1931 with one officer and four NCOs, had expanded considerably and was now handling many thousands of cases. The RAF Police took a very active part in the invasion of Europe in 1944 and received numerous commendations for gallant work. The Provost Branch has received twenty five British awards for officers and thirty-three for airmen and a solid tradition of service has been built up. The RAF Police reached its peak in January 1945, when it consisted of 468 officers, 20,300 airmen, 56 WAAF Police Officers and 400 airwomen.

In 1947, the Provost Branch was officially recognised and became a separate branch of the Royal Air Force. Amongst its many commitments today, it includes participation in 'Escape and Evasion' exercises, in which many of you have, I believe, already taken part, ceremonial parades such as the presentation of the King's colour to the Royal Air Force next month in Hyde Park, escort and convoy work including the movement of ammunition by road and sea and security cover for USAF airfields. Nor must we overlook the police dogs which are a most important and growing commitment. We now have 570 dogs and hope to go up to 900 as soon as possible. Apart from their normal duties of guarding maintenance units and patrolling airfields, they have already been used successfully on active service in Malaya.

The introduction of the new trade structure this year has done much to improve pay and prospects for the RAF Police and I feel sure that your having those two paramount qualities required of police in the services, outstanding integrity and loyalty, will continue to uphold the fine traditions which the provost branch, young as it is, has already moulded for itself.

I should just like now to make a short reference to Air Commodore de Putron, his term of office as Provost Marshal, lasting nine years, is about to end. I should like on behalf of the RAF, to congratulate him for his loyal and efficient handling of the RAF Police during this long period.

He has every reason to be proud and satisfied with his work, the results of which can be seen wherever the RAF is serving.

It now becomes my very pleasant duty to hand over to the Provost Marshal this badge, which His Majesty the King has been graciously pleased to approve. The griffin in the centre is the symbol of retribution, whilst the motto, 'Let Justice be Done', aptly epitomises the role of the Royal Air Force Police'.

In April 1951, RAF Police NCOs were established for the first time at the NATO Headquarters Fontainbleau in France, as part of an multinational military police force at the new Headquarters of the Allied Air Forces in Central Europe (AAFCE). The newly formed organisation, tasked mainly with enforcing security measures, comprised of personnel from Great Britain, the United States, Belgium, Canada, France and the Netherlands.

Air Commodore de Putron retired as the RAF Provost Marshal in May 1951, after nine extremely productive years. He was succeeded by an officer from the General Duties (Flying) Branch, Air Commodore B C Yarde CBE, who had been the station commander at RAF Gatow, during the Berlin airlift. He had been born on 5th September, 1905, at Southsea and was commissioned into the RAF in 1926. During the war, he had served in France and both the Middle and Far East. Although he was not a professional policeman, he had certainly been impressed by the work being carried out by the branch, and was extremely happy to take on his new appointment.

As Her Royal Highness Princess Elizabeth, Duchess of Edinburgh, was leaving the Royal Tournament on 19th June, she commented on the fact that the Royal Air Force Police on the carpet guard, were not accompanied by any RAF Police dogs. Her Royal Highness suggested that Her Majesty Queen Mary would undoubtedly like to see the RAF Police dogs, when she visited the tournament later that week. Accordingly, two days later, Sergeant F Holland, together with six handlers and their dogs, were presented to Her Majesty as she left the Royal Box.

It was around that period that Guy Burgess and Donald Maclean, who were employed in the Foreign Office, were exposed by the Security Services as active Soviet spies on the payroll of the Russian

Intelligence Service, the KGB. However, they both managed to escape to Moscow before they could be arrested by the British authorities. The Cold War was beginning to get even colder as relations between the east and west moved further and further apart.

Although the RAF had withdrawn its forces from India when it was granted its independence, Ceylon still remained as an RAF posting and accordingly, RAF Police were established on the island, tasked with carrying out a wide range of provost and security disciplines. As they were the only service police organisation serving there, they were responsible for carrying out duties all over the island on behalf of the Royal Navy and the British Army, as well as supporting their own service. In addition, they were also tasked with liaising with, and assisting No 41 Movements (Embarkation) Unit and the crews of all troopships, calling in at the busy port of Colombo. No 1 RAF Police District Headquarters, which at that time was under the command of Squadron Leader B D Barrett, was situated at RAF Colombo, while No 61 RAF Police Flight, under the command of Flight Lieutenant R J Horton, was situated some twenty miles further north of Colombo, at the airfield at RAF Negombo. In line with normal practice by then, the RAF Police were also supported by a force of locally recruited RAF Police Auxiliaries, under the command of Inspector T Y Dole. Ceylon, it seems, was a very popular posting for the RAF Police. It had a warm pleasant climate and a 'south seas' atmosphere about the place. There were adequate facilities for all manner of sporting activities, including, on application, membership of the exclusive Colombo Yacht Club. In addition, RAF personnel on leave also had access to the inland service recreation centre at Diyatalawa, where they could totally relax and unwind from the pressures of life.

In Korea on 10th July, representatives from both the North and South gathered at Kaesong in an effort to start peace negotiations and bring an end to the war there. Although the talks were held in an air of hostility and mistrust, some headway was established in agreeing on a stalemate which would divide the country up with a demarcation line along the 38th parallel, much as it had been before the start of the conflict.

During a parade in Cyprus to mark the occasion of His Majesty the King's birthday, a radio commentator reporting on the event announced, "Here come the RAF Police Auxiliaries, looking and marching more like trained infantry soldiers than policemen." That was hardly a surprising comment, because every member of the force had been a fully trained former serviceman. The force had been recruited principally from the disbanded Cyprus Regiment and comprised of both Turkish and Greek Cypriots. The original seventy man force, initially called RAF Wardens, had been formed on 21st October, 1946, and had been used to provide security at RAF Nicosia, under the direct control of the Cypriot Commissioner of Police. However, on 1st November, 1949, the force was taken over by the RAF Police, given the title RAF Police Auxiliaries and placed under the control of the Command Provost Marshal, with Inspector Rebjeb Halil Effendi appointed to take operational charge. The establishment had steadily increased and was used to guard and protect vital points at RAF establishments all around the island. The procedures for selecting and appointing RAF Police Auxiliaries was not taken lightly and followed strict guidelines established by Rebjeb Halil Effendi, who himself had been a firm disciplinarian, with a wide knowledge of both Cypriot police and general administrative matters. Prospective candidates had to be under thirty-five years of age, fit and over five foot, five inches tall. They had to be intelligent and had to be able to speak English. After successfully passing the interview process, they were enlisted on a month's probation before their appointment as Auxiliary Constables was finally confirmed. At that time, the main unit on the island was RAF Nicosia, which was a shared facility with the civil airport and was also home to No 12 RAF Police Flight, commanded by Flight Lieutenant W H Gerrard. In addition to the normal duties carried out by the flight, they also maintained a small detachment at the eastern sea port at Famagusta.

In the Far East, an estimated 30,000 people attended the 4th Singapore Air Display, which took place on 1st September at Kallang Airport in Singapore. Accordingly, a large number of RAF Police personnel were on duty there carrying out a wide range of police and security duties at what was undoubtedly the finest display of its kind ever seen in that part of the world. While the flying displays of various aircraft, including the Vampire, the Meteor, the Dakota and the Sunderland Flying Boat, thrilled the assembled crowds, one of the highlights of the show was of course the excellent display, staged by the local and specially trained RAF Police Dog Demonstration Team. The demonstration commenced with the six handlers and their dogs being marched onto the arena by Warrant Officer T B Whittaker from No 2 RAF Police District, and included the full range of obedience, search, obstacle and criminal work. It was an excellent display which gave a great deal of pleasure to not only the assembled crowds, but also to Air Commodore J L F Fullergood CBE, the Air Officer Commanding Malaya, who was also present throughout.

In addition to responding to special events, such as the Air Show in Kallang, the traffic sections of No 64 and 65 RAF Police Flights were kept extremely busy in Singapore. All roads on the island were patrolled and all traffic accidents involving RAF vehicles or private vehicles driven by RAF personnel were visited and fully investigated thereafter. In fact, so efficient was their response to such accidents, that the civilian police always failed to beat them to the scene. However, the liaison between the RAF Police and civilian police was nevertheless an excellent one, with the latter holding the professionalism of the former to a very high degree. In addition to attending accident scenes, the section also carried out a host of other duties on their Ariel 350cc and Triumph 500cc motorcycles, which included vehicle documentation and serviceability checks, escorting convoys and VIPs and carrying out speed checks in designated areas. Additionally, it was important to ensure that a good liaison was also maintained with the RAF Police Flights at Changi, Seletar and Tengah, the three main RAF stations on the island.

Trouble had been brewing in Egypt for some time. However, relations between Egypt and Britain worsened on the 8th October, when Egypt renounced its twenty year treaty of 1936 with Britain and reiterated its claim on the Sudan. The recently elected Egyptian Government had at first seemed friendly enough towards British interests in the region, but severe domestic problems and pressure from extremist groups within the country had combined to make the dispute with Britain a welcome distraction. Britain reacted to the announcement by refusing to accept the cancellation of the treaty, or to recognise King Farouk as the King of the Sudan. As hostility towards the British developed within Egypt, following the British statement, British military units within the Canal Zone were reinforced to deal with increased attacks and hostility against them.

On 19th January, 1952, in Egypt, two members of No 2 RAF Police Flight, Corporals Kirk and Clark, were sent in their radio-controlled patrol vehicle to assist an Army unit which had come under attack at the YMCA bridge, which crossed over the Sweet Water Canal in Ismailia. Both men responded swiftly, but shortly after their arrival, they came under heavy fire. Even so, they courageously remained at their post and continued to send back situation reports to their headquarters. However, after a short while, their vehicle took a direct hit from a terrorist bomb and the two NCOs were severely wounded. When the attack had ceased, both men were quickly evacuated to the Military Hospital in Moascar, where Corporal Clark responded positively to the treatment he received. Sadly, however, Corporal Andrew Kirk, who was twenty-nine years old, died from his injuries a week later, having only served in Egypt for two weeks prior to the attack. He was buried shortly after, with full military honours, in the British Military Cemetery in Moascar.

As trouble and rioting continued to flare up throughout the Canal Zone, the Egyptian Police, who were also openly hostile towards the British, did nothing at all to stop it. In fact, there were numerous occasions when they were observed actively inciting the trouble makers. The situation became so serious that on 25th January, British troops successfully entered and seized the Egyptian Police Headquarters in Ismailia, resulting in the deaths of some fifty Egyptians. Over the days which followed, numerous anti-British riots took place in Cairo and as a result the tension mounted.

During the same month, the RAF Police School and No 1 RAF Police Wing finally completed the move from Pershore to Netheravon, and in doing so, joined up with both the Dog Training and the RAF Police Driving Schools. In compliance with a directive from the Air Ministry, the new station, commanded by Group Captain T R Champion, was duly retitled as the Royal Air Force Police Depot. In addition, an RAF Police museum was opened there for the first time, displaying the numerous artefacts and information about the branch, which had been collected during its formative years. An official depot tie was also approved soon after, only to be worn with civilian clothes. It cost twenty-one shillings to purchase and was made of dark blue silk with small silver griffins embroidered onto it.

On 6th February, 1952, King George VI died peacefully in his sleep at Sandringham at the age of fifty-six years old, having been ill for some time. The Princess Elizabeth, who had been in Uganda at the time of his death, soon returned home to succeed her father as Sovereign and head of the nation.

By now, the RAF Police were familiar with the numerous tasks associated with trooping ships and their passengers, having carried out their duties at various ports around the world. So, given that experience, it was only natural that in February, Squadron Leader H M Shepherd, a provost officer, on route to his new posting in the Far East, should assume command of a mixed unit of around forty Military and RAF Police NCOs, on board the troopship *Empire Trooper*. Over a thousand servicemen and their families were travelling on the ship, which was bound for Japan and everywhere else along the way. His priority had been to set up the guardroom and the detention room, the latter being used almost before the ship had set sail to accommodate two sailors sentenced to twenty-eight days detention. After that, a duty roster was drawn up to provide twenty-four hour police coverage throughout the ship for every day of the trip. Soon after the ship set sail, the unit settled into their routine and during the long voyage, they dealt with a wide range of incidents, which ranged from purely disciplinary matters, thefts and a number of offences involving violence. In addition to policing the ship whilst at sea, the unit had also assisted the local law enforcement agencies ashore whenever the ship had docked. Shortly after the ship arrived at Hong Kong, Squadron Leader Shepherd disembarked and handed over all responsibility for the task to an Army provost officer who was travelling on to Japan.

Iwakuni, the largest and busiest Allied air base in Japan, was situated on the delta of the River Nishiki, approximately thirty miles from Hiroshima and fifty miles from the British Commonwealth Headquarters at Kure. A detachment from No 69 RAF Police Flight, made up a joint military police force on the air base, along with their counterparts from both America and Australia. Iwakuni had been built in 1937 and had been towards the end of the war, the training base for the infamous Kamikaze pilots. At the conclusion of the war with Japan, it had been taken over by the Allies and became the base of the RAF Occupation Force. In addition, No 75 RAF Police Flight, under the command of Squadron Leader P Crossley DFC, had taken up residence there. In 1948, the base had been handed over to the Royal Australian Air Force and shortly after became a United Nations airfield.

In June, having no further use for it, the RAF withdrew from their staging post at Asmara, in Eritrea and it was officially handed back to representatives of the host country.

In Egypt during the night of the 22nd July, a *coup d'état* took place when a group of Army officers, led by Colonel Gamal Abdula Nasser, seized control of Cairo. In an almost bloodless take over, the king was forced to abdicate and a new military government was formed under the leadership of General Mohammed Negguib, a hero of the 1948 war with Israel. The British units within the Canal Zone reacted accordingly by going on full alert to the uncertain situation.

During that year, after completing his twenty-six years service with the Blackpool Police, Squadron Leader F P McKenna (Retired) rejoined the RAF Provost Branch after being offered a short service commission with the rank of Flying Officer. He was subsequently posted to the RAF Police Depot, where he took up his appointment as a training officer, with a wealth of experience to offer both to junior provost officers and RAF Police NCOs alike.

On 3rd October, Britain tested her first nuclear weapon on the Monte Bello Islands, to the west of Australia, and two weeks later another landmark within the provost branch was reached, when for the first time, fifteen RAF Police Alsatian dogs and their handlers, from the Depot, were transported by air from RAF Abingdon to RAF Gutersloh in Northern Germany. The whole journey, by road and Valetta aircraft, had taken less than ten hours, compared to a much slower and more stressful journey for the dogs by sea.

As British reinforcements were being rushed into the Canal Zone in Egypt on 20th October, a state of emergency was declared in Kenya by the British Governor, who had been forced to act, as the Mau Mau terrorist campaign became more serious and widespread throughout the colony. Problems had been brewing in the country since 1947, when the Kikuyu tribe began to demonstrate against the British who had insisted on the cessation of female circumcision ceremonies and had inflicted their strict religious moral codes of conduct in place of traditional local customs. As they became more organised, they demanded their farming lands in the Kenyan highlands back which, they alleged, had been stolen by European settlers. During the days which followed, the suspected leader of the Mau Mau, Jomo Kenyatta, was arrested and taken into custody, charged with sedition. It was a dangerous time for the white European settlers, many of whom lived on isolated farms in remote parts of the country. There were many attacks carried out by the Mau Mau, who committed some dreadful atrocities on both adults and children alike and as a consequence, further British troops had been sent out to Kenya to reinforce the British presence and to assist the authorities in restoring law and order. By 25th November, after a number of raids throughout the country, some 2,000 members of the Kikuyu, suspected of being part of the Mau Mau, had been arrested and were in custody.

At RAF Eastleigh, situated on the outskirts of the capital, Nairobi, a number of RAF Police dog handlers had been established to enhance the unit's overall security measures. Within a short space of time, the dogs had proved themselves to be a very effective deterrent to any would-be terrorists. That was highlighted one night when a dog indicated the presence of some twenty native intruders, who had been quietly approaching a radar site. The handler located the intruders, called for assistance and challenged them but they quickly fled from the area. The dog was subsequently used to track them but unfortunately, it lost the scent near an isolated farm. As a result, the Kenyan Police searched it and seven members of the Mau Mau were duly arrested and a number of weapons and a vast quantity of ammunition were recovered. As a result of that incident, No 7 RAF Police Flight Detachment, commanded by Flying Officer F D Edge, tightened up the security measures on the station to prevent any further attempted acts of terrorism and sabotage from taking place. No chances were taken and accordingly all Africans entering and leaving the station were thoroughly searched and their identities validated. In addition to the security measures provided by the RAF Police, airmen of all trades were detailed for armed guard duties to enhance the overall security cordon.

The isolated, but nonetheless important, RAF Unit at Riyan was an airfield described as a vital staging post for defence operations. It was located a mile inland from the uncivilised and pirate-infested South Arabian coast within the Aden Protectorate. Security at the unit was undertaken by thirty-two RAF Police Auxiliaries, who had been recruited from the Yfai Tribe, the most ferocious tribe in the Sultanate of Mukalla. Indeed their feared reputation, combined with the fact that each man was a crack marksman, ensured that nothing had been stolen or sabotaged on the unit during the three years that they had been responsible for guarding it. However, that was not surprising, given the severity of the penalties for theft under Mukalla law. A thief caught in the act of stealing could be executed on the spot. If however, he was caught after the commission of the offence, he simply had his left hand amputated for the first offence and then his right hand cut off for a second offence. If, however, the thief offended a third time, then he would be publicly executed by having his head cut off. Although the Auxiliaries were under the immediate supervision of an Auxiliary Inspector, the force came under the operational command of the RAF Unit commander, who in turn was responsible for their actions to the Officer Commanding No 7 RAF Police Flight in Aden.

On the 1st January, 1953, a further district headquarters was formed in the United Kingdom, bringing the number of districts to seven. No 7 RAF Police District was duly formed at Castle Bromwich in the West Midlands.

Severe gales and floods, resulting from extremely high tides, caused widespread havoc along Britain's east coast on 2nd February, leaving many dead and thousands more homeless. Lincolnshire in particular was severely hit by the storms and the coastal RAF station at North Coates (a training unit forming part of Headquarters No 22 Group) was quickly cut off after flood water there reached a depth of four feet in a very short space of time. Because a further high tide was expected the station was quickly abandoned leaving behind a large quantity of personal and public property to its fate. In response to the situation, Wing Commander Mason, commanding the headquarters of No 3 RAF Police District, despatched a force of eighteen RAF Police NCOs, under the control of Warrant Officer T E Fraser, to the location to assist Sergeant K Dobie, the senior RAF Police NCO stationed at North Coates. The scene they found upon their arrival was chaotic. The station had been completely deserted and everything on the main part of it was under water, which included offices, hangars, barrack accommodation and both service and privately owned vehicles. However, the Guardroom, which luckily happened to be built on higher ground, had only been flooded by a few inches of water and as such, provided the RAF Police with their Incident Control Room from which to operate.

The sudden rush of water from the breached sea defences had washed away everything in its path and there was considerable work to be done in accounting for, and retrieving, all the classified and valuable material held on the unit. As a result, the team remained at the station for three days, where they were constantly working in waist-deep cold water rescuing what ever they could find. They were joined by personnel from the unit and at the end of the three days, the team, satisfied that they had successfully completed their task, handed over responsibility for the site to the station authorities. From that point on, they became responsible for drying out and cleaning up the damage caused by the water, and what a task it turned out to be.

The team, having done such a splendid job at RAF North Coates, were then tasked to assist the local police in nearby Mablethorpe, who were struggling to deal with the chaos left by the storms. When they arrived, they found that in addition to the flood water, a huge quantity of silt had been washed into the town as the sea defences had crumbled. The civil police were located in a temporary police station which had been set up in the railway yard on the outskirts of the town and while they concentrated on protecting life and property, the RAF Police detachment were employed on traffic control at the various roads within and leading into the stricken town. As the flood water subsided, the sand in places measured eight feet deep and it had covered almost everything. The RAF Police worked long and exhausting hours on the tasks and at the end of each tiring day, they returned, completely exhausted, to their temporary accommodation above the NAAFI at nearby RAF Manby. Given the magnitude of the operation, more RAF Police personnel were drafted in to assist and convoys of lorries were brought into the town to assist in moving away the sand and debris. A one-way traffic system into and out of the town was created and with the RAF Police directing and controlling the traffic, everything went very smoothly. In the end, the whole operation lasted for several days before the situation was sufficiently under control once again. At that point, the RAF Police were stood down and totally exhausted, they returned to their respective units.

However, on 5th March, the civilian authorities again asked for military assistance when a large part of the sea defences in Essex, were breached in yet another severe storm. In response, a team of around two hundred young airmen and twenty NCOs, under the control of Squadron Leader L W C Lewis of the RAF Police Depot, made their way to the River Crouch in Essex, where during the week which followed, they helped to fill in excess of 30,000 sandbags in an attempt to stem the flow of sea water.

On the same day, Marshal Joseph Stalin, the Russian leader died after ruthlessly holding onto power in the USSR for twenty-nine years. He was eventually succeeded by Nikita Khrushchev, who unfortunately continued the Soviet hard-line stance towards the West and as such, the Cold War continued to get colder.

In Kenya, on 8th April, Jomo Kenyatta was convicted by the Supreme Court in Nairobi of organising the Mau Mau terrorist campaign and was duly sentenced to seven years hard labour in prison. That was followed later in the month with the arrest, in Nairobi, of a further one thousand members of the Kikuyu tribe, all suspected of being terrorists. With their run of successful operations, it seemed that the British authorities, were by then, clamping down on the Mau Mau and gaining control again within the country.

Air Commodore Yarde was promoted to the rank of Air Vice-Marshal on 20th April, and subsequently took up his new appointment as the AOC No 62 Group. He was succeeded in post by Air Commodore North Carter CB DFC, who assumed the new title of Director of Personal Services (Provost Marshal) and Chief of Air Force Police. He had been born in Australia in 1902, and had been educated in England before joining the RAF in 1921. Prior to taking up his new appointment, he had been a senior staff officer with No 205 Group, MEAF.

In Hong Kong on the day following the appointment of the new Provost Marshal, eleven RAF Police dogs and their handlers, under the command of Flight Lieutenant G Innes, appeared on a public parade for the first time in the colony to celebrate the birthday of Her Majesty the Queen. At the end of the month, the occupation of Japan by the United States ended after being in place for seven years.

By the middle of 1953, the establishment of the PSLO at the Records Office in Gloucester had grown considerably since its formation in early 1942. However, the volume of work undertaken by the section had also seen a dramatic increase. At the beginning of the year, it was controlled by Squadron Leader D R H Jones, who was assisted in his duties by a police warrant officer, a police sergeant, four police corporals and six RAF clerks. In addition to housing the personal records of every serving member of the RAF, the office also retained those of past serving personnel as well. As such, the PSLO, maintained a close liaison with the various civil police forces around the country and dealt with hundreds of enquiries each month regarding service personnel. Liaison was also maintained with the Provost Marshal's Department, which issued identity cards and permits. In addition, the office also advised the Director of Personnel on police postings and the appointment of service personnel chosen to work in sensitive and classified areas

On 29th May, the world's highest peak, Mount Everest, was finally conquered by Edmund Hilary and Sherpa Tensing and four days after, the coronation of Her Majesty, Queen Elizabeth II, took place in Westminster Abbey. In preparation for the coronation parade, a huge military tented camp had been set up in the centre of Kensington Gardens to accommodate the 700 Officers, 1,300 Warrant Officers and SNCOs and 12,000 troops, which took part in the ceremony. Accordingly, there was a large tri-service police presence, patrolling both within the camp and around central London, maintaining the high standard of discipline amongst the service personnel on duty there. Apart from carrying out the normal provost functions on the lead up to, and during the day of the ceremony, an impressive detachment of forty RAF Police NCOs, under the command of Squadron Leader C A Mumford, also formed part of the RAF contingent in the parade. On the day after the coronation, indicating better things ahead, food rationing was finally abolished after being in force since 1942.

Serious rioting broke out in the Russian Sector of Berlin on the 16th June. The mainly working-class demonstrators waved the old German national flag and demanded that the Russians should leave Germany and go back to Russia. The protests had been largely brought about by the deteriorating standards of living in that part of the city and indeed some East Berliners were almost starving because of the lack of commodities. The Russian authorities, however, were unsympathetic and swiftly moved in to restore order in the course of which a number of protesters were killed and many more were injured.

On 15th July, Her Majesty Queen Elizabeth II, arrived at RAF Odiham in Hampshire, to review the Royal Air Force and the largest parade of aircraft ever to have been assembled in one place. The RAF Police were there in force of course, helping to control the public and the large volume of traffic attending the venue. In addition, they provided escorts and security for the visiting VIPs and point guarded some of the newly developed and still secret aircraft on display.

Two days later, after some of the longest negotiations to bring about a cease-fire, Korea became a divided country as the war there ended, and a truce was declared with the signing of an armistice at Panmunjom. Democracy prevailed in the south, while communism was rigorously enforced in North Korea. The bloody conflict had achieved little but had claimed the lives of over two million people.

In August, Flight Lieutenant B C Player, a provost officer, who had recently been in command of the RAF Police on Gibraltar, was the first RAF provost officer to successfully complete the Home Office Criminal Investigation Training Course at the Lancashire Constabulary Training School in Preston. The event opened the doors to other specially selected provost officers and SIB SNCOs to undergo the same training required of a detective in the civilian police.

Lieutenant Colonel Baldwin took up his retirement in October after thirteen years of being the inspiration of the RAF Police Dog Training School, which had, over that period, gone from strength to strength, earning an extremely high reputation. He was succeeded as the Chief Dog Training Officer by Mr Charles Edward Fricker, who himself had joined Baldwin right at the start, when the school was formed at Woodfold. Unfortunately, however, after only a year of working at Woodfold, Fricker had been conscripted to work in the coal mines as a 'Bevin Boy'. After the war had ended, he returned to the world of dogs and started his own kennels, breeding and showing Alsatians. He formed a dog display team which proved to be extremely popular and they even performed before the royal family at the Royal Inverness Show in 1948.

On 1st March, 1954, a major reorganisation of the RAF Police, serving both at home and overseas took place once again. The RAF Police Wing Headquarters system was disbanded and the RAF Police districts were renumbered and made responsible to either the Provost Marshal within the UK, or their respective Command Provost & Security Officers at their appropriate Command Headquarters overseas. As such, the Provost Marshal, through the medium of HQ P&SS (UK), retained direct control of the following RAF Police Districts, No 1, located at RAF Bishopbriggs in Scotland, No 2, located at RAF Weeton in Lancashire, No 3, located at RAF Hucknall in Nottinghamshire, No 4, located at RAF Duxford in Cambridgeshire, No 5, located at RAF Ruislip in Middlesex, No 6, located at RAF Filton near Bristol and finally, No 7, located at RAF Castle Bromwich near Birmingham.   In addition, he also directly controlled the activities of No 8 District in Gibraltar, No 9 District in Malta and finally, No 10 District in Northern Ireland.   Over in Germany, the Headquarters of the RAF Police moved from Buckeburg to Rheindahlen near Munchengladbach and was re-titled as HQ P&SS (2TAF).   No 41 District continued to operate from RAF Buckeburg, while No 42 District operated from RAF Wahn.   In the Middle East, the following districts were established, No 21 at RAF Ismailia in Egypt, No 22, at RAF Steamer Point in Aden (with a detachment in Kenya), No 23, at RAF Habbaniya in Iraq (also covering Jordan) and No 24, at RAF Nicosia in Cyprus (with a detachment in Libya).   In the Far East, the districts were, No 31, at RAF Changi in Singapore, No 32, at RAF Kuala Lumpur in Malaya, No 33, at RAF Colombo in Ceylon and finally, No 34, located at RAF Kai Tak in Hong Kong.

In the Far East in April, tragedy suddenly struck at Kallang Airport in Singapore when a Constellation passenger aircraft crashed, killing all those on board.   Consequently, the traffic section of No 31 RAF Police District provided the escort for the massive funeral procession a few days after.   In Ceylon, Her Majesty Queen Elizabeth II and His Royal Highness the Duke of Edinburgh arrived on board the SS *Gothic* for a twelve day official visit.   For the occasion, the RAF Police Auxiliaries, under the command of Inspector Dole, had all been sworn in to act as special constables of the Ceylon Police, to assist their civilian counterparts with the duties connected with the royal visit on the island.

Cyprus was captured by Richard I during the third crusade and he sold it to a French Prince.   However, some time later, the island was taken from him by Venice and later became part of the Turkish Empire.   They consequently discovered it to be an administrative burden and handed it over to Britain in return for an annual rent.   That agreement continued to work well until the outbreak of the Great War in 1914, when the Turks allied themselves with Germany.   Given the situation, Britain had no other choice but to annex the island and in 1925, it officially became a British colony.   On 1st April 1954, the Greek Cypriots, who made up fourth-fifths of the island's population, tried to make Cyprus part of Greece.   However, the Turkish Cypriots, who made up one-fifth of the island's population, Britain and the United Nations objected strongly to the proposal. As a result, the Greek Cypriot terrorist movement, Ethnike Organosis Kyprion Agoniston (EOKA), under the leadership of General Georgios Grivas, started their violent terrorist campaign on Cyprus against the British. Security at all British military units on the island was reviewed and enhanced, and both the Military and RAF Police organisations prepared themselves for whatever might happen.

In Northern Malay, just after sunrise on 23rd May, Corporal J T Elvin, RAF Police and his dog, Charlie, who were stationed at RAF Butterworth, responded to a request for assistance from the 12th Royal Lancers, who had been on jungle patrol in the state of Kedah some fifteen miles from the airfield at Butterworth. It seemed that during the previous night, the patrol had engaged a number of terrorists and a fire fight had taken place. In spite of the swift response, the gang had quickly made good their escape into the surrounding jungle and the Army patrol had lost all trace of them. However, during a search of the skirmish site at first daylight, a patch of blood-soaked earth had been discovered, which indicated that one of the terrorists had probably been wounded. After a quick examination of the scene, Corporal Elvin and Charlie, supported by the Army patrol, began tracking the wounded terrorist into the jungle. After some time, the dog stopped and started barking towards some thick undergrowth. Corporal Elvin carefully went forward and discovered the wounded terrorist, hidden at the base of a large tree. Although he was still alive, he had been shot in the thigh and had lost a considerable amount of blood. A rifle lying near him had also been damaged in the skirmish the previous night and was not capable of being fired. Nevertheless, the terrorist was promptly arrested and taken away for medical treatment and questioning. As a result of their efforts, both Corporal Elvin and Charlie were given celebrity status when the story was featured in the *Singapore Straits Times* on 26th May. In addition, Corporal Elvin also later received a commendation from the Provost Marshal for his dedication and professionalism.

On 16th June, the first four members of the United States Air Force Police arrived at the RAF Police Depot at RAF Netheravon, where they began a training programme with the Dog Training School. Although American personnel from the US Army Air Force had been trained as dog handlers, by the RAF during the Second

World War, they were the first to become qualified dog handlers with the USAF. The four eager students were named as Airman 1st Class C Crutchfield from Virginia and Airmen 2nd Class C Misner from Missouri, E Johnson from Wisconsin and finally, L Lynn from Texas.

In Kenya, the Mau Mau troubles continued to be a serious problem for the British troops trying to control the situation. Although numerous suspects had been arrested on a daily basis, the Kikuyu Tribe demanded total loyalty to their cause and as such, anyone joining their organisation was forced to undertake an oath of allegiance, which meant that there was a very strong code of silence amongst its members. However, on the night of the 21st July, Flying Officer Edge, at RAF Eastleigh, had been given reliable information which suggested that an oath-taking ceremony was going to take place on a deserted part of the airfield. At very short notice, he decided to investigate and consequently, a short time later, as he and a handful of armed RAF Police NCOs approached the area concerned, they were seen by a lookout. Although some escaped, twenty-two members of the Mau Mau were arrested and a number of weapons and literature associated with the Mau Mau cause were discovered. In recognition of his efforts, Flying Officer Edge was later awarded the MBE.

In October, Air Commodore North Carter retired as the Provost Marshal and was succeeded in post by Air Commodore H J G E Proud CBE. Air Commodore Proud was forty-eight years old and had been commissioned into the RAF in 1926. Prior to taking up his appointment as Provost Marshal, he had been the AOC, No 67 (Northern Ireland) Group Headquarters.

In Germany, during the same month, the airfield at RAF Laarbruch was opened, having taken just over a year to build. The site chosen for the 2nd ATAF base was in a densely wooded area, near the German town of Goch and close to the Dutch border and Venlo. Being the largest and most modern airfield in Europe, it was rather like a large township, being completely self-contained. During the Second World War, the area had formed part of the German defensive Siegfried Line and had been littered with trenches and all manner of discarded munitions, which of course, had to be safely disposed of before the site had been cleared and building had started.

During January 1955, the British authorities in Kenya, despite having mounted successful operations in the war over terrorism, offered an amnesty to all members of the Mau Mau, in an effort to restore order and bring to an end the state of emergency.

On the 5th May and almost ten years after the war ended, West Germany was once again given sovereignty over its own territory and consequently became the Federal Republic of Germany and a member of NATO. Although it was no longer considered a country under Allied occupation, because of the threat of invasion from the Eastern Bloc, the Allies remained at various locations throughout the new republic as a NATO deterrent. Considerable progress had been made in the Western sectors of Germany since the end of the war when the country's economical, industrial and agricultural infrastructure had been completely devastated and the morale of the people shattered. Initially, when the Allies had taken over the administration of the country, with the intention of rebuilding it, they had been faced with widespread German obstruction and hatred, which had frustrated their efforts. However, after a short period of time and a considerable effort on the part of the Allies, attitudes changed and the Germans started to co-operate with the plans to rebuild their country. In fact, the rebuilding programme had been so successful that in 1948, the Allies had taken a back seat, acting merely as advisors to the Germans who had fully organised themselves to the massive task.

As for the role of the RAF Police serving within the new republic, things were as busy as before the constitutional change. Under the German law they were made responsible for attending and investigating all traffic accidents, involving RAF personnel or their dependants, within the republic. That, of course, placed a considerable strain on the limited resources available to the RAF P&SS detachments at both RAF Wahn and RAF Sundern. However, traffic sections were quickly established, forms were prepared and specialist equipment was obtained to deal with almost any traffic or accident situation likely to be encountered. Indeed, after that, whenever an accident occurred which involved both RAF and German nationals, the civilian police sent copies of their reports to the RAF Police, who were invited to make recommendations as to any further action being taken against those involved.

On the 14th May, the Warsaw Pact was signed by eight Eastern European countries under the influence of the USSR. The pact had been largely brought as a result of West Germany regaining its sovereignty and being allowed, by the west, to form its own defence force and join NATO.

Throughout its brief existence, the RAF Police had, on a number of occasions, mourned the loss of NCOs who had been killed on duty in various parts of the world. Indeed, most of those who had been killed on duty up to that point in time, had been serving in troubled areas overseas where it was always considered a risk which went hand in hand with the job. So, on 24th August, it came as a complete shock to the branch to hear that twenty-two year old, Corporal R P Grayer, an RAF Policeman serving at RAF Manston in Kent, had been tragically killed by a twenty-three year old American serviceman, Napoleon Greene, who went berserk and had ran amok around the normally quiet unit, firing a rifle and a pistol at anyone he came across. As a result of his actions, three people, including Corporal Grayer, had been killed and a further seven had been seriously injured, before Greene finally turned his gun on himself and committed suicide. Tragedy continued after the event when Sergeant J Sutcliffe, the SNCO in charge of the RAF Police at Manston, suddenly collapsed and died later the same day at his home in Margate.

On 30th September, after talks between Turkey and Greece on the situation in Cyprus failed to produce anything positive, the troubles there worsened, violence escalated and the Greek Cypriots mounted a general strike in protest against British rule and the Turkish Cypriot terrorist organisation Volkan became involved. That was followed on 26th November by the British Governor declaring a state of emergency and all British military personnel on the island were placed on a war footing. The RAF Police and their military counterparts continued to carry out their full range of internal security patrols in close liaison with the civilian police force, dealing with all manner of incidents ranging from rioting, looting, murder and bomb attacks. Although the troubles were widespread, they didn't really affect the building of the new RAF airfield at Akrotiri, which was finished on 1st January, 1956, and made ready for operational use. EOKA terrorist activity continued at an alarming rate with the violence being directed towards not only the British but also towards the Turkish Cypriot population. On 11th February, the terrorists launched a surprise attack against the RAF airfield at Nicosia and as a result, three airman were killed and one was seriously injured. The RAF

Police were quickly mobilised and the three terrorists concerned in the attack were arrested in the area soon after. However, it did little to deter such terrorist activity and on 4th March, EOKA destroyed a British Hermes civilian transport aircraft which had been parked on an apron at Larnaca civil airport. Although there had been no casualties on that occasion, the aircraft was being used to bring troops in and out of the island, and an investigation revealed that a bomb had been loaded on board the aircraft packed inside a suitcase. Although no one had been hurt, it was still an embarrassment to the authorities and in order to prevent further attacks, the RAF Police were called in and shortly after, commenced security duties at the airport. Consequently, every piece of luggage or cargo taken onto any RAF or civilian chartered aircraft after that event was thoroughly searched. Five days after that incident, Archbishop Makarios, the Greek Cypriot leader, was exiled to the Seychelles after it was revealed that he had strong links with the terrorist organisation. As a result of his deportation, the violence against the British and the Turkish Cypriot population escalated and as a consequence, the death penalty was introduced, with a number of terrorists being hanged inside Nicosia Prison.

Tragedy suddenly struck on the island of Malta on Saturday the 18th February, 1956, when a York passenger aircraft, operated by Scottish airlines, crashed shortly after taking off from the airfield at RAF Luqa on its way to Stansted Airport in the UK.

RAF eye witnesses reported that as the aircraft left Luqa they saw thick smoke pouring out from its two engines and shortly after getting airborne and climbing to approximately two hundred feet the engines stalled and fell out of the sky and crashed in a field close to Zurrieq where it burst into a ball of flame, killing all fifty personnel on board. Military and civilian rescue services, including the RAF Police from Luqa, arrived at the scene soon after and very quickly established that no one had survived the crash.

The aircraft, chartered by the RAF and flown by Captain Frank Coker, a very experienced pilot, had originally left RAF Abu Suier in Egypt a few days before and was taking forty-four members of the RAF and one member of the Army home to the UK. The passenger list was not released for twenty-four hours but when it was, it became clear that fourteen RAF Police NCOs had been amongst those who had lost their lives on that doomed flight. The funerals of the service personnel took place on the island three days later at the Mtarfa

Military Cemetery.

After an agreement on the 17th May, between the British Government and President Nasser, all British forces were withdrawn from Egypt. The years leading up to the withdrawal had been extremely troubled. There had been widespread open hostility towards the British presence in the country, withdrawal of local labour, riots and sabotage, bordering on the outbreak of all-out war. On the 26th July, President Nasser announced to a jubilant crowd in Cairo that he was taking over control of the internationally owned Suez Canal, which would be a valuable source of income with which to finance his dream of building the Aswan hydroelectric dam. That of course brought about a serious political situation and urgent talks with Egypt were called for by Britain and France.

Following the break down of the negotiations with Egypt on 21st August, a number of specially selected RAF Police NCOs reported to RAF Innsworth, where, after being fully equipped, inoculated and armed with Sten guns, they were conveyed to an RAF base in the south of England, where they joined other personnel being assembled as a Task Force to go into Egypt and the Canal Zone. After a comprehensive briefing, the Task Force, including the RAF Police contingent, flew out of London Airport and after several hours arrived in Cyprus. After leaving Akrotiri, the force travelled to Episkopi where given the terrorist situation in Cyprus, the RAF Police quickly organised their first task of securing the building, designated as the RAF Task Force Headquarters. The security measures enforced around the building were so strict that the Commander in Chief, General Keightley, was even held up at the entrance because the officer responsible for supplying the authorised access list, had forgotten to include his name on it. Luckily, however, the General saw the funny side to the slight delay. Over the days which followed, staff officers from all three services arrived at the headquarters to plan the way ahead and they were joined by a number of senior officers from the French forces, also involved in the military operation being planned.

During September, Air Commodore Proud retired as the Provost Marshal and from the service. He was succeeded in post by Air Commodore W I G Kerby CBE. His appointment was extremely popular amongst the branch because since its formation, the office of Provost Marshal had been filled by officers of the General Duties

Branch, who, in all fairness, had done a considerable amount of work moulding and developing the RAF Police organisation. However, Kerby was the first RAF Policeman to have attained the appointment, having held every rank along the way, from aircraftsman, right up to Air Commodore. He had initially joined the Royal Flying Corps in 1917, after running away from home and lying about his age. He had automatically transferred over to the RAF in 1918, where he continued to work on aero engines up until 1920, when he transferred into the RAF Service Police and after being trained by the Military Police, became one of the first RAF Police instructors at RAF Halton. Between the wars he had served at home and abroad and quickly rose through the ranks to become a Warrant Officer. In 1936, he was commissioned and during the war served with distinction, being mentioned in despatches twice. By the end of the war he held the rank of Group Captain and in 1945 was awarded the OBE. However, in 1954, he was elevated to CBE. Prior to taking up his appointment as the Provost Marshal, he had been the Command Provost Marshal with the 2nd TAF in Germany.

In Europe on 23rd October, a political uprising began in Hungary, with organised demonstrations being held all over the country. Unfortunately, the Soviet authorities intervened and sent tanks and troops into Budapest to crush the revolt. As a consequence, many were killed and injured and considerable structural damage was inflicted on the city. The Russians demonstrated to the world what communism meant by ruthlessly placing a very tight grip on their new found satellites.

On 31st October, 1956, following the complete collapse of negotiations with President Nasser, British and French forces launched Operation Musketeer in an effort to recover and restore normality to the Suez Canal zone. The military operation had started with a successful series of bombing raids against the Egyptian Air Force. That was followed up on 5th November, by the landing of a joint Anglo and French force of paratroopers, who invaded the area of Port Said at dawn. In addition to recovering the canal zone, the operation was also described by the politicians as a policing role to restore order after the Sinai Peninsular had been invaded by Israeli forces.

Shortly after, the RAF Police Task Force in Cyprus was divided into two sections, one of which remained in Cyprus to continue providing security for the headquarters, while the other section, under the command of Squadron Leader B Barrett, was flown into El Gamil airfield, close to Port Said. As the aircraft flew over the area, smoke was still pouring from the large fuel tanks near the docks and troops could clearly be seen deploying around the town. Once on the ground, the section, using two tents for accommodation, quickly established a base from which to operate. After a short time, patrols were sent out to liaise with other units in the area and during that task, the ferocity of the brief battle to capture Port Said quickly became apparent. However, judging by the number of Russian-made tanks and armoured gun carriers which had been abandoned in the streets, the Egyptians had made a hasty retreat. Soon after, in conjunction with the Royal Military Police, a system of mobile patrols was set up covering the Port Said and Arab quarter areas. As such, over the following days, a wide variety of police and security duties were undertaken, despite being subjected to a great degree of hostility from the Arab community, who were being lead by an anti-British underground movement, called the 'Red Eagle'. Although the Army Civil Affairs Branch tried to return the area to normality as quickly as possible, most of the shops remained closed and the streets remained deserted. The normally busy port was quiet and deserted of normal shipping and the entrance to the canal was totally blocked by ships, sunk by the Egyptians. As the days passed, things gradually became more organised and the French Military police and Egyptian civil police joined the patrols being carried out by the RAF and Royal Military Police. Over that period, it was interesting to note that the majority of the Royal Military Police NCOs engaged in the task were patrolmen from the Automobile Association, who had been called up from the reserve at the start of the crisis. Accordingly, as you can imagine, they did a fine job, route-signing the city and its approaches. As things settled down and became more organised, the RAF Police moved out of their tents, which were next to a temporary cemetery for the Egyptian troops killed in the battle, and into improved accommodation provided by a beach chalet. Following the cease-fire, UN forces were eventually sent to the region to take over from the Anglo and French force. Consequently, the RAF Police Task Force were relieved of their responsibilities and left Port Said on 31st November on board HMS Salerno, a tank landing ship. The journey back to the UK took them via Malta and Gibraltar. As the ship was entering Gibraltar, the captain accorded the RAF Police Task Force the unusual privilege of manning the quarter deck, a privilege normally reserved for the Royal Marines. On 18th December, the ship finally arrived at Plymouth. Four days later, the final handover in Port Said was completed and the last British and French forces left Egypt.

Building work had started at Addu Atoll in the Maldive islands, in January 1957, to construct the new RAF airfield on the tiny island of Gan. The base was required to provide a bridge between the RAF bases in the Middle East and those in the Far East without having to rely on the turbulent mainland territory of Asia. It was estimated that the building programme would take around two years to fully complete.

In Jordan on 30th June, in the presence of King Hussein, the British Ambassador and the AOC in C MEAF, the RAF station at Mafraq was officially handed over to the Jordanian Army, bringing to an end the thirty-five years that the RAF had been stationed in the country. A guard of honour was provided by members of the RAF Regiment and the RAF Ensign and Union Jack were lowered for the last time by two RAF Police NCOs, Flight Sergeant A C G Knapp and Sergeant T Morgan. After the ceremony, the last remaining RAF personnel boarded a convoy of around forty vehicles, which then made their way to RAF Habbaniyah, 500 miles away in Iraq. The event marked the sad closure of yet another RAF station within the Middle East. However, during the eight months leading up to the closure, conditions at the unit had been very cramped and indeed, very uncomfortable. Because of the rising tension with the local Arab population, and an attempted coup in April, all British servicemen had been brought into Mafraq from their surrounding units and had been confined to camp. The families had been evacuated and many of the remaining men had been detailed for long, mundane periods of guard duty to assist in maintaining the security of the camp. In fact, over the period leading up to the closure, hardly a night had gone by without local intruders being engaged, challenged and indeed in many of the incidents, arrested by the RAF Police patrols.

Throughout the year, the British started conducted tests on their first hydrogen nuclear thermo bomb on Christmas Island, in the middle of the Pacific Ocean. The island had been discovered by Captain Cook on the 24th December 1777, and is located 1,200 miles due south of Hawaii and sits on the top of an extinct volcano which rises six hundred fathoms from the sea bed. Being the largest coral atoll in the world, it covers an area of some 350 square miles, of which, 250 square miles consist of inland lagoons. The land however, is flat with the highest point rising to only thirty feet above sea level. During the months which lead up to the tests being conducted and during the period after the test, security on the island was provided by a detachment of RAF Police, who for the first time since their formation, were established within the South Pacific region. The detachment, No 11 RAF Police District, under the command of Flight Lieutenant G Innes, operated from a disused American airfield in the northern part of the island and provided a full array of provost and security functions for all three services involved in the programme, which also included the administration of a service detention centre. In addition, close liaison was established and maintained with the small detachment of civilian police officers from the Gilbertese Police Force, who were also stationed on the island. Two of the original RAF Police NCOs who had made up the detachment were Sergeant D Chapple and Corporal R J Denny. In addition, because Honolulu on Hawaii was used as a recreational centre for the British troops, an RAF Police NCO was attached there to serve with the American Military Police at Hickham Air Force Base.

During the evening of 19th September, three RAF Police NCOs, Flight Sergeant J W S Child, Corporal C S Middleton and Corporal D L Waterman, were on duty at RAF West Raynham in Norfolk, when they suddenly saw an American Air Force B-45 Tornado Jet Bomber crash on the outskirts of the station. They immediately responded to the incident and were on the scene very quickly. However, when they arrived, the aircraft was already a raging inferno, with thousands of gallons of burning aviation fuel pouring out all over the place. In addition, the intense heat was causing the aircraft's ammunition to explode around them, making conditions extremely perilous. However, with little regard for their own safety and with no protective clothing at hand, they continued their rescue bid and managed to get to the cockpit, where they successfully brought the crew out. Their gallant efforts were only just in time, because as soon as the crew had been removed, the cockpit and the armed ejection seats erupted in flames. The successful rescue had been achieved by the prompt and gallant actions of all three RAF Police NCOs that night. Had they not been there to assist, the crew would certainly have died in the flames.

As you can imagine, the USAF were thrilled with the rescue and as a result, Colonel J G Glover, the Commander of the USAF 47th Tactical Bombardment Wing, wrote personally to each man and to the APM at No 4 RAF Police District, expressing his gratitude for their swift actions and their courage.

During that same month, the first annual RAF Police Dog, Championship Trials were held at the RAF Police Depot before a large audience. After a combination of assessments throughout the year to determine which units had the most efficient teams, twenty dogs and their handlers were rigorously tested over a two day period, before a panel of judges. In all, some twelve separate aspects of the discipline were stringently tested, emphasising that the trial was not a circus act or drill display. The standards required by the judges were very high and not surprisingly, so were the performances. Each team was put through a set routine which included basic obedience, a criminal attack under gunfire, obstacles, searching, tracking and finally the condition of each dog was thoroughly checked to ensure it was being maintained to the highest standards. At the end of a tough competition, the winner of the first trials and the Sabre Trophy was announced as Acting Corporal D Hodgson and Air Dog Cindy, from RAF Waddington near Lincoln. The trophy, donated by Lieutenant Colonel and Mrs Douglas Bain, was presented to the winner by Air Commodore C M Stewart CBE, the AOC No 27 Group. The three judges involved in the first competition were naturally, Lieutenant Colonel Baldwin DSO, who had done so much to establish RAF Police dogs in the first place, Mrs G Hester of Croydon and Mr C H Belcher of Bingley.

For a number of years, the day to day routine of feeding, grooming and exercising RAF Police dogs at the school had been carried out by members of the WRAF, who had been borrowed from the trade of Administration Orderly. Unfortunately, there had been no formal training course involved in their employment at the kennels, and that particular type of employment limited the career prospects of the girls who continued to serve in that capacity. Indeed, many of them never attained the rank of Leading Aircraftswoman but enjoyed the job so much that they were prepared, in most cases, to tolerate the many drawbacks involved. However, in 1957, as part of an overall restructuring of ground trade groups, the trade of Kennel Maid was, for the first time, officially recognised, and the sixteen kennel maids serving at Netheravon became, for the first time, part of the RAF Police trade group structure. A formal training course was developed shortly after, during which the girls were taught not only how to care for the dogs on a daily basis, but also basic treatment techniques and how to prevent the spread of diseases and finally, general dog section administration. In addition, promotion prospects were opened up for the first time, and successful candidates could if they wished, attain the rank of corporal. Although the girls who enlisted as kennel maids thoroughly enjoyed their work, it was nevertheless a difficult, and at times, a very strenuous job, especially during the winter months.

As part of the overall reorganisation of the RAF ground trades, changes were brought in, which altered the way that RAF Police NCOs, having completed their basic trade training, were chosen for future employment within the branch. Previously, NCOs had been selected for employment on either station police duties or on provost duties at the districts. Those employed on districts, under the direct control of the Provost Marshal, viewed being posted on to the strength of a station as something of a demotion, while those employed on stations, under the command of their respective station commanders, viewed those on the districts with a certain amount of envy and in some cases, with mistrust. In addition, the promotion prospects for those working on stations were not as inviting as those for the NCOs employed on the districts and as you can imagine, there was a certain amount of rivalry between the two groups. So, in an effort to redress the imbalance, all RAF Police NCOs were, from that point on, posted onto station duties for the first part of their career and after a certain period, those NCOs who showed future potential were selected for employment with the districts. However, there was no guarantee of remaining with the districts and NCOs could, and would from that point on, be freely posted between the two, in an effort to widen and enhance their overall trade abilities and experience.

Over in Cyprus, the troubles were still very much in the news headlines and the co-operation between the RAF Police and the civilian police on the island remained excellent. So, it was only natural for the Commissioner of the Cyprus Police Force, Lieutenant Colonel G White OBE, (who was also the Chief Constable of the Warwickshire Constabulary, on loan to Cyprus) to be invited by the APM, Wing Commander H M Shephard, to carry out a formal inspection of No 24 RAF Police District. It was the first time that such an inspection had taken place at the headquarters in Nicosia and accordingly, regular and auxiliary personnel from the headquarters, Limassol, Famagusta and RAF Nicosia were assembled on parade. Amongst those present, were Flying Officer McKenna OBE, the Stalag Luft 3 investigator, Inspector Redjeb Halil Effendi, the Head of the RAF Police Auxiliaries in Cyprus and Corporal M Unwin, the survivor of some twelve EOKA bomb attacks. After inspecting the parade, accompanied by the Command Provost Marshal, Group Captain S N Kettle, Lieutenant Colonel White addressed the parade:

> I would like to thank Wing Commander Shephard for asking me to come along this morning to see you on parade. I have always had a great affection and a very high regard for the Royal Air Force, and therefore it is a very great privilege to take part in a parade made up of members of the Royal Air Force Police. The other reason is that it provides me with an opportunity of expressing to everyone of you my own personal thanks for the great help which you men here this morning, and your comrades who have left the island, have given in dealing with terrorism during the last two years.
>
> I think myself that, as far as you chaps are concerned, the job that you are doing on this island since you have been here is probably the most important work that any member of the Royal Air Force Police can be called upon to perform in any place where the Royal Air Force are stationed. I can think of no other territory where your services have been more valuable, and no other territory where the work can be more hazardous, and I can think of no other territory where the work can be more interesting. This is really police work with a vengeance.
>
> I spent a good many hours a year ago when we were going through a very difficult period, particularly in the evenings, sitting in the back of a Land Rover strictly incognito, I found it difficult to sit at home, and I expect I was seeing some of you chaps frequently 'out on the job'. You and your colleagues, the Military Police, were often first on the scene of the incident and got on with the task which confronted one of you. The example which you

set at that time is one which you should all be very proud. I
was very proud indeed and I hope that you too have acquired
a certain amount of satisfaction in knowing that you did a
dangerous job well.'

After the address, the Commissioner was given a full guided tour
around the headquarters building and the operations room, which was
fitted out with three separate, up-to-date radio networks, capable of
controlling RAF Police patrols over the entire island, as well as
communicating directly with the civilian police, and was impressed by
what he saw. Later during a cocktail party, attended by numerous
senior Army, RAF and civilian police officers, he expressed his
immense pleasure and gratitude at having been afforded the
opportunity of visiting the headquarters and speaking to the RAF
Police serving on the island.

Ever since their formation, the RAF Police had always taken on
unusual tasks whenever their assistance had been called for, and in
1958, they were confronted with another unique challenge, when they
took on the major responsibility for safeguarding the nuclear weapons,
assigned to the RAF. As such, armed RAF Police NCOs found
themselves responsible for providing the constant security measures
required to protect Britain's nuclear deterrent. The assignment,
although extremely important, was nevertheless, very monotonous and
involved carrying out static guard duties, mobile patrols and convoy
escorts. Accordingly, the initial trade training specifications at the
Police School were altered to cater for the requirements of that new
commitment.

In Aden, on 2nd May, 1958, the British Governor declared a state
of emergency as Egyptian-sponsored civil unrest, violence and anti-
British protests continued to escalate within the colony. Accordingly,
security at all the British military bases was increased and further
troops were sent out to reinforce the colony and restore law and order.
The colony was situated on the peninsula of volcanic rock which juts
out at the southernmost tip of Arabia, and was one of the Imperial
ports out to the Far East, on the old Arabian spice route. During that
period, it had been a duty-free port and as such, many consumer
goods could be bought there at very cheap prices. One of the recent
additions to the colony's industries at the time had been a large oil
refinery belonging to British Petroleum, which had been built in virgin

desert. Of all the RAF stations within the command, the two largest were located in Aden. The first, RAF Steamer Point, had been home to the Command Headquarters, No 114 Maintenance Unit, the Aden Supply Depot and the main military hospital. The second, RAF Khormasksar, having had an active airfield, was home to a number of fighter, transport and helicopter squadrons. In addition to their normal role, both RAF stations had maintained large RAF Police Flights. However, Aden being a somewhat hot, dusty and barren place, also provided personnel serving there with the chance to escape from it all, down to the services leave centre at the coastal resort of Mombassa in Kenya. A similar scheme had also been introduced for the RAF Police dogs serving within in Aden. Although the Alsatians stood up to the incredible heat in the colony pretty well, they were prone at times, to suffer from various skin complaints, which proved difficult to treat in the uncomfortable climate of Aden. To resolve the problem, the dogs had to be flown out to the more temperate climate of Kenya to recover. Unfortunately, they didn't see Mombassa but instead went to the kennels at RAF Eastleigh, where they received the best veterinary treatment and were put on 'light duties' until completely recuperated.

In July, the British and Commonwealth Games were held in South Wales and in order to accommodate the competitors, the Air Ministry agreed that part of RAF St Athan could be used as the Empire Village, being ideally situated some seventeen miles from the centre of the activities in Cardiff. The planning for the village however, had been going on for some eighteen months prior to the games starting. Responsibility for providing adequate security at the site had been given to the RAF Police, who worked very well in close liaison with the Glamorgan County Constabulary. Flight Lieutenant R A Morgan was appointed as the detachment commander and RAF Police NCOs were brought in from districts all over the country to form the police unit. A six foot chain link fence had been constructed around the entire 'village' site, with an inner fence providing added security around the female quarters. Passes were produced and issued and control of entry was maintained at all entrances leading into the site. The whole area set aside for the village had taken on an incredible transformation. The Airmen's Mess was turned into the competitors' dining room, having been fully redecorated for the occasion. The NAAFI club had been equally fitted out and would not have looked out of place in any fashionable area of town and on every corner, stands had been erected which served a wide range of drinks and snacks. In addition to the usual routine tasks performed by the detachment, the RAF Police had been able to take part in the flag raising ceremony, which had been carried out when each country's team had arrived at the village. As their were thirty-four countries involved in the games, there were as many ceremonies. No 5 Regional Band, conducted by their Director of Music, Flight Lieutenant R Davies, had played each team onto the field. After a few words of welcome from the Event Commandant, Major General Cowan CB, CBE, DSO, MC, DL, a fanfare had been played and the national flag from that particular country was subsequently raised and broken at the flag mast by either Flight Sergeant Fegan or Sergeant Potter, RAF Police.

At the conclusion of the games, it was pleasing to note that both the organisers and the competitors alike had fully expressed their appreciation in respect of the professional and helpful manner in which the RAF Police had gone about their tasks. They had certainly been kept extremely busy and during the period concerned, had checked and parked around 10,381 vehicles, and produced and issued some 8,921 permanent and 1,469 temporary passes, in addition to having carried out a host of other police and security commitments connected with the event.

With nuclear war then a global possibility, 1958 saw the formation of the Campaign for Nuclear Disarmament (CND) within the UK. The organisation, headed by the philosopher Bertrand Russell and assisted by Canon L J Collins, Michael Foot MP and the writer J B Priestly, quickly gained a great deal of public sympathy and recruited numerous members throughout the country. As a consequence, it had organised the very first protest march at Easter, when thousands of peaceful demonstrators had joined forces and had marched fifty miles from London to the Atomic Weapons Research Establishment, at Aldermaston, where they had demanded that Britain should give up her nuclear deterrent and the research into nuclear missile systems.

In Cyprus, EOKA terrorist activity had finally ceased during the spring, after an agreement had been reached in London to grant Cyprus her independence as a republic. The agreement, however, made provision for Britain to create and retain two Sovereign Base Areas (SBAs) in the southern half of the island.

In Singapore on 17th May, the new combined Provost Headquarters building, located on the junction of Waterloo Street and Bras Basah Road, had been officially opened by the Colonel Commandant of the Royal Military Police and Director of Operations Malaya, Lieutenant General Sir James Cassels, KBE, CB, DSO. During the ceremony, he had unveiled a brass plaque embossed with the badges of the three British Provost services, which had been set into the wall directly behind the information desk in the reception area of the foyer. The new building had been erected to take the place of the old pre-war Nissen hut which had, until the year before, stood on the exact same site, housing the same tri-service headquarters. Consequently, No 31 RAF Police District moved into the more spacious and modern accommodation which the new complex offered.

The defence policy of the United Kingdom over that period had been based on the possession of a weapons system acting as a deterrent to any potential aggressor, which happened at the time to be the USSR and the Warsaw Pact Alliance. Consequently, in line with that policy, the United Kingdom had developed and had brought into service their own nuclear capability, in the form of free-fall bombs, operated by the RAF using the V Force Vulcan, Valiant and Victor bombers. In addition, the Blue Streak ballistic missile system capable of carrying nuclear warheads had been developed and deployed at sites on the east coast. However, during the year, in an effort to counter the increase in the Soviet weapon systems, the RAF introduced the Thor Intermediate Range Ballistic Missile into service. As a result, on Friday 19th September, reporters from all the main newspapers, together with television cameramen, gathered outside RAF Feltwell, near Thetford in Norfolk, to witness the delivery of the first missile to be handed over to Bomber Command and No 77 Squadron. The convoy, comprising the ninety-foot long missile transporter, had been escorted by the RAF Police from its storage area to the final delivery point. Although the missile was British, the nuclear warheads carried by the system belonged to the Americans and as such, were subjected to both British and American control. However, for some months prior to the delivery being made, a specially selected and trained unit of RAF Police NCOs had been formed at the station, with the sole task of providing the important 'all round security protection' for the missile system. As Thor was developed, further sites were set up at RAF North Luffenham, RAF Helmswell and RAF Driffield and guarded by the RAF Police and the US Air Force Police working side by side.

A list was published, on 14th October, which detailed the special operational honours and awards issued in respect of the emergency situation in Cyprus during the EOKA campaign. The list had contained the details of thirty-seven RAF Officers, NCOs and airmen who had been rewarded for their peacekeeping and gallant actions during the troubles on the island and from the list, a quarter of the honours had been awarded to members of the RAF Police, who were, or had been, serving with No 24 RAF Police District. The awards had included an MBE for Squadron Leader W E Cannon and BEMs for Flight Sergeant T B Grimshaw, Corporals H W Spackman and F G Wright. In addition, a number of RAF Police personnel had been mentioned in despatches (including Flying Officer McKenna) or awarded commendations from the C-in-C.

The church of St Clement Danes, in the Strand in London, had originally been built in 1681 by Sir Christopher Wren. It had been a pretty church, made famous by the children's nursery rhyme "Oranges and lemons say the bells of St Clements, I owe you five farthings say the bells of St Martins." However, on the night of 10th May 1941, it had been completely destroyed during a German air raid on London. In 1953, the church was still lying in ruins when the Air Council had accepted it from the Diocese of London, and had agreed to renovate it as the Royal Air Force Church. After four years of painstaking work, the church had been completely rebuilt and fully restored to serve as the perpetual shrine of RAF remembrance. On Sunday 19th October, a service had been held at the church, attended by Her Majesty the Queen, HRH Prince Philip and other members of the royal family, to reconsecrate it. Security, prior to and during the service, was of course, provided by the RAF Police from No 5 RAF Police District, who had carried out a full search of the building before mounting an all-night guard at the church prior to the service taking place. The following day, RAF Police NCOs had also carried out a wide range of tasks in and around the church, which had included the reception and parking of vehicles, control of entry into the church and assisting the City of London Police, with crowd control and traffic point duties.

On 1st December, the RAF Police Districts within the United Kingdom were once again reorganised and reduced from seven districts to five, covering England, Scotland and Wales. No 1 RAF

Police District was located at RAF Turnhouse near Edinburgh, No 2 RAF Police District was located at RAF Church Fenton in Yorkshire, No 3 RAF Police District was located at RAF Spitalgate near Grantham, No 4 RAF Police District was located at RAF Innsworth near Gloucester and finally No 5 RAF Police District was located at RAF Northolt in West London. The RAF Police presence in Northern Ireland continued to be known as No 10 RAF Police District.

In February 1959, a violent guerrilla campaign against the ruling Sultan, which had been going on since the mid-1950s, ended in Muscat and Oman. During that time, the RAF had been actively involved in various operations which had been mounted to support the Sultan and his forces. However, with the likelihood of guerrilla and terrorist activity being renewed in the region, the RAF were allowed to maintain operational bases at Sharjah, Salalah and Masirah in Oman. The control of those far flung stations had previously been under the wing of RAF Habbaniya and as such, had formed part of HQ MEAF. However, after 1st April, 1958, they became part of the newly created Headquarters British Forces Arabian Peninsula. The Command Headquarters had been rather unique because ever since 1928, the Colony of Aden and its protectorates had been 'garrisoned' not by the Army, but by the RAF. Accordingly, the AOC held the title of Commander and had RAF, Army and Royal Navy units under his command. From the RAF Police point of view, No 22 RAF Police District, under the command of Wing Commander G F McMahon, maintained its own headquarters at RAF Steamer Point in Aden, and was responsible for policing the extremely large geographical area covered by the Command Headquarters. That included not only the stations within Aden, but also Sharjah, Salalah, Masirah, Bahrain (RAF Maharraq) and finally RAF Eastleigh in Kenya. Indeed, the district was even more unusual because it also had a detachment of Royal Military Police NCOs working under the direct control of the RAF Police.

Elsewhere around the world, the RAF Police had been kept extremely busy with a variety of different police and security commitments. For instance, in April, Investigators from No 9 RAF Police District in Malta had been carrying out an intensive investigation into the circumstances of how a home-made bomb came to be placed up against a Valiant bomber aircraft parked at RAF Luqa. Additionally, while that enquiry was taking place, Investigators from

No 32 RAF Police District in Malaya had been carrying out an investigation into the circumstances which had resulted in a helicopter crashing, during which three RAF personnel had been killed.

On 8th June, RAF Habbaniya and Basrah were closed down and, after forty years of service in the region, the RAF finally withdraw from Iraq. It was a sad end brought about by the revolutionary government who had seized power in the country the previous year following the assassination of their king. As the overall political situation worsened, pressure had been placed on the British Government to withdraw its presence. As part of the pressure, the RAF had been denied the use of their units for flying operations and as such, there was no point in trying to keep them open. The ten horses however, which had been used so successfully by the RAF Police Mounted Section up until then, were all transferred to RAF Akrotiri in Cyprus, where they continued to give the same valuable operational service.

Since its relaunch in 1948, the circulation of the *Provost Parade* had been steadily increasing and had become a very popular magazine with almost everyone serving in the branch and even a large number of RAF personnel serving in other trades within the service. Its success again took on a turn for the best when during the 1950s, cheeky cartoons depicting the RAF Police at work, started appearing between the covers. Although contributions had been accepted from a number of budding artists, three cartoonists stood out above the rest. The first of the popular series, appeared in the November 1952 edition having been submitted by Junior Technician Clayton, an airframe fitter. However, his success no doubt inspired the talents of Sergeant S Shepherdson, an RAF Police NCO, who, in the May 1953 edition, submitted the first of his own particular brand of cartoons under the name of Shep. However, while Shep and Clayton were battling it out for supremacy between the pages, another talented cartoonist, Flying Officer G N B Miller, an armaments officer, serving at RAF Waddington, submitted the first of many rib ticklers in the August 1953 issue, using the name Dusty. His submissions were particularly cheeky and showed the RAF Police carrying out their functions as seen through the eyes of their customers. In fact his collection of cartoons were simply entitled *As Others See Us*.

Chapter VI
End of an Empire

The beginning of the 1960s marked the final stages of the close down of what was once a vast British empire around the world. It also highlighted the increasing diversity of specialist roles being undertaken by the RAF Police. The first was, of course, the detailed development of the security protection required for the nuclear weapons held by the RAF as part of the national defence deterrent and the second was the establishment and formation of what became known as Travel Control Security (TCS) measures. Up until that time, most of the troop movements around the British empire had been undertaken by huge troopships. However, as British influence around the world grew smaller and many of the British military bases closed down, it became much cheaper and faster to carry out troop movements either by RAF transport aircraft or indeed civilian aircraft, chartered for the purpose. However, the procedure was seriously prone to attack by terrorists, either hijacking the aircraft in flight or sabotaging it whilst on the ground. Indeed, there had been several such terrorist attacks mounted against civilian aircraft during the preceding years and the RAF desperately wanted to avoid similar problems. Consequently, in an effort to overcome such a threat, selected RAF Police NCOs were trained in the new role and, soon after, TCS units were formed at all airfields dealing with passengers and large freight movements.

Unfortunately, over the previous years, there had been a number of national security scandals, which understandably had caused great embarrassment and widespread alarm to the British Government and in some cases the armed forces. In addition, they had also caused grave damage to the country's reputation with her allies, mainly the United States of America, who were not at all happy with the way things had been handled and as such, a certain amount of mistrust had developed. As a consequence, the government appointed a committee, under the chairmanship of Lord Radcliffe, to examine what had gone wrong and to report on the whole subject of the state of our national security and the way it could be improved, to prevent any further embarrassment.

After a mere forty-three years of loyal service to king and country, Air Commodore Kerby finally retired from the RAF on 1st February. However, he maintained his connections with the branch in the years which followed and continued to offer his services as the President of the RAF Provost & Security Association. He was duly succeeded in post as the Director of Personal Services (Provost Marshal), by Air Commodore W S Gardner CB, OBE, DFC, AFC, who again was not a professional policeman, but a pilot. During the war years he had been an operational pilot flying bomber aircraft and it was whilst engaged in that role that he was awarded the DFC and bar and the AFC for gallantry in the air. Prior to taking up his appointment as Provost Marshal, Air Commodore Gardner had been the head of the Plans, Training and Operations Division of the Central Treaty Military Planning Organisation.

In Cyprus on 2nd February, the first ever dog-handling course to be held on the island, specially for the RAF Police Auxiliaries, was successfully completed at RAF Nicosia. In all, seven Auxiliaries, trained by Corporal P Regan RAF Police, had successfully completed their training and during the subsequent passing out parade, the Inspecting Officer, Squadron Leader A Smart BEM, of No 24 RAF Police District, congratulated the handlers and their instructor on their smart appearance, the condition of their dogs and the high standard of training which they had achieved. Shortly after, all seven took up their role as qualified handlers patrolling and guarding various RAF installations around Cyprus. In addition, because the scheme proved to be so successful, the idea was copied soon after in the Far East, where twelve volunteers from the RAF Police Auxiliaries, under the instruction of Sergeant J A Pearson, successfully completed a locally organised training course to become qualified dog handlers.

As the cold war dragged on and the USSR continued to develop and expand its intermediate range weapon systems, the threat of nuclear attack against Britain increased in size. As intelligence sources indicated that the USSR had the capability of destroying our Blue Streak missile sites before the weapons could be prepared for launch, the system was scrapped on 13th March, leaving the Thor and V Force to provide our nuclear sting. However, that did little to please the CND movement, which by then was holding large demonstrations around the country almost every weekend. The RAF had taken on the role of providing Britain's nuclear deterrent, using the Thor missile to strike into the heart of Russia and the V Bomber Force to deliver free-fall nuclear weapons. As such, the CND mounted various protest meetings at a large number of RAF stations around the country, with the aim of disrupting the operational role of the base. As you can imagine, their activities took up a considerable amount of RAF and civil police time in trying to prevent them from succeeding in their aims. As a result, RAF Police personnel from non-nuclear units were quickly drafted into the stations at risk, to reinforce and supplement the existing establishment in maintaining adequate security cover. Indeed, many of the demonstrations turned out to be quite violent affairs and most were covered by the media, who by their very presence, tended on a number of occasions to incite trouble, which of course helped to liven up their news reports.

On 1st April, after being tried at the Old Bailey, Flying Officer Anthony Wraight, an RAF pilot, was sentenced to three years imprisonment by Mr Justice Donovan, after being absent behind the Iron Curtain for three and a half years. Wraight had been commissioned into the RAF in 1953 and after successfully completing his training was posted to RAF,Chivenor in north Devon. However, shortly after arriving there he began writing to the Society for Cultural Relations with the USSR and also became acquainted with a member of the KGB employed at the Soviet Embassy in London. The case concerning Wraight had first come to notice during 1956, when during a routine security check, mail addressed to the KGB agent was intercepted by the Security Services and traced back to Wraight who had since been posted to RAF Halton. He was subsequently interviewed about the matter by a representative from the Security Services and Wing Commander J Smith, a provost officer from the Provost Marshal's Office. However, Wraight denied any involvement with the Russians or being involved in any type of espionage activity. The two investigators, unsatisfied with his answers, left Halton to conduct further enquiries and Wraight, fearing he was about to be court martialled, fled the country and went straight to East Berlin, where he received a full debrief from his KGB masters. Despite a search for him, nothing more was heard from him until he walked into the American Embassy in Moscow on 24th November, 1959 and asked to be sent back to the UK. On his arrival in London, he was arrested and subsequently interviewed by the Special Branch, the Security Services and Group Captain H D Bisley from the Provost Marshal's Office. During the interviews, Wraight continued to protest his innocence.

Later during the same month, seven members of the RAF Police, from No 1 and No 2 RAF Police Districts, under the control of Flight Sergeant B McRann, were invited for the first time to take part in an RAF recruiting campaign in Edinburgh. The team, complete with their Land-Rover and two motorcycles were invited to represent the RAF Police in encouraging potential recruits that a career in the branch was indeed a worthwhile venture. The three day recruiting campaign, organised by the RAF Careers Information Centre in Edinburgh, turned out to be a great success and throughout, the RAF Police element attracted a huge amount of positive interest in the branch and its work. In fact, the venture was so successful that the RAF Police were invited to return to Edinburgh for a similar recruiting drive being organised for June.

An estimated total of over a quarter of a million people attended the thirty performances of the 1960 Royal Tournament Show at Earl's Court, between 22nd June and 9th July. Amongst all the spectacles provided to thrill the crowds, the star of the show turned out to be a three year old RAF Police dog by the name of Judge, and the crowds loved him. The scenario for his performance happened to be a simulated RAF guided missile base being patrolled by an RAF Police dog handler and his dog. Suddenly, as the lights in the arena dimmed and the patrol commenced, the base came under a surprise attack from a group of armed saboteurs. In the initial stages, the team responded and the dog indicated the presence of the intruders. The handler, Corporal John Black, quickly challenged them and released Judge but unfortunately, as the dog made his way towards the intruders, they shot him dead, and he immediately dropped to the floor of the arena and lay there motionless. As you can imagine, nearly every person in the audience gave a loud sigh as they witnessed poor Judge cruelly gunned down. Indeed, night after night, many in the audience attempted to revive Judge by whistling at him and calling his name, but Judge remained quite still and played his part wonderfully. After the display ended and the team took up their positions in front of the royal box, Judge remained inert on the floor, then just as the salute was about to be given, he sprang to life and joined his handler in the line-up. The crowds loved him and their cheers filled the house.

On 31st July, the twelve-year state of emergency within Malaya finally came to an end. Britain had granted Malaya her full independence on 31st August, 1937, which had effectively ended 170 years of British rule in the colony. Unfortunately, that also meant the closure of RAF Kuala Lumpur, which was formally handed over to the Royal Malay Air Force soon after. Consequently, No 32 RAF Police District, based at Kuala Lumpur and No 31 RAF Police District, based at RAF Changi were disbanded, reorganised and retitled as the HQ P&SS (FEAF). In addition, the RAF withdrew from Ceylon when the remaining RAF station at Katunayake had also been formally handed over to the Royal Ceylonese Air Force.

During August and September, the RAF Police School moved home once again to RAF Debden, which was situated three miles south east of Saffron Walden in Essex. No 2 (Driving Training) and No 4 (Advanced Training) Squadrons were the first to move, followed shortly after by No 1 (Basic Training) Squadron. However, No 3 (Police Dog Training) Squadron had to be left behind at RAF Netheravon, until suitable accommodation could be built at Debden to house it. The Air Ministry Constabulary, which had been formed in 1923, had moved its training school from RAF Stafford to RAF Debden in March. Although the two schools operated quite independently of each other, the various instructional staff quickly established a close liaison and maintained co-operation with each other on a wide range of subjects of mutual interest. In addition, for the very first time since its creation, the *Provost Parade*, which at that time was being published four times a year, was circulated as the 'Official Journal of the Royal Air Force Police and the Air Ministry Constabulary'. Accordingly, the first three issues of the journal contained a detailed history of the Air Ministry Constabulary and later included articles submitted from within the force. The new Depot, under the command of Group Captain S N Kettle, had originally been opened on the 22nd April, 1937, as a fighter airfield. However, in May 1943, it was handed over to the American 8th Army Air Force, who had used it for the remainder of the war. Prior to the arrival of the RAF Police Depot, the station had been used as a technical training school.

On 21st September, Cyprus was finally granted her independence and Archbishop Makarios was allowed to return to the island, where soon after, he was duly elected as the first president of the new republic. Although Cyprus became a fully independent nation in its own right, Britain, as part of the overall independence agreement, still maintained her two SBAs. The first, protecting its bases in Dhekelia on the south-eastern part of the island and the second, protecting the area around Akrotiri and Episkopi on the south-western part of the island. The agreement had also made provision for the formation of a new civilian police force to uphold law and order within the new territory. It became known as the Sovereign Base Areas Police Force. However, because of initial manpower shortages to form the force, a request was made by the SBA Administrator for the loan of RAF Police NCOs in order to make the force operational whilst local recruits were being trained. Although resources were somewhat stretched at the time, the C-in-C MEAF, agreed to release thirty-five RAF Police NCOs for six months to assist. Soon after, the NCOs were nominated and arrangements were made to take over the former Cypriot police stations in the new SBA territory. Unfortunately, prior to leaving, the Cypriots had stripped everything out of the buildings and had left them completely gutted and bare. However, that posed no major problem and within a short space of time each of the newly acquired police stations was furnished and fully operational. The NCOs who had been selected to perform as SBA policemen wore their normal khaki uniforms and white webbing equipment, but were distinguished as SBA policemen by wearing a blue and white diced cap band around their white caps and a Metropolitan striped duty armband around their right wrists. As the task got fully under way, everything went very well for the RAF Police involved, who successfully dealt with a wide range of matters over the period concerned, earning admiration and praise from the Chief Constable and the SBA Administrator. In addition, the Provost Marshal and the C-in-C MEAF were also extremely pleased that the operation had gone so well; after all, it had been the very first time that the RAF Police had been called upon to assist in such an important way at the 'birth' of a brand new civilian police force.

On 7th November, as a reminder of the continuing tension between the East and West, the USSR demonstrated to the world her military might, when for the first time, inter-continental ballistic missiles were displayed during a parade through Red Square in Moscow. In Kenya, the state of emergency which had been brought about by the Mau Mau terrorist campaign within the country also came to an end during the year.

Much to the relief of many young men throughout the country, the last people to be conscripted into national service with the British forces were called up for duty on 31st December. However, earlier in the year, John Stewart became the last national serviceman to join the ranks of the RAF Police, when he was conscripted on 8th March. John had been born in Greenock, Scotland on 24th July, 1939 and had been educated at the Ladyburn Junior Secondary School, where for a time he had been the captain of the soccer team. In 1956 and 1957, he had been a member of the crew which had won the Scottish rowing championships. He had two older brothers also serving in the forces, one serving in the Royal Navy and the other in the Army. Prior to being called up for his military service, he had been a fireplace maker, a trade he intended returning to after his release from the RAF.

During the year there were a number of changes made to the specialist training courses being conducted at the Depot. The Special Investigation course, covering the investigation of criminal matters, was upgraded and a brand new specialist course was introduced, covering all aspects of security and counter-intelligence as it affected the RAF. Accordingly, the new breed of Security NCOs became specialists in countering the threat from espionage, subversion, sabotage and finally, terrorism. Needless to say, that before long, intense competition had developed for the limited number of vacancies being offered on either course. However the qualified Special Investigators still retained the advantage of furthering their experience, because since the late 1950s, specially selected officers and NCOs from the SIB had been attending the Home Office Detective Training courses, sponsored by the various civil police forces around the country.

On the 8th May, 1961, the British spy, George Blake was sentenced to a total of forty-two years imprisonment after being found guilty of spying for the Russians. That of course sparked off yet another security scandal and proved to be a further source of embarrassment to the government.

In order to protect her overland trade routes to and from India, Britain had, over a considerable number of years, established and maintained various treaties with the different tribes who controlled the Gulf region of the Middle East. Indeed, many of the treaties had been updated and renewed at the turn of the century in order to protect the oil deposits which were needed for the newly developed combustion engines. After the hostilities of the Second World War, and during the build up to the Cold War, the USSR had shown immense interest in befriending those oil-rich states, especially those with the potential for building Soviet naval bases with access into the Indian Ocean. As such, the whole region was one of continuing political change and tension. Tension which, it was believed by many, could have developed into the 'Third World War'.

Britain and Kuwait had of course been friends ever since 1899, and huge oil deposits had been discovered there in 1931. As a result, Britain and Kuwait agreed to set up the Anglo-American Oil Company and, of course, Britain depended heavily on the valuable oil supplies which Kuwait produced. At the time, the tiny Gulf state was the sixth largest oil producer in the world. So, during June 1961, when it appeared that Iraq was about to invade Kuwait, Britain placed her units in the Middle East on full alert and reinforcements were quickly sent into the region, ready to defend Kuwait if required. Although the invasion by Iraq never occurred, it was nevertheless a valuable military exercise in rapid response and the alert was cancelled soon after.

As economic and basic living conditions continued to worsen in East Germany, 1961 saw a record number of refugees leaving the country. With the border between East and West Germany strictly controlled, many saw their chance of freedom, by initially getting into Berlin. As a result, many obtained their freedom by simply crossing over into West Berlin. The East German authorities, alarmed at what was happening, started to fear a massive drain on their skilled workforce and took measures to prevent the situation from getting worse and on 20th August, work began to construct the Berlin Wall. The stark barrier was completed very quickly and was patrolled by armed East German border guards, with orders to shoot anyone trying to cross over into the West. A number of hopeful escapees tried but unfortunately, many lost their lives in the attempt. The building of the wall effectively cut the city into two zones and divided its population, relatives, friends and colleagues. In addition, it isolated West Berlin from the rest of West Germany and travel in and out of that half of the city was tightly controlled and directed along special 'corridors' into and out from the city. As for the Western Allies stationed in the city, the wall meant nothing and as such, they continued to exercise their right to move about within the entire area of Berlin unrestricted. Although the Western Allies recognised the correctly titled Russian Occupied Zone of Germany, they flatly refused to recognise the formation of the German Democratic Republic of East Germany. Obviously, a number of official crossing points were built in the wall and probably the most famous of them was 'Checkpoint Charlie' in the British zone. While the intense political situation continued within the city, No 3 RAF P&SS Detachment, stationed at RAF Gatow some 125 miles inside East Germany, continued to function as the only RAF Police unit operating from behind the Iron Curtain. The duties performed by the detachment were much the same as those performed by their colleagues around the world, except that by virtue of the Berlin Occupation Statues they, together with their counterparts in the Royal Military Police, were in fact the official police authority within the British zone. As such, the local civil police or other law enforcement bodies within the city had no jurisdiction over members of the occupying forces, their families or their national civilian employees. That, in effect, meant that anything which happened involving those people had to be dealt with by the Service Police.

The coming of 1962 saw the world, for the first time, on the brink of nuclear war, as the two superpowers, Russia and the USA, defiantly faced each other over the Cuban Missile Crisis. The renewed tension was suddenly increased when American aerial photographs clearly showed the deployment of Soviet missiles on the island of Cuba aimed towards the USA. As a consequence, the United States military had been put onto alert and the Navy was ordered to impose a complete blockade around the island. Shortly after, both the US and Russian Governments were locked into dialogue in an effort to defuse the situation and prevent it from developing into all-out war.

On the 16th July, Air Commodore Gardner relinquished his appointment as the Provost Marshal on being appointed Director

General of Personnel Services at the Air Ministry and promoted to the rank of Air Vice-Marshal. He was succeeded in post by Air Commodore J C Millar DSO, another pilot, who prior to taking up his new appointment had been the Commandant of the Central Signals Establishment at RAF Watton in Norfolk. He had been born in Dublin on Christmas Day in 1913 and was later educated at Malvern College and Trinity College, Cambridge. He had joined the RAF in 1934, and after flying in Army co-operation squadrons both at home and in India, he became a signals specialist. During the war he had flown Blenheims and Liberator aircraft and had been awarded the DSO for his low-level mining of the Venice Harbour and an attack on the railway sidings at Graz. After the war he had served at the Empire Radio School, the RAF Staff College, Bomber Command and at the Air Ministry.

By mid 1962, RAF Khormaksar in Aden was officially the largest RAF unit anywhere in the world, with an establishment of just over 3,000 officers and other ranks and a huge army of local civilian labourers. The busy airfield had been a shared facility with the civil airport and that of course made security of the RAF station all the more difficult to maintain. During September, Yemen had called upon the tribes in South Arabia to demonstrate and rebel against the presence of the British within the region. As a result, the incitement had provoked serious demonstrations within Aden itself, and that had been followed by periodic spates of guerrilla activity in the wild and largely inaccessible territory beyond. Accordingly, the RAF Police, who by then were getting quite used to that sort of political tension, had prepared themselves for the inevitable.

During October, the missile crisis in Cuba had been brought to a successful conclusion by the intervention of the United Nations Security Council. Their timely intervention had prevented the situation from developing into a further global conflict. Although nuclear war had been narrowly avoided, the episode added further fuel to the CND movement within the UK, who used it to promote their cause even further. However, it did little to stop the development of new weapon systems like the Blue Steel missile which was brought into service with the RAF. Blue Steel was an aircraft-launched missile capable of carrying a nuclear warhead for 200 miles when released at a height of 50,000 feet.

In December Britain again found herself involved in another terrorist campaign as the second Malaysian state of emergency was declared. Sponsored by Indonesia, the trouble began in Borneo with a number of carefully co-ordinated incidents of civil unrest and rebellion in both Brunei, a British protectorate, and the neighbouring colony of Sarawak. As the campaign developed, a violent rebel group tried to seize control of the main town and the local security forces and police found themselves hard pressed to deal with the situation. As the violence increased and threatened to get totally out of control, British troops were sent in to restore order.

By March 1963, the situation on Borneo had been brought under control and as a result, a detachment of RAF Police NCOs returned to the UK after having spent a four month tour of duty in Brunei, where they had been sent to assist the Sultan and his security forces in restoring order. During their tour of duty on the island, they had worked very closely with the local civil police, the Royal Military Police and the Royal Marines Police. In addition to providing the necessary security cover for the deployed RAF aircraft at Labuan airfield, they had been employed in maintaining the peace and restoring law and order. In doing so, the combined police units had been kept extremely busy and had dealt with numerous instances of looting, arson, robbery and violence, which had unfortunately been rather commonplace occurrences. After much effort, order was gradually restored in the town, which in effect forced the rebels out into the surrounding jungle and accordingly, the Royal Marines and the Gurkhas had been sent in to flush them out. The operation had been fairly successful and by the beginning of spring it had settled down enough to allow many of the reinforcement troops to return back to their home bases in Singapore and the UK.

During the same month, the Secretary of State for War, John Profumo, denied to the House of Commons that he had engaged in an affair with Christine Keeler, a woman described by the media as a prostitute. However, when it was later revealed that he had lied, and that Keeler had also been involved with the Soviet Naval Attaché, Eugene Ivanov, Profumo resigned in the midst of yet another embarrassing security scandal for the government. Then as if that particular episode hadn't been embarrassing enough, it was followed soon after, on 1st July, with Kim Philby being named as the 'third man' in the Burgess and Maclean spy affair.

On Saturday 29th June, RAF Waddington in Lincolnshire, received, at very short notice, the President of the United States, John F Kennedy, who paid a brief official visit to the station. As you can imagine, given such short notice, security arrangements were hastily, but successfully provided with the help of RAF Police reinforcements from the neighbouring RAF stations at Scampton, Hemswell Conningsby and Finningley. After a rather hectic but successful day, the President flew out of the station on board his Boeing aircraft and everything on the station quickly reverted back to normal again.

It had by then become common practice to staff the smaller and less important RAF stations with a single RAF Police NCO, who was responsible for policing his territory by working a flexible shift pattern. As such, the posts quickly became known as 'village constable' establishments, and although the terminology accurately described the community policing being carried out, it wasn't unfortunately, appreciated by everyone, which included the Provost Marshal. He disliked the term so much that on 26th July, he wrote a personal letter to the AOC at each of the home command headquarters and the Command Provost Marshals overseas, asking for their assistance in stamping out the terminology. In his letter, Air Commodore Millar described the term as being associated with that of a "fat old flatfoot, bending his knees outside the village pub". A quaint image it might have been, but it certainly wasn't the impression that he wanted the RAF community to have of the RAF Police. However, despite his concerted efforts, the terminology remained and became even more widespread, even if the Provost Marshal's description of the 'village constable' didn't.

In 1963, with brand new facilities having been completed, the RAF Police Dog Training School joined the Depot at RAF Debden and soon after on 31st July, RAF Netheravon closed. After settling into their new accommodation, Mr Charles Fricker introduced the competition known as the Annual Working Dog Trials. To obtain the results, he had to travel to every RAF station which had RAF Police dogs established on it and subject both the handlers and their dogs to a number of efficiency tests. As soon as the results were known, the best teams were invited to the Depot, where, to compete for the title 'RAF Police Dog Champion of the Year', they demonstrated their skills before an assembled audience. To present the prizes, Mr Fricker, enlisted the assistance of the Provost Marshal and other notable officers of air rank, and before long the trials proved to be a very popular annual event, so much so that similar events were subsequently organised in every overseas command.

On 12th December, Kenya was granted her independence from Britain and on the same day further north, in Libya, RAF El Adem was busy celebrating its twenty-first anniversary. At the time, the station was probably one of the best known in the region, having processed some 70,000 transit passengers through it, on their way out to the Near, Middle and Far East. In addition, another 10,000 RAF personnel had visited the station in connection with various detachments, trials and exercises which had taken place in the region. As part of the overall celebrations, the RAF Police stationed there had formed a Mounted Police Section to patrol the station perimeter fence which covered just over seven miles, across difficult terrain. The idea of forming the section had first been suggested a few months previously by the Station Commander, Group Captain N Briggs, and as a result, the resident provost officer, Flight Lieutenant W Sheppard, decided to have the section up and running in time for the Annual Formal Inspection by Air Chief Marshal Sir Denis Barnett, KCB, CBE, DFC, MA, the Air Officer Commanding in Chief, NEAF. In order to accommodate the section, stables were built by a number of police personnel in their off-duty time, and of course the necessary equipment was obtained to support the new concept. Once fully established, two fine looking horses, by the names of Shepp (Sheppard) and Briggie (Briggs) were purchased and handed over to Corporal T Walls, RAF Police and Constable Said, RAF Auxiliary Police, who became the first two members of the newly formed section.

By the end of the year, the Thor intermediate ballistic missile system had been withdrawn from service in favour of the newly developed Polaris deterrent and all the Thor nuclear warheads were duly returned to the USA. The RAF however, retained the V Force and their free-fall nuclear weapon systems, for which the RAF Police continued to provide 'around the clock' security protection.

As the Cold War continued between the East and West, an investigation which had been carried out in 1961 by the Security Service MI5 and the Special Branch, ended with the successful arrest of a number of Soviet spies, amongst them was the leader, Gordon Lonsdale, a top agent in the KGB. He, along with the others, was subsequently tried, convicted and sentenced to a lengthy prison sentence. However, during the following year, Greville Wynne, an alleged British agent was arrested in Russia, tried as a spy and finally sentenced to eight years imprisonment. The Russians were keen to get Lonsdale back and offered to exchange Wynne for him. After much negotiating, an agreement was reached and in 1964 Lonsdale was flown out to Berlin where the exchange was to be made. He was taken to RAF Gatow, where the RAF Police, under the command of Flight Lieutenant G D Whitney, were tasked with providing additional security arrangements for their temporary guest. Accordingly security arrangements at the station were increased to prevent the media and anyone else not on official business from gaining entry to the unit. The exchange of prisoners was successfully carried out during the following day at Checkpoint Heerstrasse on the Berlin Wall, after which Greville Wynne was taken straight to RAF Gatow to rest before embarking on his flight home. The huge security operation had been successfully carried out without encountering any problems and the officials at the Foreign Office in London later wrote to the Station Commander commending the whole operation and the way security at the station had been organised and maintained.

Following the release of the much awaited Radcliffe report on security during the year, a number of radical recommendations were quickly brought into being by the Air Ministry. The changes included the formation of a Directorate of RAF Security within the Provost Marshal's Department and the appointment of a new Director of Security (RAF), in addition to the appointment held by the Provost Marshal. As a result, the first officer appointed to the post was Air Commodore J Pike and although he held equal rank to the Provost Marshal, he was solely responsible for security matters and not RAF Police matters, which continued to remain under the firm control of the Provost Marshal, albeit a very fine line divided the two appointments. From that point on, all aspects of security took on a higher status and the RAF vetting system for identifying those thought to be vulnerable to pressure from hostile intelligence agencies was reviewed and updated. In addition, security staff were established within the Air Ministry, as well as at the Command and Group Headquarters and security officers were appointed on each RAF unit to provide specialist assistance and guidance to station commanders on security matters.

On 18th March, 1964, a multinational United Nations taskforce, comprising of, amongst others, civilian police officers from Australia and New Zealand, were sent to Cyprus to restore peace between the Greek and Turkish Cypriot population after violence had broken out again on the island. The Turkish Air Force had control of the skies above Cyprus and their Navy was only prevented from invading by the low-key intervention of the American 6th Fleet, which at the time, happened to be in the Mediterranean. In addition, the UN peacekeeping force was made up of specially selected RAF Police NCOs, under the command of a former colonial police officer, Squadron Leader R Truscott. So the RAF Police found themselves very much on the front line as the conflict escalated once again. However, on that occasion, their familiar white hats had been replaced by the standard UN blue beret. As for the RAF Police stationed within the SBAs, they once again put into practice the security measures quickly learnt from the EOKA troubles a few years before.

In Singapore during the evening of the 31st May, Indonesian terrorists launched an attack against the technical area of RAF Changi. The resulting noise of the explosion was heard by RAF Police Auxiliary Sergeant Sharif Bin Mohamad Isa, who was, at the time, off duty at his nearby home. However, he responded and quickly made for Changi village, where he mingled with the curious villagers looking for strangers. After about an hour, he saw a man who was an obvious stranger and so he challenged him and the man responded by getting into a taxi, which then drove off at speed. At that precise moment, the local APM, Wing Commander Pink was driving his car back from Changi when he saw the sergeant trying to flag down vehicles. The APM stopped and picked the sergeant up and whilst they continued to drive, the sergeant unfolded his story. Eventually, the taxi was forced to stop and the passenger was arrested and taken back to Changi where he was handed over to the civil police. After a further search of the area around the station, a second suspect was discovered and duly arrested. Eventually both men were tried, convicted and sentenced to death for causing the explosion. However, had it not been for the positive actions taken by Sergeant Sharif Bin Mohamad Isa, the two terrorists would certainly have made good their escape that night.

During the same period, the British Government was experiencing further problems of colonial unrest and upset around the world. Over in Aden, further British troops had been sent in to reinforce the colony as the violence there continued to escalate and the struggle went on to restore order. Even on the island of Malta, which Britain had always thought of as an extremely loyal territory, the population were forcefully but peacefully demanding their total independence from Britain. As those matters caused further problems for the government and the Foreign Office, British troops were sent into British Guyana to assist the authorities in restoring law and order following serious rioting and looting there. The colonial problems continued to develop the following month when the Prime Minister of Britain's last colony in Africa, Ian Smith, threatened unilateral independence, in response to Britain's insistence on full rights for the African majority. As he moved to enforce his threat, Britain responded by introducing sanctions against Rhodesia.

On 14th October, the Soviet leader, Nikita Khrushchev was unceremoniously ousted from power during a Kremlin coup, while he was away from Moscow on holiday. As a result, he was replaced by Leonid Brezhnev.

Diplomatic relations between Britain and Spain reached an all-time low on 3rd February, 1965 over the disagreements regarding the sovereignty of Gibraltar. In response, the Spanish Government closed their border and tried to impose a blockade on the colony. In the Far East during the month which followed, American troops were sent into Vietnam in an effort to stop the communist take-over in the region and that was followed in August, when Singapore finally broke away from the Malaysian Federation.

On 23rd September, 1965, trouble had become so serious within Aden that the British High Commissioner dissolved the constitution and imposed direct rule on the colony. His action, of course, provoked not only further unrest within the colony, but also from Egypt, where President Nasser fully supported any action which could result in the expulsion of the British from the region. The constitution which had governed the colony had been rather complicated and had been drawn up after agreements had been reached with the various ruling sheikhs, who at the time had controlled the population. Great Britain had been anxious to hold on to the colony because of its strategic importance within the region. However, nationalist strikes and terrorism, backed by the Egyptians, had steadily increased over the previous few years and had been further complicated by incursions from Yemen, where a bloody civil war had been raging since their republican revolution in 1963.

In November, Air Commodore Millar DSO, retired from the RAF and was subsequently succeeded in post as Provost Marshal by another former pilot, Air Commodore W I C Inness CBE OBE ADC. During the same month, the political situation in Rhodesia took on a new twist when Mr Smith, its Prime Minister, demanded total independence from Britain.

The RAF community in Aden were stunned when, two days before Christmas and without warning, terrorists attacked an RAF officer's married quarters, where a party was being held. A grenade was thrown into the house and as a result, the daughter of a senior RAF officer was killed and four other teenagers were seriously injured. It was a senseless attack which sickened and angered the entire RAF community. However, the repulsion did little to suppress the activities of the terrorists and from that point on, similar terrorist attacks took place throughout the seventy-five square mile area which formed Aden. As a consequence, RAF security was again increased and strengthened in an attempt to counter the threat of further attacks. Unfortunately, the airfield at Khormaksar, which at that time was under the command of Group Captain A Humphries, proved to be a nightmare as far as security was concerned, because it was a shared facility with the civil airport. However, working in harmony together, the RAF Police, under the command of Flight Lieutenant J McCarthy, and the RAF Regiment quickly overcame the problems and eventually brought in some very effective measures to improve their security problems. One of the measures they introduced included a 'four colour alert state' system, together with detailed instructions of what counter measures and actions were to be taken on the declaration of each state.

In Germany on 31st December, Hermann Glemnitz, the German interpreter serving with the RAF Police at RAF Gatow in Berlin, finally retired after a successful and rewarding career. During the Second World War, he had been employed as an interpreter at the Stalag Luft 3 Prisoner of War Camp and although he was absent on leave at the time of the Great Escape, he clearly remembered the Commandant being told by the Gestapo that the fifty officers had been shot. At the camp he had been responsible for briefing newly arrived prisoners on the rules and regulations. In doing so, he had to read off a list of items which the Germans had considered useful in aiding escapes. After reading out the list, the new arrivals had to declare having any such items and then surrender them to the guards. On one occasion, he remembered that a couple of RAF officers asked him, sarcastically, what they should do with their "Tommy guns and revolvers". Herr Glemnitz carefully and calmly scanned the list in front of him, looked up with no expression and replied, "Such items are not listed, so you may keep them." As you can imagine, the two RAF officers were flabbergasted.

After ten years of existence, No 10 RAF Police District, based at Sydenham in Northern Ireland, was quietly disbanded on the very same day that Herr Glemnitz retired. The district headquarters, commanded by Squadron Leader R T W Laing, had ceased to be an independent unit after that date but instead remained within the province as a detachment of No 1 RAF Police District. As such, nothing really changed in respect of its role, which carried on as normal, operating within the six counties.

On 1st July, 1966, following the withdrawal of France from the NATO military alliance, the Headquarters moved from Fontainbleau in France to a new home in Brussels, where RAF provost officers and Police NCOs continued to serve within the NATO multinational police and security organisation. In August, Indonesia called off its confrontation with Malaysia, bringing an end to the second state of emergency in the region and in the NEAF, RAF Nicosia in Cyprus and RAF Idris in Libya finally closed.

At RAF Changi in Singapore, the RAF Police again found themselves carrying out another unusual commitment, following the decision of the Singapore Government to appointed ten members of the branch as Deputy Assistant Controllers of Customs, Immigration and Revenue. The unique task had not been carried out by the RAF Police anywhere else in the world. At that time, over 10,000 passengers were passing through the airport every year, but no doubt, very few of them ever realised that the Customs and Immigration Officers who had dealt with them were in fact members of the RAF Police, working in civilian clothes. In carrying out their duties in that capacity, the NCOs were responsible for collecting all the customs revenue on behalf of the government.

For a number of years, Bugis Street in the heart of Singapore had gained quite a reputation as a vice centre offering a wide variety of sexual offerings to the British servicemen who were visiting or permanently stationed in the region. Accordingly, the area was heavily patrolled and supervised by anti-vice units from both the civilian and service police organisations who worked extremely hard in trying to control the uncontrollable. In addition to female prostitutes, the area was infested with catamites who, despite looking like handsome and enticing young ladies, were in fact homosexual men. In fact, over the years, many a young man has learned a valuable lesson when suddenly confronted by more than he had bargained for on an evening out. On one such occasion, a young airman reported to the RAF Police that his wallet had been stolen whilst in Bugis Street. During the interview which followed, he told the RAF Police that he had been in Bugis Street alone and had met a beautiful young lady and together they had gone off to spend the night at her home. Unfortunately, it was not until they were in bed together that he discovered that the beautiful young woman was in fact a catamite. Obviously shocked by the experience, he leapt out of the bed, grabbed his clothes and hastily left the premises. If it hadn't been for the fact that his wallet containing his identity card and his money was missing, the event would have gone unreported. However, his identity document was accountable and therefore he had no choice but to report the matter. At the time the RAF Police Anti-vice section kept a photograph album of all the registered catamites and luckily the young airman was able to identify the one who might have stolen his wallet. The catamite was subsequently located and taken to the police station and interviewed. It transpired that as the young airman removed his trousers and placed them on the bed, a second catamite, who was hiding under the bed reached up and stole the wallet. The identity card and wallet were later recovered and the two thieves prosecuted.

Regrettably, the P&SS Detachment at RAF Eastleigh in Kenya was disbanded on 1st December, 1966, when the RAF station was formally handed over to the Kenyan Air Force. However, a number of RAF Police NCOs remained in Kenya, on loan, to continue training the newly formed Kenyan Air Force Police, which had been formed the previous year. In Rhodesia, three weeks later, the Prime Minister, Ian Smith, declared that Rhodesia was an independent republic, no longer under British control.

In Aden, the violent terrorist activity by the National Liberation Front (NLF) and the Front for the Liberation of occupied South Yemen (FLOSY) continued to rise to an unacceptable level. On Christmas Eve, two RAF Police NCOs using an X-Ray machine were badly injured in the civil freight shed at Khormaksar when a bomb, placed inside a mail sack was detonated by the terrorists. Even allowing for that incident, casualties amongst the RAF were reasonably light, while the Army continued to suffer the most victims. However, during the early months of 1967, the situation in Aden became extremely serious and savage terrorist attacks continued against British servicemen and their families. In fact, the situation became so bad that the wives of servicemen were, for the first time, armed with machine guns to defend themselves and their children. In addition, the military authorities had been given primacy over the local police, in an effort to restore law and order, but it was hopeless. At the end of June, eighteen British soldiers were killed when the civil police in the colony mutinied and as the situation deteriorated, a decision was made to evacuate all the service families from the region and a massive airlift was mounted to execute the plan. However, while it was in progress, the Six Day War between Israel and Egypt broke out and hostilities against the British in Aden escalated and a general strike was called. The airlift continued and by 20th July, all the service families had been successfully withdrawn. As the weeks went by, the colony became totally ungovernable and the British Government decided to withdraw and grant it unconditional independence. As a result, all military personnel were steadily withdrawn into the safety of RAF Khormaksar and by 29th November, all British military personnel had been successfully airlifted from the colony. The RAF had served for forty-eight years in Aden.

On a cold and misty morning at RAF Halton on 12th November, a flight sergeant was out walking his dog in one of the large wooded areas which adjoined the camp. Suddenly, his dog became excited at something hidden in the undergrowth and as he went to investigate, he was confronted with the partially clothed body of a young airwoman, later identified as Rita Ellis, who had been brutally murdered. Within a short space of time, the normally quiet location had been transformed into a hive of activity as a murder investigation commenced on the camp. Although the local civilian police claimed jurisdiction over the investigation, they asked for assistance from New

An RAF Police NCO and members of the local security force on patrol in Iraq – circa 1956.

RAF Police Auxiliaries on parade at RAF Changi in Singapore – circa 1957.

Members of the WRAF Police driving an RAF Police escort Landrover – circa 1960.

An RAF Police Auxiliary member (possibly Constable Said) of the Mounted Section at RAF El Adem in Libya – circa 1964.

Sergeants Greavey and Billows RAF Police, provide an escort through the London traffic for an RAF pilot taking part in the 1969 *Daily Mail* Transatlantic Air Race.

RAF Police from the Headquarters Provost Security Services (UK) Support Squadron deploy under field conditions – 1970.

An NCO from the RAF Police Mounted Section at RAF Akrotiri in Cyprus, on patrol at the main gate to the station – 1971.

HRH The Princess Margaret carries out her inspection during the first Royal Review of the RAF Police and Provost Branch at the RAF Police Depot, Debden – 1973.

Sergeant Davies RAF Police, provides a VIP escort vehicle for General Scheidel, the USAF Provost Marshal, during an inspection at RAF Fairford – 1987.

An RAF Police mobile patrol speaking to an airman on the flight line of an RAF station – 1989.

An RAF Police 'Quick Reaction Force' employed on nuclei security duties, practising their deployment skills – 1989.

Members of the Royal Air Force Police Dog Demonstration Team with their dogs and coach – 1992.

Members of the RAF Police on a counter terrorist foot patrol as part of the Station Security Guard Force (SSGF) – 1994.

RAF Police NCOs from the HQ P&SS (UK) Support Squadron with their latest Police Mobile Operations Vehicle (PMOV) on deployment – 1995.

Brassards of office worn by the Provost Marshal (PM), the Deputy Provost Marshal (DPM), Assistant Provost Marshals (APM) and Warrant Officers and NCOs of the Royal Air Force Police (RAFP).

The RAF Police are back in the Guardrooms, RAF Shawbury – 1996.

Scotland Yard and P&SS. As a result, investigators from No 5 RAF Police District, under the command of Flight Lieutenant E Whitfield and Warrant Officer J Murphy responded. Although the murder 'incident room' had initially been set up in the main guardroom, it had been forced to move into larger accommodation within a barrack block as the investigation grew to deal with the massive enquiry.

Elsewhere in the world, the people of Gibraltar, still cut off by the Spanish, voted unanimously to remain under British sovereignty and the border between the colony and Spain remained firmly closed. In Cyprus, calm had been restored by the presence on the island of the peacekeeping force from the United Nations.

On 17th January. 1968, eight members of No 18, Basic RAF Police Training Course, successfully completed their training and passed out as Leading Aircraftsmen with the unpaid rank of acting corporal. In doing so, they became the first members of the RAF Police to pass out of training with two chevrons on their arms since the practice had been stopped by the Air Ministry some years before.

The RAF Police involvement in the Rita Ellis murder inquiry at RAF Halton came to an end on 8th March, when the team was finally stood down and returned to normal duties. During the investigation, the RAF Police had played a valuable part in pursuing thousands of enquiries both within the UK and at units overseas. However, the civilian police continued the search for her killer, linking it to a similar style attack on a civilian nurse at Tring, a village not far from Halton.

Chapter VII
Fifty Years and Beyond

On 1st April, 1968, all around the world, the Royal Air Force and of course, the RAF Police, celebrated their Golden Anniversary in a number of different ways which had been organised to mark the occasion. Despite being the junior service with uncertain beginnings, the RAF had achieved an incredible amount and had earned for itself a first-class reputation during its brief and rather colourful fifty-year history. Likewise, in parallel, the RAF Police organisation, had also grown from very humble beginnings to become a well-disciplined and professional branch, working at all levels within the service and in every theatre around the world. Despite the occasion, the RAF Police were kept fully employed over the celebration period, carrying out their various police and security commitments at all the various functions which had been laid on to mark the special occasion. The largest event by far took place at RAF Abingdon in Oxfordshire on 14th June, when Her Majesty the Queen, Prince Philip, The Queen Mother, The Duchess of Gloucester, Princess Marina and some 25,000 former and serving members of the service attended the largest RAF exhibition ever assembled. An incredible amount of work had been put into organising it and not surprisingly it turned out to be a huge success and a superb way of celebrating the occasion and accordingly, it was enjoyed by everyone who took part in it. To promote the occasion even further and to add more sparkle to the celebrations, the feature film *The Battle of Britain* produced by Mr Harry Saltzman, and starring Kenneth Moore, was also being filmed over the same period at the RAF Police Depot at Debden and at RAF Duxford. Accordingly, a number of RAF Police NCOs, eager no doubt to make the correct impression, were 'recruited' into the production as film extras.

Unfortunately, not everything during the year was cause for celebration and that was made obviously clear when Chief Technician Douglas Britten, a member of the RAF for nineteen years, was sentenced at the Old Bailey to a total of twenty-one years imprisonment, after pleading guilty to espionage charges. The charges had been brought against him after a lengthy investigation carried out by the Security Services and the RAF Police, uncovered his damaging activities and exposed him as a spy who had, since 1962, been supplying the KGB with highly sensitive and classified information. He had been recruited in the UK by a KGB agent known as 'Yuri' whom he had supplied with an RAF radio transmitter in return for cash. Shortly after that, Britten was posted to Cyprus as a linguist at a highly sensitive RAF signals unit, and the KGB assigned him to one of their local controlling officers, who blackmailed him into handing over further sensitive information in return for more cash. Because Britten's lifestyle had put him into considerable debt, the money from the Russians helped him to sort out his finances. Unfortunately, once he did that, there was no turning back and the KGB continued to demand more and more classified material from him and he continued to supply it. After a while, it came to the notice of the British Security Services that the Soviets were in possession of material which could only have come from the RAF in Cyprus. As a result, the RAF Police were alerted to what was happening and an investigation commenced. Soon after, Britten was posted back to RAF Digby in the UK, where the KGB continued to pressure him into handing over further classified material. Things continued for a while, but the RAF Police investigation team, under the command of Wing Commander G Innes, were quickly closing in on him. In February 1968, he was photographed by the Security Services delivering a message to the Soviet Embassy after his KGB master failed to appear at an arranged meeting. Special Branch and Wing Commander Innes were alerted and working together, they soon uncovered Britten for what he really was. Obviously, the case highlighted further room for improvement in respect of security procedures and education, and they were soon actioned. However, as a matter of procedure in all espionage cases, the enquiries continued long after Britten's conviction, in order to assess exactly to what degree he had damaged and compromised the security of the nation.

On 20th August, 1968, the USSR showed her aggressive nature to the world once again when Soviet and other Warsaw Pact troops invaded Czechoslovakia, in order to crush the liberal regime, headed by Alexander Dubcek.

Air Commodore Inness retired as the Provost Marshal on 1st October and was succeeded in post by Air Commodore A D Panton OBE DFC. He had been born in Calcutta and educated at Bedford School before joining the RAF in 1936, to train as a pilot. During 1939, he had been awarded the DFC for flying reconnaissance missions over Germany and was subsequently shot down three times. On the first two occasions, he had managed to evade capture and had returned to the UK. However, on the third occasion, he had sustained serious burns and had been captured by the Germans. After being treated for his injuries he was imprisoned at Stalag Luft 3 until the camp was liberated by the Russians in 1945. Prior to taking up the appointment of Provost Marshal, Air Commodore Panton had been the Project Director organising the RAF Golden Jubilee celebrations.

In an effort to reduce defence costs, the government's White Paper on Defence, which had been issued in July, announced the closure of some twenty RAF stations, both within the UK and around the world. In addition, the structure of the RAF command headquarters system had also been streamlined to make them more efficient and cost-effective and in line with that policy, the Provost Marshal had received authority from the Air Force Board, to restructure the RAF Provost & Security organisation within the UK. As a result, the five UK RAF Police Districts were totally abolished and replaced by three new RAF Police Regional Headquarters, which provided both SI and CI resources for the RAF stations they supported in their respective areas. P&SS Northern Region was based at RAF Linton-on-Ouse and became responsible for service interests in the area north of a line drawn between Hull and Liverpool, including the counties of Yorkshire, Lancashire and Cheshire. It was also responsible for two detachments, one in Scotland and the other in Northern Ireland. P&SS Central Region, based at RAF Spitalgate near Grantham, became responsible for the territory below that line, south to a line drawn between Bristol and Colchester, which included Wales and the counties of Gloucester, Warwick, Northampton, Huntingdon, Cambridge and Suffolk. Finally, P&SS Southern Region, based at RAF Northolt, assumed responsibility for the territory below that line.

The restructuring also saw the creation at RAF Debden, on the 1st October, of a brand new RAF Police squadron entitled The Provost and Security Services, Support Squadron (P&SS(SS)). It comprised sixty professional RAF Police NCOs, under the command of Squadron Leader A L C Thompson, and was formed as a task force, to provide experienced RAF Police assistance wherever it was needed. The squadron was fully self-supporting with all the vehicles and necessary equipment required to undertake a wide variety of tasks anywhere around the world. In addition, it was made up of NCOs, qualified in undertaking SI or CI investigations, together with NCOs qualified to drive heavy goods vehicles and motorcycles. Some of the duties undertaken by the squadron included VIP security, travel control security measures, convoy escorts and public order duties at major public ceremonial events and CND demonstrations, tasks which had all previously been carried out by the staff of the former RAF Police Districts. Finally, the reorganisation also involved the transfer of the tasks previously undertaken by the Police & Security Liaison Warrant Officers and the RAF Police Dog Inspectors, from the Districts to the various Command Provost & Security Officers.

At the end of October, Flight Sergeant D Barfield, RAF Police, returned to the UK having spent just over three years 'on loan' to the Kenyan Air Force. He had been tasked with forming an Air Force Police Flight there and training the seventy-five African trainee policemen who had been selected to run it. The flight, once established, was organised on similar lines to those used by the RAF Police around the world and comprised of a Guardroom, a Provost Section, a Criminal and Security Investigation Section and of course, a Dog Section. While it had been hard work, the whole task had nevertheless been a most successful venture and the Kenyan Government had been very pleased with the commitment that Flight Sergeant Barfield had shown throughout his attachment. As a result, on his return to the UK, he was awarded a commendation from the Provost Marshal.

In West Germany and in West Berlin, things were fairly calm and relaxed and it was termed a very good posting for the majority of personnel who served there. In addition, both airmen and their families enjoyed the luxury of cheap alcohol, cheap entertainment, cheap petrol, fast roads and cheap but powerful cars during their tour of duty. In isolation, none of those factors presented too much of a problem, but whenever they were mixed together, they usually ended up with serious and often fatal results. Unfortunately, it was all too common for the RAF Police to attend the scene of horrific accidents involving service personnel and their families. The casualty numbers for traffic accidents were rising steadily and it was clear that something had to be done and done quickly to prevent the problem from getting totally out of hand. As a result, a number of road safety campaigns were launched throughout the command, by the RAF Police, in an effort to curtail the problem. In addition, the number of traffic patrols mounted by the RAF and Royal Military Police throughout the areas used by British service personnel, and the penalties for offenders were dramatically increased.

Following the Defence Reviews in 1968, the RAF Police organisation within the UK underwent further restructuring during 1969 and as such, the appointments of Director of Security and Provost Marshal were combined to form one single appointment. In addition, with the ending of conscription and the continuing good liaison with the civil police, there was no longer a need for uniformed RAF Police town patrols to roam around the country, enforcing RAF discipline. After all, the remaining professional, and above all career-minded personnel within the RAF at that time, seemed less likely to involve themselves in the sort of criminal activity which had been commonplace amongst some of the National Servicemen. Accordingly, from that point on, all offences involving RAF personnel outside RAF stations, were dealt with by the civil police or referred to the nearest P&SS region for assistance.

To celebrate the Golden Anniversary of the first non-stop flight across the Atlantic Ocean, *The Daily Mail* newspaper staged a transatlantic air race at the beginning of May 1969, involving some 375 competitors. The race from the UK, started at the Post Office Tower in London and finished at the Empire State Building in New York, and had to be completed as quickly as possible in order to win. Along with the other two services, the RAF entered three separate teams who flew a Harrier jump jet, a Victor SR2 and a VC10 during the race. After much planning and to cut down the time taken to travel from the Post Office Tower to their waiting aircraft, the Harrier jump jet was successfully landed at a disused coal yard at St Pancras railway station. Although the landing site was as close as possible to the tower, the London traffic still presented a frustrating delay to the aircrew and to overcome the problem, a number of RAF Police motorcyclists, riding BSA 650 Lightnings, were enlisted to convoy the pilot, Squadron Leader Lecky-Thompson, to his waiting aircraft. The mission turned out to be a complete success and no doubt contributed to the RAF Harrier's victory. The RAF Police NCOs who played such an important role in getting the crew to the aircraft at the start of the race were Sergeants J Greavey and N Billows together with Corporals D Fayers and R Cooke, all of whom must have been very proud of the part which they played in the competition.

Sadly, on 24th May, at the age of sixty-seven and after a long illness, Wing Commander W Bowes OBE, the officer who had headed the famous Stalag Luft 3 murder enquiry, quietly passed away at his home at Margate in Kent. He had retired from the RAF in 1954, after thirty-five years dedicated and loyal service. Unfortunately, his death was followed a month later by that of Group Captain C R Richdale, another well-respected and founding member of the branch, who passed away at his home in Natal, South Africa.

On 8th June, General Franco, once again closed the border crossing between Spain and Gibraltar after relations between Britain and Spain deteriorated, over the future of the colony. Once again, the service personnel and their families stationed in Gibraltar were denied direct access into Spain and her nearby holiday resorts. Over in Northern Ireland, the situation was rapidly deteriorating after the continuing sectarian violence had escalated out of all control. As a consequence, additional British troops were sent into the province by the British Government to assist the civil authorities there in restoring law and order.

The RAF Police Dog Demonstration Team had become so popular by that period, that towards the end of the summer, the Parachute Regiment, who were organising a public relations tour around Canada and the United States of America, extended an invitation for the team to join them. The Provost Marshal duly approved the request and later in the year the trip went ahead. Accordingly, as they worked their way through the hectic but enjoyable tour schedule, it proved to be a very successful venture indeed and as a result, the public on that side of the Atlantic showed their great warmth and admiration for the British Military and in particular, the RAF Police Dog Demonstration Team, at every venue in which they performed.

In Cyprus on 22nd December, hailstones the size of large marbles bombarded the town of Limassol and the surrounding countryside, sending people fleeing indoors for cover. That unusual climatic event was followed shortly after by a large destructive tornado which first struck the RAF station at Akrotiri, causing considerable damage to a large number of buildings and vehicles. Although some forty odd service families were made homeless during the storm and a number of people were injured, it was fortunate that no loss of life was incurred. However, as the tornado left the station, it made its way across the bay towards Limassol and struck the Turkish quarter, inflicting major damage to a large number of the old and somewhat frail buildings there. Although the storm moved quickly over that part of the town, it nevertheless left a tremendous trail of damage, with over four hundred houses so badly damaged that they were declared unfit for habitation. Luckily, once again, there had been no loss of life and only a small number of people were injured. However, the area was a wreck, which left many roads blocked and the civil authorities unable to cope with the situation. As a result, military assistance was requested and medical and rescue teams were quickly sent into Limassol from both Akrotiri and Episkopi. The RAF Police from all over the island were also mobilised to assist the civil police in coping with the situation, as well as reassuring the large number of RAF families who at the time, were accommodated in private dwellings within the town. In addition, a number of radio-equipped RAF Police Land-Rovers were also deployed at various locations inside the town to provide a vital communication link between the Civil Rescue Centre, the Police Headquarters and the rescue crews operating on the ground. Everyone involved in the operation worked well and after a hard night's work by the rescue crews, order and calm had been restored to the area and therefore the military teams were all stood down.

By the end of 1969, the number of WRAF Police NCOs had seriously declined, despite assurances from the recruiting offices, that there was still good interest being shown in the branch by prospective candidates. During that period, there were no WRAF Police NCOs employed at RAF stations within the UK. Instead, the practice at that time was that as soon as female recruits had completed their basic police training, they were automatically given either a specialist CI or SI course and then posted to one of the regions or to HQ P&SS(UK).

As competition for those courses was intense it was quite understandable when male NCOs demonstrated resentment towards their WRAF colleagues, especially if they left the service soon after to get married and start families. At the end of the year, the last female provost officer, Flying Officer D Lewis, left the branch after sixteen years of service

In January 1970, the Provost Marshal advised the MOD about the increased involvement of service personnel in the abuse of illegal and dangerous drugs. Throughout the hippie decade of the sixties the RAF Police had been monitoring the use of illegal and controlled drugs by society in general and had become alarmed with the increased ease at which the drugs could be obtained and used. At that time, drug abuse happened to be a major problem within the United States' own armed forces and the problem continued to grow. To prevent that situation from developing within the RAF, the Dog Training Flight at the Depot was tasked with training two RAF Police dogs in the detection of the drug cannabis in all its associated forms. However, before training began, liaison was established with the Metropolitan Police who had, for a number of years, been successfully using their dogs to detect the drug. In response to the approach, they provided invaluable advice and assistance to the RAF Police NCOs tasked with setting up the training programme, which it was envisaged would take between ten to twelve weeks to complete. As the experiment quickly proved successful, the training moved on to include the detection of other dangerous drugs and as a consequence, Her Majesty's Customs and Excise began to show a particular interest in the breakthrough.

In February a re-designed and detailed course for 'non professional' RAF security officers was held at the RAF Police Depot for the first time. With security matters high on the agenda, a large number of officers from outside the Provost Branch had been appointed to fulfil the appointment of both station and unit security officers. Although the officers filling those posts had previously received a basic level of instruction at the Air Ministry in London, it was felt that with the increase in numbers, the Depot would be far better placed to offer the correct level of professional and up to date instruction. Indeed, it was envisaged from the very start that around seventeen courses would be held at the Depot each year, accommodating some two hundred and fifty officers.

In Libya on 31st March, the RAF finally withdrew from their airfield at El Adam as a result of political changes within the country. Those events had been brought about in the previous September, when Colonel Muammar Gaddafi and his Revolutionary Command Council had launched a bloodless *coup d'etat*, overthrowing King Idris. Although there had been no immediate hostility towards the British forces who were stationed within the country, it soon became very clear that the British would have no choice but to leave.

In May, RAF Seletar in Singapore finally ceased to operate after fifty-one years of occupation by the RAF. Work to construct the airfield there had begun in 1927, and after final completion, it became Singapore's first civil airport. In January 1930, it became one of the largest RAF stations at the time, with a large RAF Police section, commanded by a flight sergeant. In February 1941, the station had been taken and occupied by the Japanese Navy, which continued to operate it throughout the war. In September 1945, the RAF returned to find that their once proud station had fallen into a serious state of dilapidation in their absence; however, it was quickly renovated and the RAF continued to operate a wide variety of aircraft from the base over the following years. As the station finally closed, the Guardroom, and the focus of all former RAF Police activities at the unit, was formally handed over to representatives from the Singapore Armed Forces by Sergeant R Chester, the last remaining RAF Police senior NCO serving there.

Sometime during the summer of 1970, two valuable silver maces were stolen from the RAF Church of St Clement Danes in central London. The maces had originally been presented to the Parish Beadle in the eighteenth century by the parish constables whom he had employed. He in turn had presented them to the church and they had been in the possession of the church until the day they were stolen. Although extensive enquiries into the theft had been carried out by the civil police and the thief had later been arrested, the whereabouts of the maces were unfortunately never discovered. Some time later, Group Captain A Smart, the Command Provost Marshal, FEAF, suggested to the Provost Marshal that as logical descendants of the St Clement Danes law enforcement body, it would be a fitting gesture if two replacement mace heads were donated by the RAF Police. The Provost Marshal approached the Chaplain-in-Chief with the idea and he readily agreed with the proposal and an urgent appeal for funds went out to all RAF Police personnel serving around the globe.

Since the end of the last war, with the introduction into service of much heavier and more sophisticated aircraft, the flying stations became pretty much static bases, comprising the airfield and runway, and the technical, operational and domestic areas. As such, the overall routine security commitment at that type of unit was relatively easy for the RAF Police to maintain on a day to day basis. However, with the introduction into service of the Harrier V/STOL jet fighter aircraft, that principle quickly changed along with the required security measures needed to protect the new aircraft. The Harrier, being capable of vertical or short take-off and landings, didn't require conventional runways and airfields from which to operate from and could be deployed into and out from any location away from its parent station. In Germany for instance, the aircraft were based at RAF Wildenrath as part of NATO's first line of defence against the threat of invasion from the Eastern Bloc Alliance. However, as part of the constant preparation for war, the aircraft and their supporting elements were regularly deployed around Germany, taking part in the numerous military exercises throughout the year. Consequently, nominated RAF Police NCOs from both Wildenrath and other units within Germany found themselves living under canvas in field conditions, whilst providing the necessary police and security support to the field air commander at their assigned site. During those exercises, the aircraft regularly operated out of military training areas, woodland, farms and even from closed-off sections of the autobahns to demonstrate their full potential. In addition to providing static security guards for the aircraft, RAF Police NCOs at each of the deployment sites, under the control of a SNCO, carried out foot and mobile security patrols of the areas using RAF Police dogs as well as maintaining a control of entry system into the site for visitors. In addition, whenever public roads were being used as temporary short take off runways, the RAF Police were empowered by the German authorities to close them off to normal traffic while the aircraft took off or landed. Obviously, the deployment site, together with its aircraft and all the associated activity, attracted considerable interest from the local population, who in many cases, were keen to get a closer look. Consequently, the RAF Police were kept extremely busy in maintaining the security of both the aircraft and its supporting elements in many unusual locations.

In the Far East on 18th February, 1971, the RAF Police Auxiliaries, stationed in Singapore, and the FEAF celebrated the Silver Anniversary of their formation at RAF Changi. Since 1946, the establishment of the force had grown considerably with some 400 multiracial officers and other ranks being employed on a wide range of duties at various stations throughout Malaysia and Singapore. During their brief but very successful history, the force had worked extremely hard from humble beginnings to earn the highest respect from their regular RAF Police counterparts and the remainder of the RAF. Indeed, they had continually distinguished themselves in all manner of ways and some 800 members of the force held the General Service Medal for their valuable campaign service in Malaya, the Malay, the Malay peninsular and in Borneo. In addition to their combined contribution to the emergency situation in the region, reports of individual distinguished service had also been rewarded. Two British Empire Medals had been awarded, one to Sub-Inspector Mohamed Kassim Bin Mahat in 1956 and the other to Inspector Abu Hassin Bin Haji Ibrahim in 1965. Additionally, commendations from the AOC, the Air Commander and the Provost Marshal had also been awarded to ten other members of the force.

The occasion was marked with a splendid parade made up of four flights, including the dog section and reviewed by Air Vice Marshal N M Maynard CB, CBE, DFC, AFC, RAF, AOC FEAF, accompanied throughout the day by the Command Provost Marshal, Group Captain A A Witherington. The parade was followed by the beating of the retreat, performed by the band of the Australian Army, who had kindly offered their services for the occasion. The Parade Commander was Assistant Superintendent Tajri Bin Haji Ali, assisted by Sub-Inspector Abd Samad Bin Said, the Parade Adjutant, and Sergeant Tahir Bin Awang, the Parade Warrant Officer. After the conclusion of the parade, the reviewing officer was presented with an inscribed outsized truncheon (of the type first issued to the auxiliaries in 1946) by Sergeant Tahir Bin Awak and in turn, the reviewing officer presented each member of the force with a copy of their famous cap badge, mounted onto a wooden shield. The formal ceremony was followed later by the 'Ronggeng', the Malay festival of feasting and dancing, to which everyone taking part in the parade, together with the spectators and their families were invited. Although the day's celebrations turned out to be a great success, they did unfortunately herald the start of the intended withdrawal of the RAF from that region of the Far East.

During the spring, a dedicated team of RAF Police NCOs from the recently formed P&SS Support Squadron arrived at the RAF College, Cranwell, where they quickly established and maintained the required standard of security in and around the station, while His Royal Highness The Prince of Wales, who had recently been commissioned into the RAF, completed his training to become a pilot.

In early April, the Provost Branch was saddened to learn of the death of Colonel J W Baldwin, DSO, the founder and 'father' of the RAF Police Dog organisation. Although he had been in retirement since 1953, he had continued to maintain his strong links with the branch and was immensely proud of his connection with the service and of course, the highest standard of achievement which he had worked so hard to attain during the time spent working with the RAF Police. Five years after he had retired and as a mark of gratitude and respect for all that he had done, a room in the RAF Police Museum, dedicated to the dogs which he loved so much, was named as 'The Baldwin Room'.

The appeal to replace the mace heads in St Clement Danes Church became a huge success with the princely sum of £1,200 being raised by members of the branch. Mr Leslie Durbin, an eminent London silversmith was commissioned to design and prepare the replacements and on 20th June, when the work was completed, representatives from the RAF Police presented them to the RAF Chaplain-in-Chief in a ceremony at the church attended by over four hundred people. The mace heads, simply inscribed, 'Presented by the RAF Police – 20th June, 1971', are housed in secure display cases by the west door, where they can be viewed by visitors to the church.

In July, following a trial at Leeds Assizes, Nicholas Prager, a former RAF Chief Technician, was sentenced to twelve years imprisonment for espionage after he had been identified as a spy by Josef Frolik, a former member of the Czech Intelligence Service, who had defected to the CIA when the Russians invaded Czechoslovakia. At the time of his birth in Czechoslovakia in 1928, Prager's father, a Czech national, had been employed as a clerk in the British Embassy. However, in 1948, he retired and became a naturalised British subject.

Accordingly, Nicholas Prager claimed British citizenship and moved to the UK, where, after lying about his background history, successfully joined the RAF as a radar technician. In 1956, he was posted to RAF Wittering, where he passed to the Czech Intelligence Service details about the top-secret radar-jamming equipment used by the nuclear V Force bombers. He continued to pass on classified information to the Czech Intelligence service until he left the RAF in 1961 to take up employment with the company English Electric.

As September approached, HQ P&SS (FEAF), under the command of Group Captain Witherington, disbanded and faded away to become just another chapter in the history of the branch. The last few remaining staff who had organised the closure were either posted back to the UK, absorbed into the RAF Police Flight at RAF Changi or were posted into the RAF Police unit with the British Commonwealth ANZUK (Australia, New Zealand & UK) Force. In addition, the RAF base at Tengah, which had first been built and occupied by the RAF in 1939, was also formally handed over to the Singapore Armed Forces as the RAF withdrew on 15th September. The complete withdrawal of the RAF from the region was steadily gaining momentum.

Air Commodore Panton retired as Provost Marshal on 16th October and was succeeded in post by Air Commodore H M Shepherd OBE MBIM, who became the second provost officer to have reached the top appointment within the branch. Air Commodore Shephard had been born on the 15th August, 1918 in Wanstead, Essex and had been educated at St John's in Leatherhead. His career to some extent had been influenced by family connections with the police. His great grandfather had been a superintendent in the Essex Police and his uncle had served in the British South African Police. Consequently, he had joined the Metropolitan Police in 1937 and served in West London until released to join the RAF in July 1941. After initially training as a pilot, he was commissioned into the Administrative & Special Duties Branch in September 1943 as a provost officer. During the remainder of the war he had served as a DAPM in Lincoln and with the SIB in London. In March 1945, he went over to Germany, where, for two years, he had worked as a police prosecutor with the Public Safety Branch of the Control Commission, located at Essen. In 1947, he served with the SIB at No 2 RAF Police Wing, BAFO until returning in March 1950 to take over command of the RAF Police

School. After a brief tour of duty in Hong Kong, he had returned to the Air Ministry as head of PM 1. In 1957, he became both the Command Provost Marshal and Commanding Officer of No 24 RAF Police District at Nicosia in Cyprus, during the time of the EOKA terrorist campaign and was awarded the OBE as a result of his work there. After leaving Cyprus, he completed further tours of duty with No 4 RAF Police District, the Air Ministry, the Police School and the FEAF. Prior to being promoted and taking up his appointment, Air Commodore Shephard had been serving in Germany as the Command Provost & Security Officer.

With the closure of further overseas bases, the RAF finally withdrew from RAF Changi in Singapore on 9th December and from RAF Muharraq in Bahrain a week later. The two closures were followed shortly after by the closure of RAF Sharjah in Oman.

By that time, the majority of the guardrooms on RAF stations within both the UK and Germany, formerly staffed by the RAF Police, had been completely taken over by the Station Warrant Officer and personnel from Trade Group 10 (General Duties & Trade Assistant General). Guardrooms at RAF stations outside the UK and in Germany however, continued, for the time being, to be staffed by the RAF Police. The move had been largely brought about by a general shortage of RAF Police NCOs and the increasing number of security commitments being undertaken by the RAF Police, at the larger operational stations. Even the RAF Detention Unit, which up until the start of 1972 had been staffed by the RAF Police had been taken over by Trade Group 10 staff. Indeed, there was such a shortage of RAF Police NCOs to cover all the required security duties that stations which were considered as low security risks, had no RAF Police personnel established at all, but instead, were protected by members of the Ministry of Defence Police. The move out of the guardrooms and into the newly styled and isolated 'Security Control Centres', situated on the airfields or in other equally isolated areas within the station, was unpopular amongst a large proportion of the branch who were suddenly 'exiled' from the domestic areas of the camp to concentrate on their more important security commitments. The guardrooms and the RAF Police had, since the beginning, been associated with the maintenance of discipline and high personal standards amongst RAF personnel. They saw the importance of being in the guardrooms with their fingers firmly on the pulse of life, being taken away from their control. However, what was done was done, but unfortunately, their views soon proved to be correct as the overall standards of discipline and deportment amongst the younger element of the general RAF community quickly started to decline.

During April 1972, the RAF finally made their withdrawal from Singapore, bringing to an end yet another important era. In addition, because of the rising costs of maintenance, the last RAF Police Mounted Section was sadly closed at RAF Akrotiri on Cyprus. Atlas, ridden for the last time by Corporal B Gribble and Hercules, ridden by Corporal J Keir, were the last two horses used by the RAF Police and were donated to the RAF Cyprus Saddle Club, where they lived out their retirement in comfortable style. The horses had been a familiar sight at the station where they had helped to patrol the more awkward areas of the twenty-five square miles which the station covered.

On 2nd June, at the officers mess at RAF Debden, the RAF Provost Branch, celebrated the silver jubilee of its official formation. The Provost Marshal, Air Commodore Shephard and his wife received the guests which included many VIPs, former and serving members of the branch. The celebrations continued later on into the month with a formal dinner, held in the Cafe Royal in London. During his after-dinner speech, Air Chief Marshal, Sir Lewis Hodges, the Air Member for Personnel, announced that the Air Force Board had approved a request from the Provost Marshal for a royal review of the RAF Police, which was to take place the following year.

Although military reinforcements had been trying to restore law and order within Northern Ireland since being sent there in 1969, the situation was still extremely serious at the beginning of 1972. Since the outbreak of the Troubles, the RAF Police stationed within the province had been largely employed with maintaining the internal security of the RAF bases there, which left the Military Police to patrol the territory beyond. However, at the beginning of October, the Provost Marshal received a request from his Army counterpart for RAF Police NCOs to assist the Military Police in carrying out their task within the province. Subsequently, on 17th October, fifteen RAF Police NCOs from Strike Command stations within the UK, assembled at the Aldershot Headquarters of No 160 Provost Company, Royal Military Police. The NCOs formed the advance party of a much larger RAF Police detachment destined for the streets of Northern Ireland, serving in Belfast, Lisburn, Londonderry and Armagh. After being briefed on the nature of their task, the RAF Police detachment were sent out to the province on the 27th October, to assist No 1 Regiment, Royal Military Police, with their role. As soon as the detachment had been settled into their new surroundings and had been given a very detailed tour of familiarisation, they were posted to their respective platoons to commence their duties, which involved assisting the RUC with their patrols, the protection of VIPs and the investigation of all complaints made against the military security forces. Those investigations could range from an allegation of verbal abuse by a member of the Security Forces to the actual shooting of a suspected terrorist. As a matter of interest, the RMP formed an additional regiment, No 2 Regiment, in Northern Ireland later on and its first commanding officer was Squadron Leader C Burghope, an RAF provost officer.

As 1973 approached, the branch prepared itself for the impending royal review and as such, there was much to be done and everyone was kept extremely busy, especially at the Depot where the review was to take place. In March, after being at the RAF Police Depot for thirteen years, the Ministry of Defence Police Training School, left Debden and moved into new accommodation in Redhill, Surrey.

After much hard work and effort, the 5th of June finally arrived and Her Royal Highness the Princess Margaret, Countess of Snowdon, arrived at the Depot by helicopter, to carry out the first ever Royal Review of the RAF Police and only the fourth Royal Review of the RAF. The weather for the occasion was magnificent and as Her Royal Highness stepped out from the aircraft, she was met by Air Marshal Sir Harold Martin KCB DSO DFC AFC, the Air Member for Personnel, the Provost Marshal, Air Commodore Shephard, Colonel Sir John Ruggles-Brise Bt CB OBE TD JP, the Lord Lieutenant of Essex, Group Captain R D England the station Commander and the officer in charge of the parade, Group Captain Witherington. At that point, the Queens Colour Squadron of the RAF Regiment came smartly to attention and presented the Royal salute as the RAF Southern Band played the national anthem. After being welcomed to the Depot, she was invited to inspect the smartly turned out provost officers and RAF Police NCOs on parade, who represented the RAF Police and the RAF Police Auxiliaries serving around the world. With the sunlight glinting from the polished brasses and row upon row of white hats, Her Royal Highness carried out a full inspection, stopping to chat to NCOs from every group of the parade. After the ceremony, she was taken on a tour of the Police School where she viewed an impressive exhibition of photographs, models and static displays depicting the RAF Police at work. She then moved on to the Griffin Club where members of the RAF Police and their families were presented to her during an informal gathering. After lunch in the officers mess, a group photograph was taken to mark the occasion, after which she was presented with a unique solid gold brooch of a griffin, which had been subscribed to by every serving officer in the branch. Finally, she was shown around the Dog Training School and was clearly delighted with the demonstration arranged for her visit by Mr Charles Fricker. At the conclusion of a most successful day, Princess Margaret returned to her helicopter and finally left the station, having had an extremely enjoyable and interesting day.

The RAF Police detachments to the Royal Military Patrol in Northern Ireland continued successfully and without incident until suddenly, without warning, tragedy struck on 25th July. A joint foot patrol comprising of two young corporals, one from the RAF Police and the other from the Royal Military Police, was carrying out a routine patrol through the notorious Bogside area of Londonderry. Suddenly, they were confronted by a gang of youths who at first shouted abuse at the patrol and then started throwing bricks in the direction of the two men. Faced with the hostility, which was quite normal given the area they were patrolling, the two NCOs remained calm but nevertheless tried to get away to the safety of some nearby shops and the Rossville Flats. However, as they were making their way there another angry crowd appeared and so they changed direction and made their way to Waterloo Place, where they hoped to find some safety in the nearby shops. Unfortunately, before they could make it there, they were both shot in the back and fell onto the pavement seriously wounded. As they lay there unable to move, a crowd assembled and thankfully, someone called an ambulance to the scene. Luckily, both men survived the attack, although Corporal J Phillips, the RAF Police NCO, a married man with two children and twelve years service, still carried the .38 bullet firmly embedded in his shoulder when he returned to work some months later. Unfortunately, his RMP colleague was more seriously injured in the attack and spent several more months afterwards undergoing specialist medical treatment to recover from the ordeal.

In a further tragic incident, over in Belfast, another RAF Police NCO, Corporal D Ianson, narrowly escaped serious injury when unfortunately his dog, trained to detect the presence of explosive substances, was killed in an explosion. The incident happened when they were summoned by the army to search a derelict house which they suspected had a hidden cache of explosives. Although dangerous work, it was quite a routine task for the experienced handler and his dog. They had cleared the ground floor of the building without finding anything and were just about to check upstairs. However, as the dog climbed the stairs, it triggered a trip wire and a booby trap bomb went off killing the dog instantly. Luckily, the handler had been at the bottom of the stairs and around a bend at the fatal moment, otherwise, he too might have been killed by the powerful blast.

Although 1973 saw the ending of the Vietnam war, the Troubles continued in Northern Ireland and tension was further escalated when the Irish Republican Army (IRA) moved their bloody bombing campaign onto the British mainland, with a view of bringing their struggle closer to the minds of the British people and of course blackmailing the government into withdrawing their troops from the province.

In January 1974, Air Commodore Shephard retired as the Provost Marshal and was succeeded in post by Air Commodore B C Player CBE, another professional provost officer, who prior to being promoted and taking up his appointment, had been the RAF Germany Command Provost & Security Officer. Air Commodore Player, an ex-member of the Hampshire Constabulary, had been commissioned into the RAF in 1942 and after qualifying as a pilot, became a provost officer in 1947. During his career, he had seen service at home and overseas in India, Gibraltar, Aden, Cyprus and finally in Germany.

The Government review into reducing the defence budget was at its height and accordingly, soon after taking up his appointment, Air Commodore Player recognised that, in common with the whole of the British armed forces, the RAF P&SS organisation could expect to suffer serious cuts in manpower and other resources. As a result, he tasked Group Captain Innes, the Commanding Officer at HQ P&SS(UK), into conducting a detailed study into ways of streamlining the provost element of the organisation to make it much more cost effective. Although it had to operate in the most economical and efficient manner, it still had to provide the traditional services and high level of support which had always been offered to the RAF, by the Provost Marshal and his staff. The establishment and effectiveness of the RAF Police serving on individual stations however, remained the responsibility of their respective station commanders and their command headquarters staff.

In April, Sergeant Drummond A Window, a former member of the RAF Police who had retired from the service in 1966, became the first member of the RAF Police or indeed the Royal Air Force, to be appointed to the Queen's Body Guard of the Yeoman. The hand picked Yeoman of the Guard (which should not be confused with the body of Yeoman Guards established to protect the Tower of London) had been formed by King Henry VII in 1485, after the battle of Bosworth Field and have since that date been responsible for protecting the Sovereign at home and on the battlefield, although their present-day role is more symbolic and ceremonial.

In June, trouble broke out once again on the island of Cyprus. The Turkish Cypriot minority were being victimised by the Greek Cypriot majority and Turkey protested to the UN and the Security Council, but nothing happened and the situation deteriorated. The overall situation became more serious when on 20th July, Turkish forces, fearing a Greek take-over within Cyprus, launched an invasion on the island to prevent it from taking place. Within a very short time, the invaders had taken forty percent of the northern territory, and were well established inside the capital, Nicosia. During the chaos which followed, it was unclear to those on the outside exactly what their final objectives would be. Unfortunately, the United Nations peacekeeping force, stationed on the island, were powerless to stop the invasion and could only observe and report what they saw taking place. While no military action was directed towards the British Sovereign Base Areas (SBA), service families, who were accommodated outside the SBAs, had to be quickly protected. Consequently, over the days which followed, things settled down and it seemed that the Turks were happy with occupying just the northern part of the island. However, the service families who were living outside the bases were quickly assembled and brought onto the Army and RAF units within the SBAs for their own protection. Accordingly, both the Military and RAF Police were heavily committed during the operation, ensuring that no danger came to the convoys which were carrying the families to safety. Given the seriousness of the situation, it was decided soon after to evacuate all the families and all non-essential British civilian employees off the island altogether, and a huge airlift was quickly organised and undertaken by the RAF. During the invasion, large numbers of Greek Cypriots had been arrested by the invaders and subsequently transported back to Turkey. Consequently, a large number of Greek Cypriots, fearing for their lives, fled into the SBAs from the Turkish Cypriot areas, looking for asylum. That placed a considerable strain on the meagre resources of the British military authorities but the refugees were taken in and accommodated close to Episkopi in tented camps. As a result of the protection offered to the refugees, there were violent protests at the main entrance to Akrotiri, during which a number of vehicles were set on fire and a youth was murdered by the demonstrators. The whole situation began to look very ugly indeed and wasn't improved any when a large number of locally employed civilians were dismissed from their jobs within the SBAs. In Nicosia, two members of the branch, Squadron Leader R Chasemore and Flight Sergeant W B Oldroyd, attended a serious fire, which it was suspected had been started by an explosive device. Although at risk, they quickly took control of the situation and managed to bring the fire under control. In recognition of their swift and positive action, they were both subsequently awarded the Queen's Gallantry Medal.

Later in the year, the RAF Police School moved from RAF Debden to RAF Newton, near Nottingham. Unfortunately, the Dog Training School remained behind for a while longer, until work on a new kennel complex had been completed. Unfortunately, with the move to RAF Newton, the title 'RAF Police Depot' was lost once again and the school reverted to being just another lodger unit, occupying space on the station.

At the end of the year, due to establishment reductions and priority commitments elsewhere, the four month RAF Police detachments to assist the Royal Military Police in Northern Ireland ceased. During the successful two-year operation, there had only been two RAF Police casualties, the NCO who had been shot in the back and the dog handler who had been injured when a bomb went off, killing his dog. It had been an interesting time for those NCOs involved in the detachments and many in the branch were sorry to see an end to the task.

In February 1976, Air Commodore Player retired from the service and was succeeded in post as the Provost Marshal by Air Commodore G Innes CBE MBIM, another professional provost officer and one of the RAF investigators who had arrested the RAF spy Douglas Britten in 1968. Air Commodore Innes had been commissioned into the RAF in May 1943, and after successfully qualifying as a pilot, he became a provost officer in October 1945. In 1975, while serving as the Officer Commanding HQ P&SS(UK), he became the first provost officer to be appointed as an aide-de-camp to Her Majesty, Queen Elizabeth II and had also been tasked with reviewing the overall function of the RAF Provost & Security Services within the UK.

In the spring of 1976, in line with further defence cuts, both RAF Gan in the middle of the Indian Ocean and RAF Masirah, located on a small island just off the southern coast of Oman, were closed and the RAF made yet another sad withdrawal, leaving the local population to re-organise their lives, which for so long had revolved around both RAF stations. The population around Gan seemed to be the worst affected by the closure and the RAF Police Auxiliaries, under the command of Flight Lieutenant M Cammeron, were disbanded after years of loyal service and assistance to their regular counterparts.

At around the same time, a startling directive from the Ministry of Defence sent a shudder running through almost everyone in the branch, when it was announced that the RAF Police and the RAF Regiment were to be combined to form a single RAF Security trade group. Relief however, was soon evident when it was discovered that the combination was merely for administrative purposes and that the two separate disciplines would more or less continue to operate much as they had done before the announcement. The only significant change which the 'amalgamation' brought about was that an Air Vice-Marshal was appointed to act as the Director General of RAF Security (DG RAF Sy), with two Air Commodores to assist him. One became the Director, RAF Regiment, whilst the other was the Provost Marshal, retitled as the Deputy Director of Security and Provost Marshal (RAF) (DD Sy & PM (RAF)). Consequently, Air Vice Marshal A Griffiths CB, AFC, RAF, was appointed as the first DG RAF Sy, and from that point on, the RAF Regiment, RAF Fire

Service and RAF Police were brought together to form the new Security Trade Group, known collectively as Trade Group 8.

As part of the same overall defence rationalisation, the former, Fighter, Bomber and Coastal Command Headquarters, were amalgamated into the newly formed Strike Command Headquarters, located at RAF High Wycombe in Buckinghamshire. In addition, Training, Transport and Maintenance Command Headquarters, were also amalgamated into the newly formed Support Command Headquarters located at RAF Brampton, near Huntingdon. As part of the new staffing establishment a senior provost officer was appointed to act as the Command Security Officer at each of the new command headquarters with a staff of provost officers and RAF Police NCOs to assist him in his inspectorate role.

In September, Mr Charles Fricker retired and handed over his appointment and responsibilities as the Chief Training Officer (Dogs) to Mr Terry McHaffie, who had been his deputy for many years. During his time in charge of training police dogs, Mr Fricker had ensured that the dogs had been exposed to as much publicity as possible, which had included many appearances on television at home and abroad. Over the years his methods had been extremely effective. The public at large had a very healthy respect for the branch and its dogs, which they had continued to donate to the RAF over the years. Indeed, whenever the RAF Police Dog Demonstration Team appeared in public, as they frequently did around the country, the shows were always very well attended and that in itself proved to be one of the organisation's best public relations exercises.

Basic training for new RAF Police recruits had recently been reviewed and modified to take into account the fact that many of them would be engaged mainly on security-related tasks for the first few years of their careers. As such, from early 1977, all RAF Police NCOs who held acting rank and who were selected for promotion to the rank of substantive corporal, were required to successfully complete a three week further training course at the RAF Police School. The course expanded the basic training they had received and prepared them for the supervisory responsibilities required of their new rank. In addition, candidates who were selected to undertake the course were issued with a pre-course study package to work on at their units to ensure that each student arrived on the course with the same level of trade knowledge. As the system developed, it became most successful.

During the previous year, a large number of RAF Police NCOs had been wearing locally manufactured and purchased forms of trade insignia on their uniform epaulettes together with their badges of rank. Although they were unauthorised patterns of dress, they were nevertheless more practical than wearing brassards for everyday use. In addition, being a much smaller version of the red and black brassard, they looked smarter and made RAF police NCOs easily recognised if they were not wearing brassards. Although their introduction and use was initially frowned upon and indeed discouraged by some senior officers of the branch, they were eventually sanctioned, produced and issued to all NCOs. While those worn by RAF Police warrant officers and NCOs had the letters RAFP marked on them, the ones issued to provost officers were marked with the letters, APM, denoting Assistant Provost Marshal. The title of DAPM had long since been discontinued.

In June 1977, as a result of the review carried out by the Provost Marshal, both HQ P&SS(UK) and the Provost Marshal's Department vacated their cramped and expensively rented accommodation in the Government Buildings in Acton and went their separate ways. The Provost Marshal's Department moved initially into the Norman Shaw Building, which was formerly the home of New Scotland Yard and then into permanent accommodation in the Metropole Building in Whitehall. HQ P&SS(UK) on the other hand, set up in a beautiful stone manor house at RAF Rudloe Manor, just outside Corsham in Wiltshire. Shortly after, P&SS Support Squadron and P&SS (Southern Region) also moved to Rudloe Manor from RAF Northolt. Once organised, the headquarters comprised of two wings, each under the command of a provost wing commander. Vetting Wing was responsible for all security vetting matters concerning the RAF and the issue of identity documents, passes and permits. Support Wing, on the other hand, was responsible for an assortment of operational and support functions. It included Support Squadron and the Flying Complaints Cell, which had been formed to investigate, on behalf of the MOD, complaints from the public in respect of military flying. Southern Region however, remained as an independent unit under the command of a Wing Commander. Group Captain A L C Thompson, the officer who had formed the Support Squadron in 1968, was appointed as the Officer Commanding HQ P&SS(UK) and station commander of RAF Rudloe Manor.

As part of the nationwide Silver Jubilee celebrations to commemorate the reign of Her Majesty Queen Elizabeth II, the largest ever Royal Review of the RAF took place on the 29th July, at RAF Finningley near Doncaster. Her Majesty and HRH Prince Philip arrived at the review accompanied by five other members of the royal family. In addition, a huge number of her government ministers, ambassadors and high commissioners, members of the Air Force Board and a host of other VIPs had also been invited to attend the review, along with some 10,000 servicemen and their families and five hundred members of the media. From the RAF Police perspective, the police and security planning aspects of the review had started some twelve months beforehand, when Wing Commander G E Winch, the then Commanding Officer at P&SS Northern Region, was appointed to act as the RAF Police & Security Operations Commander. To enable him in carrying out all of his preparations and the commitments on the day, he was allocated twelve provost officers and two hundred and ten RAF Police NCOs to assist with the task. During the planning stages and throughout the review, the RAF Police once again established and maintained an excellent working relationship with the other service bodies involved in the review and of course the South Yorkshire Police and the British Transport Police at Doncaster. The review at Finningley comprised a ceremonial parade, followed by the royal party and the VIPs being given an escorted tour around the impressive indoor exhibition, after which they were entertained during a formal luncheon. After lunch, the royal party conducted an informal walkabout where they had the opportunity to meet and speak to some of the invited quests. Then finally, the royal party and the assembled guests were entertained by an impressive demonstration by a Harrier 'jump jet' and a full flying display.

At the end of the day, the RAF Police on duty at the review had carried out all their duties smoothly and effectively without encountering any major problems. In addition, they had also erected and manned three static display units in the exhibition hall, depicting the RAF Police involvement in aircraft security, dog handling and special investigations. Indeed, as the royal party were shown around the displays, both the Queen and the Queen Mother were delighted with what they saw and spoke at length to the NCOs manning the stands. At the end of the review and after an extremely busy day, the RAF Police remained in place and braced themselves for the arrival the following day, of some 200,000 cars, coaches and motorcycles, carrying the vast number of people who attended the RAF Finningley Public Day which also turned out to be a huge success, both from the display and security aspects.

Following a very successful two year trial period during which two RAF Police drug detection dogs, on secondment with their handlers, had proved their effectiveness in combating the illegal importation of illicit drugs, HM Commissioner of Customs & Excise decided to form a national force of drug detection dogs to detect the smuggling of heroin and cannabis. In May 1978, the RAF Police School was selected as the most suitable and qualified establishment in the country to undertake the programme of training the forty additional Customs handlers and their dogs, required for the task. A new training cell was quickly established within the Dog Training Flight and soon after, the fourteen week training programme commenced under the watchful eye of Flight Sergeant J Coulson.

During the same month, Air Commodore Innes retired as the Provost Marshal and was succeeded in post by Air Commodore I Young MBE FBIM, who up until his promotion had been the RAF Germany Command Provost & Security Officer.

In the rundown to the RAF withdrawal from the Island of Malta, in view of the political situation, RAF Safi closed on 27th October, having been in operation since 1942. The closure left RAF Luqa as the only remaining operational RAF station on the island, and that was destined to close by March the following year.

During the year the tiny British colony of British Honduras, situated in Central America, south of Mexico, came under the threat of invasion from her neighbour, Guatemala. Guatemala had been in conflict with the British Government for some time over her claim to the 8,870 square miles of territory forming the colony. Unfortunately, British Honduras was a poor country unable to mount a resistance to such an invasion and so British troops were sent to the region as a deterrent. However, as the political situation continued to deteriorate, the RAF sent out a number of Puma helicopters and Harrier jet aircraft to support the army operations. Accordingly, an RAF Police Flight under the control of a Sergeant, was quickly established at Airport Camp to provide the necessary security protection for the aircraft which were deployed on immediate readiness in hastily constructed hides at the international airport outside Belize City.

As 1978 drew to a close, industrial relations between the unions and the government deteriorated and the Fire Brigade nationwide were amongst those who went out on strike, causing considerable problems for the senior fire officers and the police who were left to cope with the situation. War time 'Green Goddess' fire engines were brought out from storage facilities around the country and the military were called in to man them. Accordingly, a large number of RAF Police NCOs from RAF stations nationwide were detached onto fire-fighting operations during the strike.

Sadly on the 31st March, 1979, in accordance with an agreement between the British and Maltese Governments, the RAF finally withdrew from RAF Luqa, its remaining station and airfield on the island of Malta. The withdrawal brought to an end another era in the history of both the island and the British military connection with it, stretching back over many years.

During an informal ceremony at HQ P&SS(UK) Rudloe Manor on the 3rd April, Air Commodore Young was invited by Group Captain Thompson to unveil the newly authorised unit badge for HQ P&SS(UK). The idea of obtaining an official badge for the headquarters had been started the previous year to mark its silver jubilee. A number of possible design variations were forwarded to the Inspector of RAF Badges for approval, after which, the one thought to be most suitable was produced by the College of Arms. In keeping with the unit's role of providing specialist investigatory, protective and advisory services in the field of crime and security to all RAF units within the United Kingdom, the badge depicting "a demi griffin issuant from the battlements of a tower and gorged with an ancient coronet" was graciously approved and signed by Her Majesty the Queen. The demi griffin in the badge relates to the griffin in the badge of the RAF Police, while the coronet is indicative in heraldry of the specialist and elite role of the unit. The battlements of the tower symbolise the headquarters status and the adopted motto, "Without Fear or Favour", proclaims the impartiality with which the unit performs its role, regardless of rank or location.

In Northern Ireland, the terrorist campaign was still active and the IRA continued to mount damaging attacks around the province. Their activity was highlighted on 27th August, when the IRA carried out two sickening and murderous attacks which shocked the nation. In the first, Earl Louis Mountbatten, his grandson and a local boy were killed and others were injured, when a bomb on his boat was detonated while they were fishing off the Irish coast. In the second attack, the IRA killed and injured a number of soldiers during an ambush at Warren Point, close to the border with Eire.

Earlier in the year, Vietnamese forces had occupied the Kampuchean capital, Phnom Penh and the country's former dictator, Pol Pot and his Khmer Rouge henchmen had fled the country, leaving behind a bloody trail and total devastation. During his evil government, Pol Pot had executed millions of his fellow countrymen as serious opponents and had totally destroyed the economical and industrial fabric of the country. Consequently, the surviving population were on the point of starvation and the United Nations and the International Red Cross were called in to assist.

In the early hours of the morning of 8th October, an RAF Hercules transport aircraft took off from RAF Lyneham for an undisclosed location. An RAF Police NCO, Flight Sergeant J Wood, from the P&SS Support Squadron was onboard and had been detailed to act as the Air Transport Security (ATSy) NCO. In addition, the aircraft also contained a team from the UK Mobile Air Movements Squadron and a couple of aircraft painters. Soon after taking off the team were informed that the aircraft was going to take part in the International Red Cross Mercy mission into Kampuchea. After stopping off in Cyprus, Bahrain and Sri Lanka, where all the military markings had been removed and the aircraft had been repainted with the distinctive Red Cross insignia, it arrived in Bangkok to be loaded with food. Flight Sergeant Wood accompanied the first flight into Phnom Penh, where he was left to establish and run the ATSy system on the ground, required to receive the aircraft and its cargo each time it landed. Consequently, he quickly made his introductions to the Red Cross officials there, and found himself in charge of a team of willing Kampuchean coolies who unfortunately didn't speak or understand a word of English. However, Flight Sergeant Wood quickly adapted to his unusual surroundings and through patience and dedication, made his instructions understood by the team. Consequently, during the remainder of the highly successful operation, both he and his team continued to work most effectively in achieving their objectives. As a result of his sterling efforts, operating under extremely primitive and difficult conditions, he was commended upon his return to the UK by the International Red Cross for his hard work and dedication.

At the age of 86, Air Commodore O W de Putron, the Provost Marshal who had achieved so much for the branch during its formative years, died at his Devonshire home on 17th February, 1980. Throughout his retirement, the Air Commodore had maintained a lively and tireless interest in the activities and progress of the branch.

At the beginning of 1980, shortly before Rhodesia was granted her independence from Great Britain and renamed Zimbabwe, a small detachment of RAF Police NCOs from the P&SS Support Squadron flew out to the capital, Salisbury, to form part of the Commonwealth force, sent to monitor the cease-fire agreed by the various political factions fighting for power in the country. Although the team enjoyed yet another new experience, the detachment passed off without incident.

During the summer months, members of the P&SS Support Squadron took part in Operation Golden Eagle, the security operation set up to provide the necessary security measures required for the protection of HRH the Duke of York, who had recently been commissioned into the Royal Navy, while he completed his five months of basic flying training. The task was similar to that undertaken by the squadron some years previously for his brother, HRH Prince Charles. However, unlike his brother, Andrew was based at the Royal Naval Elementary Flying Squadron, located at RAF Leeming in North Yorkshire. The RAF Police NCOs involved in the operation worked very closely with the resident RAF Police Flight, officers from the Metropolitan Police Royal Protection Squad and the North Yorkshire Police and spent four weeks at a time at Leeming and its sister unit, RAF Topcliffe, guarding the aircraft used by the prince and enhancing the security measures in and around the two stations.

In October, following a breakdown of negotiations between the Prison Officers Association and the Home Office, the prison officers commenced industrial action and refused to accept further prisoners into the system, which resulted in many prisoners being confined in cells at police stations all over the country. As the situation seriously deteriorated and the system was on the point of collapse, military assistance was requested by the government and Operation Ruddock was quickly put into action. In order to relieve the acute problem of prisoners being held within police cells, a temporary prison was hastily established and secured at Rolleston Camp, an Army deployment encampment, located on the bleak Salisbury Plain. Although the RAF Police NCOs involved in the task were not employed on duties inside the prison, they nevertheless provided the necessary outer security cordon. As such, the custodial tasks remained the responsibility of the senior prison staff and both Army and RAF personnel detached in from the military detention centres. As the operation got underway, a large number of RAF Police dog handlers were detached into the camp to carry out external security patrols to prevent escapes from succeeding. Although the RAF Police dogs are extremely well trained, in comparison to the dogs used by the Prison Service, they quickly gained the reputation amongst the inmates of being rather savage beasts. Accordingly, no escape attempts were made throughout the entire five-month operation. Rollestone, however, quickly filled up to capacity with the new prisoners who arrived there on a daily basis. In an effort to resolve the problem, the Home Office decided to use, ahead of schedule, the newly commissioned and partly completed prison at Frankland in Durham. Obviously, the Prison Officers Association wanted no part in establishing and staffing the partially built complex and so the military were drafted in to run it. At one point, a number of RAF Police NCOs were detached there and additional manpower from the P&SS Support Squadron were about to be detached there to assist with the custodial duties, but at the eleventh hour they were not required, because the prison officers called off their industrial action.

Towards the end of the year, serious inter-tribal conflict had erupted on the small South Pacific Island of Vanuatu. The population there were fighting, rioting and looting everything they could lay their hands on and the fragile system of law and order had quickly collapsed under the strain. As a result and in an effort to restore normality on the island, both the British and French Governments decided to send out a peace-keeping force. The French sent in their finest, the Foreign Legion, and the British despatched theirs, the Royal Marines. The latter were flown out to the region via Fiji and, accordingly, four RAF Police NCOs from the P&SS Support Squadron accompanied them on the RAF Hercules transport aircraft from Lyneham. Two of the RAF Police NCOs were subsequently dropped off in Fiji to prepare an airhead there, while the other two, Sergeants M Tracy and F Gibbons, flew on into Vanuatu to set up a similar operation. As a result, they remained in the region for three months, before the situation had calmed down enough and the four RAF Police NCOs were able to return home again to the UK.

At RAF Uxbridge in West London, during the evening on 8th January 1981, a young RAF musician noticed the smell of petrol coming from somewhere inside his barrack accommodation. When he went to investigate the source of the smell, he was shocked to find two large plastic containers filled with petrol, hidden under the stairs of the ground floor. As he made a closer inspection, he noticed a canvas satchel lying between the containers and although he really didn't have any idea what he was looking at, he suspected the worst. He quickly raised the alarm and had the three storey building evacuated. The brick building, of solid pre-war construction, happened to be the closest to the perimeter fence and beyond it was a bus stop, a busy dual carriageway and a large number of private residential properties, which were all placed at risk. As a result, the musician, together with the Station Warrant Officer and an MOD Police Constable, went into the building and working together quickly removed the petrol containers, leaving only the satchel inside. Given the circumstances and a lot of hindsight, it was a rather risky thing to do and as it happened, they only just made it in time, before a large explosion ripped through the entire building. Although the accommodation was extensively damaged, luckily no one was hurt as a result. As it was suspected to be the work of the IRA, the Metropolitan Police Anti-Terrorist Squad was quickly on the scene and shortly after setting up their incident room, began enquiries. They were joined a little later by a number of RAF Police investigators from P&SS Southern Region, who had been sworn in as special constables by a local justice of the peace, to assist in the enquiry.

It had been the first time that the IRA had actually attacked an RAF station on the mainland and accordingly it sent shivers up the spines of a number of high ranking officers. Apparently, the terrorists had been able to take their bomb into RAF Uxbridge with no trouble whatsoever, the main gate had been wide open and there was no real form of controlled entry being exercised. However, that wasn't unusual on any RAF unit at the time. As a result of the attack, a number of policy changes were quickly introduced and strict control of entry measures were brought into being at all the RAF stations throughout the UK, in an effort to increase the level of security and of course to prevent a reoccurrence.

Air Commodore Young retired as the Provost Marshal on 11th December, and was succeeded in post by Air Commodore M J David OBE FBIM, who, prior to taking up his appointment, had been the Deputy Director of Security at MOD. Educated at Rye Grammar School, he had joined the RAF in 1953 on national service but shortly after took a short service commission in the RAF Regiment before transferring to the Provost Branch in 1956. During his early years as a young provost officer, he had been the personal assistant to Air Commodore Kerby, the Provost Marshal. In 1966, he had attended the staff course at the RAF Staff College and in 1981, he became the first provost officer selected to attend a course at the Royal College of Defence Studies.

On 2nd April, 1982, Argentinean forces invaded and occupied the Falkland Islands, a British dependency in the South Atlantic Ocean. While the British Government made their strong representations to the United Nations Security Council, the Prime Minister, Margaret Thatcher, assembled a task force to recover the islands by force if required. As part of the process, RAF Police NCOs from the P&SS Support Squadron were placed on standby.

In May, while the task force was preparing to recover the Falkland Islands from Argentina, Pope John Paul II paid his first visit to Britain and part of his programme involved a visit to Scotland where he was scheduled to visit Edinburgh. In order to provide increased security for his arrival and to avoid any congestion at Edinburgh airport, it was decided to receive and park his aircraft at RAF Turnhouse, which quite conveniently was located on the southern side of the airport at Edinburgh. Additionally, the Pope had also utilised RAF Leeming during his flight out from visiting York and as a result of both visits, teams of RAF Police NCOs from the P&SS Scottish Detachment and Northern Region, were sent into the units to assist in establishing and providing the required security cover for both his aircraft and the station during his brief but well-publicised visits.

On the 14th June, after a number of fierce battles, the Argentinean forces occupying the Falkland Islands finally surrendered to the British Task Force and the islands were once again placed firmly under

British control. Soon after, a number of RAF Police NCOs from the P&SS Support Squadron, under the command of Squadron Leader J Styles and the control of Flight Sergeant Wood, together with personnel from the Royal Military Police and the Naval Provost Branch, quickly organised themselves in and around Stanley and prepared for the variety of tasks which followed any conflict. Some of those tasks involved dealing with prisoners of war, securing the massive amount of surrendered weapons and in the case of the RAF Police, setting up the airhead security facilities at Port Stanley airport.

As a result of the increased violence in the war being waged over in Beirut, it had been announced in early June that all British and other friendly nationals, if they wished, were to be evacuated as quickly as possible from Lebanon and taken to safety on the island of Cyprus. At the start of the operation it was anticipated that the rescue mission would involve some 1,500 refugees and as such, plans were quickly drawn up to deal with all expected contingencies. RAF Akrotiri had been placed on standby to provide accommodation and RAF P&SS (Cyprus) had been tasked to provide a number of RAF Police NCOs to assist with the passenger embarkation process. Accordingly, a team of eight NCOs under the control of Flight Sergeant T Sheehan were detailed and briefed to undertake the task. Initially, the operation was to be carried out using two ships, HMS *Leander* and the MV *Royal Prince*. However, as plans were drawn up, the former vessel was recalled for operational duties, leaving just the MV *Royal Prince* to carry out the task. On 23rd June, under cover of darkness, the vessel quietly left Cyprus but as it approached the Lebanese coast, it was hastily intercepted by an Israeli gunboat and, after a slight delay, was allowed to proceed. However, after a short time, two hostile MIG aircraft flew over it, closely pursued by an RAF Phantom aircraft which fired off two missiles and brought both aircraft down. The ship continued and just after dawn, it sailed into Jounieh Port, where members of the crew landed and established contact with officials from the British Embassy. Shortly after, the RAF Police disembarked and after liaising with the Lebanese Militia, set up their Travel Control Security post on the wharf at La Crea Marina. Within a short time, the refugees started to arrive, whereupon their documentation was carefully checked and they were thoroughly searched by the Police before being ferried out to the waiting ship. At half-past midnight on 25th June, the last refugee stepped on board the ship and shortly after it set sail again for Cyprus. However, as the ship made its way back, the RAF Police continued to assist Embassy officials on board with interviewing the passengers in preparation for landing in the Republic of Cyprus. The rescue mission had been very successful and all in all, a considerable number of refugees from some thirty different countries had been dealt with during the day.

Shortly after the Falklands conflict ended, two RAF Police SNCOs, Sergeants J Caldicott and D Anderson, established another RAF Police section on Ascension Island, in the South Atlantic, where they took over the policing role from the Naval Provost Branch. However, after a few months they were reinforced with a number of junior NCOs to assist with the large volume of work being undertaken there. As the island happened to be a 'bridge link' between the UK and the Falkland Islands, huge numbers of troops passed through it each week, either going to, or coming from the south. As the weeks went by, it soon became apparent to the authorities that attempts were being made, by troops and merchant seamen, to smuggle illegally acquired weapons and munitions home to the UK. As a consequence and in order to stop that from happening again, all troop ships returning from the Falkland Islands and landing on Ascension Island were boarded by RAF Police NCOs. They had been tasked to search the luggage of every passenger before they disembarked to board the aircraft waiting to take them home. During the months which followed, a large quantity of weapons, munitions and other dangerous and prohibited items were impounded during the continuing and successful operation.

During September, the CND movement, which had grown from strength to strength since the late Fifties, established their first 'Women's Peace Camp' outside RAF Greenham Common, near Newbury in Berkshire. The unit had been leased to the United States Air Force and had been chosen for the protest because it was suspected of housing Tomahawk cruise missiles capable of carrying nuclear warheads. Indeed, during the week which followed the arrival of the women, a number of demonstrators broke into the less sensitive areas of the unit in an effort to prove just how poor the security arrangements were at the base. Their activities of course did no actual harm, but nevertheless attracted considerable attention from the media, who gave the story a very wide distribution. As a result of the embarrassing coverage, a decision was taken for an RAF Police Flight to be established at the base, to assist the hard pressed Ministry of Defence Police in maintaining security. Accordingly, RAF Police NCOs from stations all around the country suddenly found themselves being detached to Greenham Common for short periods thereafter. During a huge demonstration at the base in December, some 20,000 mainly women protesters linked their arms to encircle the entire nine-mile perimeter fence. The entrances were blocked, movements in and out of the base stopped for a while and in some places, the sheer weight of the protesters brought down the fences. As you can well imagine, a huge proportion of personnel from the RAF, USAF, Thames Valley and Ministry of Defence Police, were kept extremely busy throughout the day, trying to control and contain the situation under the watchful eyes of the media. However, the protest continued long into the night.

In addition to the large RAF Police presence at RAF Greenham Common, another nine RAF Police NCOs along with an RAF Regiment squadron, had been posted into the unit and onto the strength of the USAF Security Police Group, to assist with in securing and escorting the mobile launchers of the 501st Tactical Missile Wing on their way to deployment sites around the country. The RAF Police contingent, under the control of a flight sergeant, were all qualified motorcyclists, equipped with the latest Norton Interpol motorcycles, which were used to good effect when escorting convoys around the country.

The RAF Police had by that time been working with dogs for some forty years, and had earned for itself a reputation second to none. Not only were patrol dogs being trained but the specialist training of the dogs used to detect the presence of drugs and explosives had been a very successful venture. It was therefore, rather pleasing to see that during 1982, a well-wishing member of the public kindly donated the 10,000th dog into service with the branch.

During the year which followed, demonstrations in Poland continued to call for the restoration of the illegal trade union known as 'Solidarity'. As the pressure mounted and gathered momentum, the worried Polish authorities lifted martial law, which had been established in an effort to crush the union and its support. However, further east, the Russians once again demonstrated their aggressive tendencies to the world, when in September, without warning, they shot down an airliner belonging to Korean Airways, which had apparently strayed, unwittingly, into their airspace, close to a sensitive military installation. In all, 269 people who were travelling on the aircraft on that fateful day were killed.

At the beginning of 1984, trouble flared up once again in the Lebanon, stranding and placing at risk a number of British and foreign nationals. As a result, another rescue evacuation operation was authorised and military personnel from Cyprus were once again alerted to carry it out. As with the previous mission, a number of RAF Police NCOs and a female member of the Royal Military Police, based in Cyprus, were tasked to accompany the rescue vessel, which turned out to be an old flat-bottomed car ferry, the *Sol Georgios*, which had originally been used on the Rhine in Germany. After finalising the arrangements, the team left Cyprus on 8th February and after a rather rough crossing, arrived off the coast of Lebanon the following day and quickly began their task. However, due to the terrible weather conditions at the time, all the refugees had to be airlifted off the quayside by helicopter and taken to the Royal Fleet Auxiliary ship, the *Reliant*, which had been sent out to assist. On 11th February, after the operation had been successfully completed, the team returned to Cyprus on board the *Sol Georgious*.

Up until 1984, there had only been one provost officer established to act as the Drug Abuse Prevention Officer (DAPO) within the RAF and he was based at HQ P&SS(UK). He was indeed a very busy man, responsible for touring the RAF world, lecturing to all members of the RAF and their families on the dangers involved with drug abuse, as well as offering constructive advice to station commanders on the matter. However, he was but one man and with the rise of drug-related offences, both within the RAF and in civilian life, a further four DAPOs were established, one at each of the UK P&SS Regions and the other with HQ P&SS in Germany. The HQ P&SS(UK) DAPO however, retained responsibility for the rest of the RAF world, while the newly created DAPOs took over responsibility for lecturing within their respective areas and in the case of the DAPO in Germany, he took on responsibility for all mainland Europe. In addition, for the first time, they also took over operational control of all drug investigations and intelligence gathering activities within their regions.

Having enjoyed a very interesting and exciting career in the Provost Branch, Air Commodore David retired from the RAF in June, and Air Commodore A E G Hales, who had previously been the RAF Germany Command Provost Marshal, was subsequently promoted and appointed as the new RAF Provost Marshal.

In August, Sergeant B Flynn RAF Police, serving with the P&SS Support Squadron, commenced a four-month exchange of duties with the Royal Australian Air Force Police, during a deployment known as 'Exercise Airwave'. Although the exercise had been developed in 1982, involving other trades within the RAF, the RAF Police had not taken any part in it until 1984 because of other operational commitments. However, as those commitments began to ease slightly, the MOD gave their approval for the branch to select one SNCO to take part in the exchange. It was the first time that the RAF Police had taken part in an exchange programme with the RAAF. Consequently, as Sergeant Flynn flew south to Australia, his exchange counterpart, Sergeant K Dusting RAAF Police, arrived at RAF Rudloe Manor and was introduced to the P&SS Support Squadron, where he was employed on a wide variety of provost and security tasks during his detachment.

At the time, Sergeant Flynn wasn't the only RAF Policeman detached to a pleasant and unusual location oversees, because Warrant Officer T Figgins and Sergeant Geordie Rowe from the RAF Police School were detached to Thailand. Their successful three-month visit had been brought about following a request from the Thai Government for the RAF Police to assist them, to train a number of their Air Force dogs to detect firearms and explosives. Throughout the detachment the two NCOs had been hosted by the Royal Thai Air Force at Korat, situated some two hundred kilometres north of the capital, Bangkok. After quickly settling in to their new environment, the two men had prepared their intensive training programme, which to complicate matters slightly, had involved learning enough of the Thai language so that the basic commands could be given to the dogs being trained. The occasion however, hadn't been the first time that the RAF Police had operated within Thailand. During 1963, a four-man team under the control of Sergeant D A Window RAF Police, had been detached from RAF Changi in Singapore to take part in a commonwealth training exercise at Ubon Ratchathani, close to the Laosian border. During the period of the exercise the team, besides carrying out the normal routine range of provost tasks, provided, at the request of the Thai Provincial Commander, Colonel Dejt, security cover for the aircraft carrying the King of Thailand during his inspection of the troops involved in the deployment.

Over in Germany, HQ P&SS (RAF Germany) were honoured when Her Majesty the Queen graciously approved a unit badge for the headquarters. In keeping with the style of the standard RAF unit badge, it comprises a golden griffin passant set against a wreath of twisted silks of the German national colours. The adopted motto, *Recht und Gerechtigkeit* is freely translated as 'with justice and humanity'. The badge had originally been proposed in 1983 by Group Captain Hales and the suggested design, forwarded for approval, had been painted by Flight Sergeant P Tucker RAF Police.

At RAF Rheindahlen on 2nd October, HQ P&SS (RAF Germany) were further honoured when the Wilkinson Sword of Peace for 1983 was formally presented to the unit. The award had been introduced during 1966, after Wilkinson Sword Limited had approached the MOD with the idea of presenting the sword each year to the unit achieving the highest performance in fostering good relations within the area or territory in which they served. The award was available to all three arms of the British forces and the winner was selected each year by the MOD, acting on the recommendations presented to them by the Admiralty, Army and Air Force Boards. Although other units within the RAF had won the award on previous occasions, it was the first time that it had been presented to a unit within the Provost Branch. During the ceremony, Air Chief Marshal Sir Thomas Kennedy KCB, AFC, ADC, RAF, the Air Member for Personnel, received the sword on behalf of the RAF from Mr Ronald Ellis, the President and Managing Director of the Industrial Group of Wilkinson Sword, before presenting it to the Provost Marshal. The citation for the award clearly stated why the unit had been recommended by the Air Force Board:

> Provost and Security Services, RAF Germany, have made an outstanding contribution towards sound community relations within Germany. It is a small unit with a Headquarters at RAF Rheindahlen and detachments at RAF Gutersloh and RAF Gatow. The unit's 184 officers and men were fully committed throughout 1983 to police and security roles in north-western Europe with tasks in direct support of RAF stations in Northern Germany and Berlin. Good

community relations are an essential ingredient in effective police work, and this unit has for many years exploited every opportunity to further an excellent rapport between servicemen and civilians. All ranks have devoted much of their spare time to forging sporting and social links with the local community, including the organisation of demonstrations on road safety measures and running a campaign to highlight the dangers of drug abuse. This small group of service personnel and their families also participated in a variety of fund-raising events to raise sufficient money to allow three children to have life saving operations at the Westminster Medical School Bone Marrow Transplant Project. The appeal achieved double the target and the success was largely due to the Provost and Security Services, who raised about half of the £29,000 presented to the Westminster Medical School Project. In 1983, this small unit's contribution in the field of humanitarian activities has had a major effect on the lives of numerous people abroad. The unit has done so much to further the good name of the Royal Air Force amongst allied forces and the local communities, and is a deserving winner of the 1983 Wilkinson Sword of Peace.

It was a very proud and rewarding occasion for everyone serving at the unit and after the splendid ceremony, supported by the RAF Germany Band, a reception was held at the unit's headquarters. It was attended by numerous invited service dignitaries and guests from the German Civilian Police and Customs Service and their Dutch counterparts.

On 12th October, the IRA struck once again on the British mainland, when a bomb they had planted in the Grand Hotel in Brighton exploded during the early hours of the morning. At the time the Prime Minister and other members of her cabinet, who had been attending the Conservative Party conference, were staying in the hotel. Margaret Thatcher survived without being harmed but unfortunately, others staying in the hotel that night were killed and injured as the front of the building collapsed with the impact of the terrific blast.

The King's Flight of the Royal Air Force had been formed at Hendon on 21st July, 1936, to provide air transport for the King and other members of the royal family. At RAF Benson on 1st August, 1952, following the coronation of Queen Elizabeth it was renamed as the Queens Flight and some time later a number of RAF Police NCOs joined it to provide the twenty-four hour security cover for the aircraft both on the ground at its home base and whilst away on operations. After eight years of loyal service with the flight and having flown on five hundred royal flights around the world, Warrant Officer K Broddle MVO, RAF Police, retired from the RAF at the end of the year. He was the first member of the RAF Police to have attained that number of flights to his name and to mark the occasion, he was granted a private audience with the Queen at Buckingham Palace and became the first member of the flight to have received such an honour.

With the rapid introduction of various small computer systems into the service and the potential security risks they involved, a basic training course had been produced by the Police School to cope with the problem. However, as the subject became more complex, it quickly became apparent that additional information was urgently required to keep up with the changing technology involved. As a result, a training course design team began work at the RAF Police School in January 1985 to produce an adequate computer security training course for suitably qualified CI trained personnel, who would, from that point on, be expected to conduct investigations into breaches of computer security. Although the policy and the training objectives had been produced by the sponsors, the team was nevertheless heavily engaged in the mechanics of producing a course which would fulfil all the requirements necessary to equip the RAF Police in dealing effectively with the complex subject of computer security matters.

At the beginning of 1985, following their success in Kampuchea, the RAF became involved in famine relief operations once again. On that occasion however, it was in Ethiopia where as a result of the civil war and the lack of rain, the harvest had once again failed, leaving most of the population without food and water. As a result, thousands of people died each day from the effects of starvation, leaving the various aid agencies operating in the country unable to cope on their own. Consequently, in line with their other European partners, the British Government agreed to assist by sending in RAF transport aircraft to assist with the distribution of the food and medication. In keeping with the experience obtained from the Kampuchea operation,

RAF Police NCOs from the P&SS Support Squadron, assisted by Police NCOs from various other UK RAF stations, were sent out to Addis Ababa for three week detachments throughout the year to provide the necessary security cover for the aircraft and support equipment being used by the RAF during the operation.

In February, many in the branch were shocked by the tragic news that a coach, carrying members of the RAF Germany Band, had been involved in an accident on the autobahn in Germany while on tour. As details became clearer, it seemed that the coach had apparently crashed into a petrol tanker which burst open and the escaping fuel was instantly ignited. As a result, a large number of those travelling on the coach were killed and many more were injured as they tried to escape. Amongst those passengers killed was Corporal George Crawford, an RAF Police NCO from HQ P&SS (Germany) who had been assigned to the band as their security NCO for the tour.

In Belize (formerly British Honduras until 1981 when it became independent) the threat from Guatemalan invasion lingered on and the RAF continued to provide air support for the British Army and the Belizean Defence Force. The RAF Police Flight at Airport Camp, under the control of Sergeant S R Davies, however, were producing a number of successful results in their own battle against the large scale theft of both military and personal property which had taken place during the previous nine months. As a result of intensive enquiries and a number of large scale searches carried out in the jungle surrounding the camp and the local village, a great deal of the property concerned was discovered hidden in secret caches and recovered. As the investigation continued, with the assistance of the local police, evidence indicated that one small gang of youths had been responsible for all the thefts which had taken place on the camp. As the enquiry continued, one of the gang was arrested and confessed to all the outstanding offences. In addition, he assisted further by leading the RAF Police to the site of further hidden caches in the surrounding jungle, where more stolen equipment was recovered. Unfortunately, before the remainder of the gang could be arrested, they fled from the area, but there were no further intrusions into the camp.

Chapter VIII
The Thawing of the Cold War

On 11th March, 1985, after a succession of leaders had come and gone, Mikhail Gorbachev, a little-known Russian politician, became the leader of the Soviet Union. As the Western world looked on, it was clear from the very start that he did not have the same 'hard line' attitude as the previous Soviet leaders. That was further demonstrated later in the year when Gorbachev and the American President, Ronald Reagan, attended a summit organised in Geneva. Towards the end of the talks, the Western world was amazed to hear Gorbachev announce that the USSR and America would be co-operating, from that point on, to reduce their ever-growing stockpiles of nuclear weapons.

At RAF Brampton, near Huntingdon, on 23rd October, an RAF Police SNCO raised the alarm when he discovered a fire in the building which housed the Headquarters of RAF Support Command. However, by the time the emergency services were on the scene a short time later, the top floor of the large three-storey building was well ablaze and the fire quickly spread to other areas of the complex. In all, some twenty-five fire appliances and one hundred and thirty fire-fighters attended the scene and battled for several hours into the night until the fire was eventually brought under control. Even so, sixty per cent of the two hundred and odd offices within the building had been destroyed by the fire or the effects of the water and the smoke. In response to the incident, a large number of RAF Police NCOs from the P&SS Support Squadron and investigators from P&SS Northern Region were sent to the unit to safeguard the area and establish exactly what had happened.

As daylight broke, the vast scale of the damage became apparent. The investigation team had set up their incident room in the nearby Brampton Park Officers Mess and shortly after began their enquiries. The first task had been to cordon off the entire area and then establish

221

when the fire had actually started. One of the first questions to be asked was what was the reason for the fire? Had it been accidental or had it been deliberately started? If it had been started deliberately, then why? Could it have been to cover up the theft of classified information or other attractive items? Over the days which followed, a very detailed search of the gutted building was painstakingly carried out, during which the position of every filing cabinet and cupboard throughout the building, which had contained classified information was established and mapped. As the massive and complicated task of recovering and accounting for all the classified documents got under way, things began looking better. Although the task had been easier in the rooms which had sustained only smoke and water damage, the rooms which had been completely gutted by the fire also produced a surprising number of positive results. This had been possible because the documents inside some of the filing cabinets had been packed so tightly that they had not been able to accommodate enough oxygen to sustain the fire. However, they were all still very hot and as soon as their contents were exposed to the air they erupted, in many cases, into flame and had to be dealt with quickly. Indeed, some of the cabinets had been completely soaked during the operation to save the building and were incredibly heavy and almost impossible to move manually. However, as each filing cabinet and cupboard was gradually recovered, they were thoroughly examined and a record was established, indicating where they had been found. To accommodate the process and provide sufficient storage space for the items, the station gymnasium was used as a sorting area. Eventually, after a great deal of work by the investigation team and the huge number of airmen drafted in to assist them, most of the classified material was accounted for. In addition, during the detailed search of the building, a considerable amount of both military and personal property was recovered intact and either returned to the owners or used to refurnish the temporary accommodation needed by the headquarters staff, who were trying desperately to sort the confusion out. As the large complex had contained two inner courtyards containing ornamental pools, the luckiest survivors of the fire were the goldfish which lived there and who seemed to have been totally unaffected by the incident. Although the P&SS enquiry into the cause of the fire continued for some time, the entire building was quickly condemned and demolished and plans were prepared to provide a replacement home for the Support Command Headquarters.

At the end of the year, the Officers and Airmen Aircrew Personnel Committee (OAPC) agreed to a proposal which had been submitted by the Provost Marshal, that female officers would, after an absence of some sixteen years, be once again accepted into the Provost Branch with effect from the beginning of 1986.

Although it appeared that relations between America and the USSR were beginning to warm up considerably, things elsewhere were not quite so comfortable. On 15th April, 1986, America launched an air raid against Libya from airfields within the UK. The attack was in retaliation for various terrorist activities which had been sponsored by Libya. Simultaneously, the RAF stations in both Cyprus and Gibraltar went on full alert, in case the Libyans launched a counter-attack. Within twenty-four hours, RAF Police reinforcements from around the UK had been sent out to RAF Akrotiri and RAF Gibraltar, to assist the resident Police and RAF Regiment in securing both stations against any form of terrorist attack.

Later during the same month, six members of RAF and two soldiers who had been serving with the RAF at a signals unit in Cyprus, were brought to trial at the Old Bailey Central Criminal Court in London. They had each been charged with espionage, an offence against the Official Secrets Act 1911. The matter had come to notice on 6th February, 1984, when one of the men who had been serving with the signals unit at the time, was placed under arrest for a serious breach of security. During questioning, he later admitted passing classified information to his girlfriend, who it was alleged, was working for the Eastern Bloc intelligence services. Given the serious implications of such a disclosure, an immediate investigation by the P&SS unit stationed on the island was ordered. During the intensive enquiry which followed, another seven members of the unit were also implicated in the matter, having been blackmailed following their alleged involvement in sex and drug parties. Consequently, a major investigation ensued, involving the RAF Police, the Royal Military Police and officers from the Metropolitan Police Special Branch, who had been flown out to the island to take charge. While the wheels of progress gathered pace, the defendants were held in military custody at various British military establishments around the island until they were flown home to be tried.

The controversial trial eventually started after various challenges and objections had been made by the defending councils against the assembled jury. However, as the proceedings got under way, the defending councils alleged that each of their clients had been grossly mistreated during their interviews and whilst being held in military custody. After considerable legal wrangling, the allegations were upheld by the judge and as a result, the confessions made by the defendants were held as inadmissible and subsequently thrown out of the case. Indeed, both the trial and, more importantly, the allegations of RAF Police ill-treatment attracted intense media interest and the story of terrifying interrogations made headline news in most of the daily newspapers for some time, daubing the investigators as 'Mr Nasty and Mr Nice', for having used frightening psychological methods during the course of the investigation. Unfortunately, the branch could do very little to counter the allegations until they had been thoroughly investigated. It was a particularly tense time for all those involved.

On 1st May, the newly commissioned RAF station at Mount Pleasant on the Falkland Islands became fully operational and took over from the makeshift facilities at RAF Stanley, which had been operational since the end of the conflict. As such, the new unit, situated thirty-two miles from Stanley, became home to the Falkland Islands Garrison Police Unit (FIGPU), commanded by Major B Atkinson RMP and became responsible for provost operations throughout the region, while the RAF Police Flight, commanded by Flight Lieutenant D Wilson, became responsible for internal policing and security matters on the unit.

In Cyprus, despite the allegations being made at the Old Bailey in London, the RAF Police were quietly carrying out their commitments as normal, when on Sunday 3rd August, without warning, terrorists launched an attack against RAF Akrotiri and the nearby Ladies Mile Beach, which was being used at the time by RAF families, local people and a number of tourists. Although a number of mortar bombs were initially fired at the station, no one was killed but two RAF wives were nevertheless injured by shrapnel. After the mortars had been discharged, the terrorists drove their car along the Ladies Mile beach, firing their automatic weapons over the heads of the terrified families and the tourists who had no means of escape. Luckily, once again, no one was hurt in the cowardly attack and the alarm was quickly sounded. Although an RAF helicopter was promptly scrambled to locate the terrorists, they had unfortunately made a swift get away.

Towards the end of October, the trial at the Old Bailey of the eight Cyprus defendants charged with espionage ended when they were all acquitted of all charges. The collapse of such an important trial was a complete disaster, and so serious were the allegations of ill-treatment against the defendants, that on 29th October, the government announced that there was to be a full-scale inquiry into the matter.

In October, with the end of his rather turbulent term in office, Air Commodore Hales retired as the Provost Marshal and was succeeded in post by Air Commodore G E Winch FBIM. He had been born in July 1935 and had been educated at Bedford School and University College London. He had been commissioned into the RAF in 1956 as a fighter controller and had completed tours in the UK and the MEAF, before transferring into the Provost Branch in 1961. As a provost officer, he had completed tours of duty in the UK, in Germany, in Cyprus, at SHAPE and prior to taking up his appointment as Provost Marshal, had been Deputy Director of Security (RAF)(DD Sy (RAF)) at the MOD.

During the same month, the long-awaited 'Service Police Codes of Practice', issued as part of the Police and Criminal Evidence Act 1984, came into force and brought about a full-scale change in the way that the police carried out their investigations and the interviewing of suspects. Basically, they had replaced the 'Judges Rules' and being a statute, gave direction, amongst other things, for the treatment, questioning and identification of suspects. From that point on, all interviews with persons suspected of having committed offences had to be tape recorded and then transcribed for the courts. The change had largely been brought about in an effort to prevent miscarriages of justice and to protect the police from damaging allegations of mistreatment as well as protecting the legal rights of suspected persons. Consequently, every RAF Police NCO had to be trained in the new procedures which the codes demanded by law.

On 11th November, Mr David Calcutt QC, was appointed to inquire into the serious allegations of mistreatment made by the defendants in the Cyprus spy trial against the RAF Police investigators. Consequently, the branch braced itself as the full inquiry commenced soon after.

After visiting Cyprus and interviewing all those concerned in the case, with the exception of those making the allegations, Mr Calcutt concluded his inquiry and his much-awaited report was published on 27th March, 1986. Much to the relief not only of those involved in the original investigation, but to all serving members of the branch, the allegations were found to be unsubstantiated and the investigators concerned were totally vindicated of any foul play or improper conduct. Unfortunately, in contrast to the accounts of the original allegations, the media gave very little coverage of that important vindication.

On 6th March, 1987, disaster suddenly struck when the cross-channel ferry, the *Herald of Free Enterprise*, capsized as it was leaving the harbour at Zeebrugge. As the ferry system was used extensively by members of the British forces serving within Europe, it was suspected that a large number of Army and RAF personnel and their families had been on board and had perished in the vessel. As a result, a provost officer and a number of RAF Police NCOs were quickly sent from the P&SS Support Squadron to assist the Kent Constabulary in their unpleasant task of identifying the victims thought to have had service connections. In addition, two 'scene of crime' RAF Police NCOs from P&SS (Germany) were detached to the investigation for six weeks to assist in the identification process. For their efforts, Sergeants D Hands and C Bassett were awarded commendations from the Provost Marshal. Unfortunately, two hundred people were killed in the disaster that morning, including a large number of service personnel and their relatives.

As the drug culture continued to develop within the UK, evidence suggested that in order to avoid being detected, some service personnel who were involved in the abuse of drugs were no longer taking them onto their units to use. Instead, it was suspected that they were conducting their illegal activities off base where they had much more freedom and the risk of getting caught was slimmer. Indeed, even if they had been caught by the civilian police at the time in possession of user amounts of most illegal drugs, they would probably have been cautioned for the offence and released. The RAF on the other hand took drug abuse amongst its personnel very seriously and offenders, if convicted, were imprisoned and discharged from the service. In April, in an effort to overcome the problems of detecting the off-base users, the RAF established two Drug Intelligence Teams, one with P&SS Northern Region and the other with P&SS Southern Region. The system of using young but well-trained police NCOs on covert drug operations had been used very effectively by the Royal Military Police during the previous few years. Shortly after the teams went operational, they quickly proved themselves to be an effective system for gaining the valuable intelligence and evidence required by the investigators employed within the Drug Abuse Prevention Flights.

On the Falkland Islands during the same month, the former tri-service Falkland Islands Garrison Police Unit and the RAF Police Flight at RAF Mount Pleasant amalgamated under the new title of Joint Service Provost and Security Unit (JSPSU), under the command of Squadron Leader J Styles. Consequently the new unit became responsible for all service police and security matters affecting all three services which were stationed on the islands.

Well behind the Iron Curtain, West Berlin continued to function quite normally and the P&SS Detachment stationed there were kept fairly busy with a wide spectrum of provost and security tasks. Although West Berlin was completely surrounded by the wall, life in the city for the P&SS staff was fairly comfortable and rather pleasant and of course, the wall which divided the two halves of the city itself didn't exist as far as the Western allies were concerned. As the complex structure of the Berlin Wall had developed over the years, the number of escape attempts across it from the east had been reduced dramatically. However, on 15th July, a daring and successful escape ended at RAF Gatow, when a light private aircraft, flown by eighteen year old Thomas Kruger from East Germany, suddenly landed on the runway. Up until his defection to the west, Kruger had been a trainee East German Air Force pilot at a paramilitary school at Schonhagen and had decided to make good his escape during his second solo flight. After take off he had complied with the requirements of his flight plan and his pre-flight briefing for fifteen minutes before suddenly changing course for West Berlin. Ignoring the repeated radio messages ordering him to return to his base, he had quickly crossed over the heavily guarded border and entered the airspace of West Berlin, where he prepared for his landing at RAF Gatow. The Air Traffic Controllers there quickly realised that a defecting aircraft was about to land on their runway and alerted, amongst others, the P&SS Detachment, who immediately despatched a patrol to investigate. A short time later Thomas Kruger was escorted away from his aircraft by the RAF Police and as he was being initially interviewed by Squadron Leader G Castle, the Officer Commanding the P&SS Detachment, the unit was besieged by the media who had quickly learned of the defection. To avoid the limelight, Kruger was secretly smuggled off the unit by P&SS and quietly handed over to the West German authorities. After completing the usual formalities he later joined his relatives who were living in West Germany.

By the middle of the year, the first three female provost officers to join the branch again, had completed their initial training courses and had been posted out to their first operational units. Flying Officer K Bennett was posted into the Headquarters Strike Command at RAF High Wycombe, Flying Officer S Mawson was posted to RAF Coltishall near Norwich as their new station security officer and finally, Flying Officer J Risely-Pritchard took up her post as station security officer at RAF Leuchars in Fife, Scotland.

On 14th September, after six long years, the RAF Police detachments to RAF Greenham Common finally ended, when overall responsibility for the security of the unit was handed over to the MOD Police. During the period, a considerable number of provost officers and RAF Police NCOs from RAF stations all around the UK had completed tours of duty on the task of keeping the CND peace protesters out of the unit and away from the Americans. The operation had in the main been a fairly successful one, which had helped to foster positive relations with the Thames Valley, MOD and USAF Security Police throughout.

At the beginning of December, Sergeant S R Davies, an SI NCO from P&SS Southern Region, returned to the UK, having completed a four month exchange of duties with Sergeant P K William of the Royal New Zealand Air Force Police (RNZAFP). It had been the first time that an RAF Police NCO had served with the RNZAFP in New Zealand, as part of 'Exercise Airwave'. During the exchange, Sergeant William had been mainly employed with the P&SS Support Squadron, touring the UK and flying around the world. Sergeant Davies on the other hand, had been given the opportunity of spending some time at all seven RNZAF bases located within New Zealand during his hectic detachment. In doing so he established a very positive working and social relationship with both the RNZAFP and the New Zealand civilian police.

At RAF Gibraltar on 14th December, Corporal A Bruce, the Dangerous Drug Search dog handler, who had been serving with P&SS (Gibraltar), was asked by the Gibraltan Customs Service to assist them with searching the voluminous luggage belonging to a Moroccan passenger, who had arrived in the colony on the hydrofoil from Tangier. The officers had suspected the passenger of carrying controlled drugs, but had been unable to locate any during their initial search. Corporal Bruce and his dogs responded and after a short time, both dogs indicated that there were drugs concealed inside six pairs of deer antlers which were mounted onto wooden plinths. In spite of the protests from the owner, the antlers were duly split open and a total of 6.3 kilograms of Pakistani black cannabis resin, with a then current street value of £18,000, was recovered. The RAF Police drug dogs had once again proved their worth and as a result, the Moroccan was subsequently charged by the authorities with attempting to smuggle controlled drugs into the colony.

As 1987 came to an end, so did the longest close protection operation ever mounted by the RAF. It was finally concluded after His Royal Highness Prince Feisal Bin Hussein of Jordan successfully completed his training with the RAF and had qualified as a fighter pilot. The operation had been running since 1st June, 1985, when the Prince had first arrived at the RAF College Cranwell, to complete his initial officer and basic flying training. As his training programme progressed he had moved across the country to RAF Valley on the island of Anglesey and then down to RAF Chivenor near Barnstaple, where he completed his advanced flying training. The team which had been selected for the lengthy operation had not come from P&SS, which up until that point had been the normal practice, but had been selected from the Police School and a number of RAF stations around the country. Originally formed by Warrant Officer C L Crossan RAF Police, the team was directly responsible to the Command Provost & Security Officer, located at the HQ RAF Support Command for all of their commitments. When Warrant Officer Crossan retired from the RAF in December 1986, he was replaced by Warrant Officer J C Reade, who had joined the fourteen man RAF Police Team in September. As always in operations of that type, an excellent rapport was quickly established and maintained throughout the period with the Metropolitan Police Special Branch and police officers from

Lincolnshire, North Wales and Devon & Cornwall, who were also involved in the lengthy but very successful task.

On 7th March, 1988, Gibraltar went onto full alert when three members of an IRA Active Service Unit, who had been planning to carry out terrorist activities within the colony, were shot dead by members of the Special Air Service, who, acting upon intelligence reports, had been tracking them ever since they set out for the continent. In retaliation for the shootings, the Provisional IRA stepped up their campaign of terror in Northern Ireland by attacking a minibus and a coach containing soldiers. In addition, two members of the Royal Signals Regiment, who had strayed by mistake into a crowd attending an IRA funeral, were horribly attacked and murdered by an angry republican mob. Unfortunately, the media were covering the funeral at the time, so the full horror of the incident was broadcast live on mainland television, and was watched by thousands of stunned people.

As the Cold War between the East and the West continued to thaw, the co-operation between the British and Soviet authorities in the war against the importation of contraband and illicit drugs, went from strength to strength as the number of successful customs operations increased. Consequently, a most unusual and prestigious visit took place at the RAF Police School on 14th September, when the First Deputy Chairman of the Soviet State Customs Board & Council of Ministers, Mr Vitaly Konstantonovich Boyarov, accompanied by Lieutenant General Pankin of the Soviet Ministry of the Interior, were entertained at the Dog Training Squadron. The visitors had been very impressed by the training carried out by the Dangerous Drug Search Dog Cell at the school and had asked, during their week-long visit to the UK, to see it for themselves. After being met by the Station Commander, Group Captain R E Holliday and Wing Commander A V Schofield, the Officer Commanding the RAF Police School, they were given a full briefing and a demonstration of the techniques used in the training of the drug detection dogs by the search cell staff. At the end of the visit, Mr Boyarov, impressed by what he had seen, presented a Soviet State Customs Board Medal to the RAF Police School, where it is now displayed in the 'Baldwin Room' at the RAF Police Museum.

In December, while President Gorbachev was on route to Washington to attend a summit meeting with President Reagan, he stopped off at RAF Brize Norton for talks with the British Prime

Minister Margaret Thatcher. The subsequent meeting between the two leaders was held in the Officers Mess on the unit, while the RAF Police provided the required security measures within the station. As a continuing sign of the changing times and a further thawing of the Cold War, it was the very first time that a Soviet leader had stepped foot inside an RAF station in the UK, together with his KGB protection team.

On 22nd December, disaster struck once again, when a Pan Am jumbo jet which had taken off on a scheduled flight from London's Heathrow Airport en route to New York, crashed onto the small Scottish village of Lockerbie, after a terrorist bomb had exploded on board. The disaster devastated the tiny village and over three hundred people were killed in the incident, with the wreckage being spread over a very wide area.

During the early part of 1988, the IRA active service units began a terror campaign in mainland Europe, by targeting British servicemen and their families stationed on the continent. A number of off-duty soldiers had been shot dead in separate 'close-quarter assassination' incidents and bombs had been placed at the Headquarters British Army on the Rhine (BAOR) and a number of other army units within Germany. Unfortunately, at the time, the terrorists had been able to target British service personnel with relative ease, because their privately owned cars had been easily identified by specially designed 'British Forces' vehicle registration plates. The attacks against the RAF started on 1st May, when in separate incidents, four off-duty members of the RAF Regiment from RAF Bruggen were killed at Roermond in Holland, close to the German border. Two had been the victims of a bomb placed under their car, while the other two had been gunned down as they sat in their car talking. As the attacks continued, RAF Police reinforcements had been swiftly detached into Germany, to assist HQ P&SS (Germany) in maintaining the patrols designed to counter the terrorist threat.

Following the recent authorisation of unit badges to a number of P&SS units within the UK and Germany, authority was granted to P&SS (Gibraltar), allowing them to adopt their own unit badge. Adopting the normal RAF badge pattern, the design displays "a griffin passant, holding a key all gold set in front of a roundel per fess wavy argent and azure" together with the motto *Ministerium et Securitas*. The dominant element in the badge, the griffin, is taken from the badge of the RAF Police. The unit's location is indicated by the key and the roundel, the former being taken from the crest of the city of Gibraltar and the badge of RAF Gibraltar and the roundel, tinctured argent and azure, refers to the Straits of Gibraltar. The motto freely translates as 'service and security'.

The beginning of 1989 brought about that great moment in history, which finally signalled to the world the end of the Cold War between the East and West. This was the signing of a peace accord between the American and Russian superpowers to reduce the arms race and with it, their massive stocks of nuclear and conventional weapons. As a further gesture of goodwill, President Gorbachev announced to the world that he would be making a substantial number of radical changes within the USSR, creating a new policy of openness or 'perestroika' as it became known. His announcement was followed shortly after by the withdrawal of the last Soviet troops from war-ravaged Afghanistan, which had been occupied by the USSR for nine years.

On 20th February, during the early hours of the morning, an armed IRA active service unit placed a bomb against an occupied accommodation block inside Clive Barracks at Tern Hill, in Shropshire. Although the terrorists were spotted and immediately challenged by a roving guard patrol, because of the arming policy at the time, the guards were unable to open fire at them because the magazines containing their ammunition were sealed and not fitted to their rifles. As a result, the terrorists effectively used their own weapons to aid their escape. However, the alarm was quickly raised by the guards and the accommodation was rapidly cleared just before the bomb exploded. Although nobody had been killed in the attack, the event definitely brought about an urgent change in the arming policy for all personnel guarding military installations on the UK mainland and that included the RAF Police. From that point on, the RAF Police and the guard force alike, who were stationed on RAF units, started patrolling with magazines containing live ammunition, fitted to their weapons.

In March 1989 Air Commodore Winch retired as the Provost Marshal after a rather busy period in office, and was succeeded in post by Air Commodore A C P Seymour, who had originally joined the RAF as a secretarial officer, before transferring across to the provost branch in 1967. Prior to taking up his appointment he had been the Officer Commanding HQ P&SS(UK) at RAF Rudloe Manor.

Based at Rudloe Manor, the specially trained RAF Police investigators who make up the small but very busy HQ P&SS(UK) Flying Complaints Flight, are responsible for the investigation of all complaints involving military aircraft which could include anything from general noise and annoyance to members of the public right through the spectrum to damage caused by sonic booms, low flying or breaches of restricted flying areas. The complex and sometimes sensitive inquiries are carried out on behalf of the Ministry of Defence to establish whether or not military aircraft were the cause of the complaint and if so, to what degree. At the conclusion of the investigation, the detailed reports collated by the unit are often used as a basis in deciding the amount of compensation to be paid out to genuine complainants who may have sustained damage to property, personal injuries or injuries or death to livestock. In addition to carrying out that type of enquiry, the unit is also responsible for carrying out surveys of areas restricted to military aircraft or which might be used for training aircrew in the skills of low flying. It is a difficult task, but during the later part of the 1980s the unit made use of a particularly valuable piece of equipment to determine whether military aircraft were breaching restricted airspace or flying below the prescribed height limits. It was an anti-aircraft directing unit for an Oerlikon Gun, which had been captured from the Argentinian Forces during the Falklands conflict and was capable of covertly monitoring low-flying military aircraft. The information provided by the unit was automatically recorded onto video tape and could be used by the investigators to plot the ground track of the aircraft and to determine whether or not it had breached the flying regulations for the area concerned.

As the year progressed, terrorist activity continued to be directed against the British Forces and in Germany on 26th October, the RAF Police responded once again as the IRA launched another bloody attack, against an off-duty RAF corporal, Maheshkumar Islania, his wife and their six month baby daughter, as they drove into a car park, outside a popular fast food facility, close to RAF Wildenrath. During the brief but murderous attack, the corporal's wife escaped unhurt as the terrorists raked their car with a hail of bullets before making good their escape, but unfortunately, both the corporal and their baby daughter were instantly killed in the sickening incident. As the hunt for the killers got under way in Germany, Holland and Belgium, various options were discussed in an effort to prevent further attacks of that type from taking place. Over the days which followed, the story was given very wide coverage by the European media, which described it as a cowardly and sickening attack against a defenceless family and a six month old baby.

As a more relaxed political attitude prevailed in Moscow, the world watched in amazement during October as the people of East Germany and Czechoslovakia suddenly turned their backs on communism and demanded their political and democratic freedom. Shortly after, the borders between East and West Germany were opened on 9th November for the first time since the start of the Cold War and over two million people from the East entered West Germany. In addition, arrangements were quickly established to dismantle the Berlin Wall and the Iron Curtain which had divided the East and West completely for so long. In December, both the American and Soviet leaders announced to the world that the Cold War had officially ended and with it, the threat of global nuclear war, which had seemed a very real possibility up until that point. As a result of the announcement, the various hardline regimes within Eastern Europe quickly crumbled as revolution took hold in various forms. In Romania, the democratic uprising quickly took hold and unlike in other parts of the former Warsaw Pact countries, fierce fighting broke out in the capital and the surrounding countryside. As the revolution gathered pace, the hardline, seventy-one year old communist leader, Nicolae Ceausescu, was captured and together with his wife, were tried for crimes against the people, found guilty and executed by firing squad. Thereafter, one by one, the former Warsaw Pact countries denounced communism and new democratic assemblies were formed and the first free elections, for forty years in some cases, were organised.

In December, Her Majesty The Queen graciously approved the award of two further unit badges to RAF P&SS units. The first was to P&SS (Scotland) and displays the griffin on a background of the St Andrew cross with the Gaelic motto *Ar Durachd Seirbheis* which freely translates into 'our wish is to serve'. The second was presented to P&SS (Cyprus), which had been formed in 1975, succeeding the former P&SS (NEAF). The badge depicts "in front of a sunburst a griffin sable winged gules" and displays the motto *Justitia in Solibus*, which may be freely translated as 'justice in the sun'. Shortly after, during a ceremony at the P&SS Headquarters, the badge was formally handed over to the P&SS Commander, Wing Commander V Burgess by Major General John Friedberger, the Commander British Forces in Cyprus.

Chapter IX
A Time for Change

In Malaysia on 7th March, 1990, six RAF Tornado aircraft from No 5 Squadron RAF Coningsby and No 27 Squadron RAF Marham, landed at the Royal Malaysian Air Force Base Butterworth (formerly RAF Butterworth) as part of a month-long deployment exercise to the Far East. Throughout the detachment, a small section of RAF Police NCOs, from Marham, Conningsby and Honington, under the control of Flight Sergeant B Finbow, accompanied the aircraft to provide the required security protection whilst they were on the ground. The journey from the UK to Malaysia, in a Hercules transport aircraft had taken three days to complete but had been broken up with overnight stops in Cyprus, Saudi Arabia and Oman, where the RAF Police team established and maintained their security cordon around the aircraft.

As the USSR continued to reduce the threat of attack on the west by withdrawing her troops from positions deemed to be intimidating, the British Government once again began calling for massive reductions in our own defence budget. Consequently on 25th July, a paper entitled *Options for Change* was presented to Parliament which outlined a number of ways of reducing the country's defences in line with the declining threat to our national security. At the time, the authorised establishment of the RAF was 89,000 and the paper called for a reduction in numbers, over a two year period to 75,000 personnel. Although it was a significant reduction, the RAF, compared with the other two services, suffered quite lightly in the arrangements. However, as the RAF began to study areas where the reductions could be made without affecting efficiency, events in the Middle East were beginning to stir once again.

During July 1990, the Iraqi Leader, Saddam Hussein, who was desperate to build up his country's economy after losing the war with Iran, made it very clear to the world that he once again wanted to take possession of Kuwait, which he considered to be Iraqi territory. During a powerful speech, he fiercely attacked the tiny state for producing too much oil which had in turn, forced down the overall world prices. Political tension between the two countries quickly mounted and as in 1962, Kuwait placed her meagre military forces on full alert as the threat of military action increased. However, despite all the preparations put into place, Iraq invaded Kuwait shortly after midnight on 2nd August, 1990, with a force of 100,000 troops. Unfortunately, Kuwait was powerless to thwart the attack and the invaders quickly took control of the entire country, including the valuable oil fields. Although both the invasion and Saddam Hussein were immediately condemned by the international community and the United Nations Security Council, Iraq continued her occupation and plunder of Kuwait. In addition, Iraqi troops moved towards the border with Saudi Arabia and as a consequence, Saudi Arabia, fearing that Iraq was about to invade her territory as well, placed her forces on full alert and quickly invited the Americans and the British in to repel the threat of any impending attack. As a result Operation Granby and the American Operation Desert Storm rapidly assembled troops and equipment into the region. In line with current practices, a number of RAF Police NCOs accompanied every RAF transport aircraft throughout the duration of the massive airlift and were also deployed within the region to provide a full array of both police and security services to the respective field commanders. In addition, towards the end of the month, a number of RAF Police NCOs, trained to provide close personal protection, were deployed to Saudi Arabia to provide the necessary personal security cover for General Sir Peter de la Billiere, Commander of the British Forces Arabian Peninsular and other senior RAF officers.

In Central America on 6th December, 1990, diplomatic relations between the British and the Guatemalan Governments warmed considerably when the RAF, stationed in neighbouring Belize, were invited to take part in the Guatemalan National Air Force Day celebrations. It was quite an honour and clearly demonstrated the closer co-operation between the two countries, who after all, had not been the best of friends over the sovereignty of Belize. In fact, up until that point in time, the British military had not operated inside Guatemala since the war between the Spanish Conquistadors and the British pioneers in the 17th century. During the previous years the country had been viewed as a hostile and somewhat foreign power, which had been placed out of bounds to all British service personnel serving in the region. The detachment which flew into the Aurora Air Force Base, located just outside Guatemala City, comprised of thirteen RAF personnel, one RAF Puma helicopter and two RAF Harrier jump jets and of course two RAF Police NCOs, Sergeant P R Baker and Corporal P Blanchard, who provided the security cover for the aircraft. In fact, when the aircraft arrived at the base they were given a very warm welcome by the crowd which had assembled. At first, the task of the two RAF Police NCOs seemed impossible, until the Base Commander placed twenty-six conscripted airmen at the disposal of Sergeant Baker, to guard the three RAF aircraft for the duration of their two-day stay. At the end of the detachment, the very first personal meeting between the RAF and the Guatemalan Air Force had been deemed most successful in improving diplomatic relations between the two countries.

On the 7th January 1991, a NATO satellite was successfully launched from Cape Canaveral in Florida. However, since the 30th September 1990, an RAF Police detachment from the P&SS Support Squadron, under the command of Flight Lieutenant P D'Ardenne, had been operating within the launch base, providing the high-level security protection required during the assembly stage and during the period prior to the launch of the satellite. The NATO IVA had been the first of two military satellites which had been built for NATO by the firms British Aerospace and Marconi. It had been yet another peculiar task which had been entrusted to the RAF Police and once again they had successfully risen to the challenge, demonstrating their remarkable flexibility in coping with the unusual.

In the Middle East Gulf region, political tension was still particularly fraught as a 700,000 strong coalition force, under the command of American General Norman Schwarzkopf, assembled within Saudi Arabia and the neighbouring Gulf States. Saddam Hussein however, continued to defy the UN Security Council's resolution to quit Kuwait, which was gradually being stripped by his army, of every asset which could be plundered. Diplomatic negotiations continued and a deadline was set by the UN for the full withdrawal of Iraqi troops from Kuwait. However, Iraqi troops continued their occupation as the deadline expired, and as a consequence, the coalition forces began their offensive attack on the

15th January, by launching air strikes against key targets in both Kuwait and Iraq, in an effort to defeat the Iraqi forces and recover the territory of Kuwait. As the air strikes continued over the weeks which followed, the RAF Police working in close co-operation with their coalition counterparts, provided and maintained their usual wide range of support services at all the forward operating bases being used to launch RAF air strikes. However, in response to the coalition attacks, Saddam Hussein threatened to use chemical and biological weapons and launched his deadly Scud missiles against the closest bases inside Saudi Arabia and against Israel, whom he hoped to entice into the conflict.

Although seriously battered by the sustained air attacks and the continued campaign of propaganda being waged against them, the Iraqi army remained within Kuwait and Saddam Hussein proved to be as defiant as ever. On 24th February, the coalition ground offensive into Kuwait began and after only four days, the territory was liberated and the Iraqi forces swiftly defeated. As the overall operation was completed in a very short space of time, a huge number of Iraqi prisoners of war were suddenly captured by, or surrendered to, the coalition forces, making the task of guarding them a momentous commitment. To assist in overcoming the problem, RAF Police dog handlers were instantaneously deployed to the POW compounds, where they were effectively used to patrol the perimeter wire of the enclosures containing the captured Iraqi troops. The cost of liberation had, however, been very expensive indeed with almost all of Kuwait's oil producing industry being destroyed and set alight by the retreating Iraqi army. The results were devastating, producing both economical and environmental chaos within the region.

During March 1991, a new organisation known as the Provost Marshal's Standards Unit was formed at the RAF Police School under the command of Squadron Leader B Rice, assisted by Flight Lieutenant R Miller and three RAF Police NCOs, Flight Sergeant G Barker and Sergeants K Wileman and D Russell. The unit was functionally controlled by the Provost Marshal and had been set up as the "centre of excellence and best practice for the RAF Police". In short, they were tasked to circulate to RAF Police formations both at home and abroad, changes in policy matters and the law as and when they occurred. In addition, they were also required to assist units by clarifying points or resolving problems resulting from those legal or policy changes.

With the ending of the Gulf conflict, accounts began to emerge of atrocities being carried out by the Iraqi secret police against captured British POWs and British workers who had been employed in both Kuwait and Iraq at the start of the conflict and who had then been held in Iraq by Saddam Hussein, as a 'human shield' against the threat of attack by the coalition forces. Some of those concerned had been treated very badly by their captors, being imprisoned, beaten, tortured and robbed of all they possessed. As the witness accounts began to mount, it was decided to fully record them in the hope that one day Saddam Hussein and his henchmen could be brought to answer the allegations at a War Crimes Tribunal. As a consequence, Operation Castle was authorised and an investigation team comprising of both Royal Military and RAF Police was assembled to undertake the massive task of collating the evidential data from all the complainants and the witnesses involved.

After a most unpopular directive from the Ministry of Defence, the RAF Police Dog Training Squadron, after much protest to prevent it from happening, finally merged with the Royal Army Veterinary Corps on 1st April, to form the Joint Service Defence Animal Centre. The Headquarters of the new formation was located at Melton Mowbray, under the command of an Army Officer, Lieutenant Colonel P A Roffey RAVC, with an RAF provost officer, Wing Commander P F Leeds as his deputy. The new unit was divided up into two separate wings. The Army wing, which looked after the army's horses and the dogs used to detect firearms and explosives, remained at Melton Mowbray, while the RAF Police Dog Training Squadron was retitled as the Dog Training Wing (Newton) of the Defence Animal Centre and remained at RAF Newton, training the general patrol and drug detection dogs. In addition, the Newton Wing continued to train dogs for HM Customs & Excise, the Royal Navy, the Scottish Prison Service and for the American Forces who were stationed within the UK.

During the same month, as a result of the continuing terrorist activity on the UK mainland, discussions were held at the MOD by the Provost Marshal, with a view to increasing the internal counter-terrorist measures at a large number of RAF stations around the country. Although the use of patrol dogs was thought to be the most efficient way of providing that deterrent, a substantial increase in the establishment of large dog sections at every station would have proved very expensive indeed and would have been totally rejected right from the very start. As an alternative, a proposal was accepted to trial the use of a small number of specially selected High Profile Counter-Terrorist (HPCT) RAF Police dogs at three RAF stations over a three month period. The trial at Shawbury, Cranwell and Uxbridge was subsequently organised and controlled by the Provost Marshal's Dog Inspector and started in July 1991. The new concept of using RAF Police Dogs in the HPCT role was quite simple and extremely cost-effective to operate. Each station was allocated two trained dogs which were teamed up with qualified RAF Police dog handlers, already established on the strength of the unit to carry out general police duties. Up until that point, RAF Police NCOs who were employed as dog handlers had been specially established purely for that role and as such, conformed to a special shift pattern which worked alongside those of their colleagues employed on general police duties. However, during the trial period, the NCOs handling the HPCT dogs were incorporated into the normal pattern of shifts, accompanied by their dogs whenever they carried out the regular foot and mobile patrols around the station. At the end of the trial period, the venture was deemed to have been highly successful and their use in that role continued to be operated and expanded to other RAF stations around the country.

Once again, many of the veterans associated with the branch were saddened to learn of the death, on 12th October, 1991, of Group Captain A A Newbury OBE, who passed away just a few weeks before his ninetieth birthday. The group captain or 'Uncle Bert' as he had been affectionately known as in the branch, had enlisted into the RAF Police in 1920 and had risen to the rank of warrant officer before being commissioned during the early stages of World War II. In 1947, as the commanding officer at the RAF Police School in Staverton, he had been instrumental in launching the *Provost Parade* and for persuading his son-in-law, Wing Commander McMahon, to design the RAF Police crest. He had been a very popular member of the branch who had a reputation for fairly treating both his officers and his men alike.

In former Yugoslavia, violence erupted in numerous Bosnian cities on 2nd March, 1992, following the results of a referendum which had supported total independence for the state of Bosnia. Unfortunately, the proposal was rejected by the Orthodox Serbs, who formed a minority of less than one third of the population. However, unlike the Catholic Croats and the Muslim majority, the Serbs were far better organised when it came to military matters and had the support of the Yugoslav National Army in their cause. Despite the outbreak of trouble in the region, Bosnia-Herzegovina quickly gained its independence and was duly recognised by the majority of governments around the world as a new and independent country. That however, did nothing whatsoever to suffocate the activities of the Serbs, who quickly escalated their violent guerrilla campaign within the region and as a result, the UN Security Council was forced to condemn the violence which soon developed into full-scale civil war. As the conflict continued in Bosnia, many atrocities were carried out by either side and many villages and areas were cut off, causing widespread misery and starvation. UN relief airlifts were organised to take food, medicines and other humanitarian supplies into the worst affected areas and a number of RAF Transport aircraft were deployed to assist in the operation. Accordingly, in line with normal operating procedures, each RAF aircraft carried an RAF Police NCO to carry out Air Transport Security duties. In addition, a number of RAF Police NCOs from the P&SS Support Squadron, on secondment to the UN and wearing the standard UN blue berets, were deployed within the region at the various airheads, carrying out a variety of police and security tasks.

By the start of 1993, RAF Police NCOs from both the UK and Germany were being detached for four month periods to fill a number of newly created but unestablished multinational police and security posts in both Europe and the Middle East. In Southern Turkey and at Muharraq in Bahrain and Dhahran and Riyadh in Saudi Arabia, the RAF had been deployed in support of Operation Jural, the policing of the restrictions placed on Iraq by the UN following the end of the Gulf conflict. At Dhahran International Airport, where the RAF combat aircraft were based, a small detachment of RAF Police NCOs, under the command of a provost flight lieutenant, were responsible for briefing newly arrived RAF personnel on the strict local rules and regulations concerning religious matters and the poor standard of driving in the country. They were also tasked with carrying out Air Transport Security and inbound customs checks on behalf of the Saudi authorities, on all military aircraft operating in support of the operation. The main concern of their Saudi hosts in respect of the customs checks, was apparently the illegal importation of pork, alcohol and pornographic material. In addition, the RAF Police also carried out the full range of police and security tasks in support of the RAF detachment commander, in Saudi and in Kuwait if the need arose. Although RAF tanker aircraft were operating out of Muharraq, a small team of RAF Police NCOs were also established there to patrol and police the immediate areas on the island used by the British forces on local leave. At Ancona in Italy and in Bosnia, the RAF had been deployed to assist the UN in providing the essential humanitarian relief to the victims of the civil war being waged in former Yugoslavia. Once again, the RAF Police had quickly established themselves as part of the team and as such, played a very important part in the overall operation at each location. At Ancona for instance, the RAF Police, as part of the multinational police section, provided security at the UN relief agency freight compound and carried out both ground and airborne Air Transport Security tasks in addition to their normal range of policing duties. In carrying out those tasks, they dealt with numerous high-ranking officials from the UN, government ministers, ambassadors and other VIPs, moving in and out of Bosnia by air. In addition, two RAF Police NCOs accompanied each RAF aircraft entering Bosnia to provide extra eyes to warn of the threat of attack by surface to air missiles as well as providing the essential security protection for the aircraft while it was on the ground.

On 1st April, the Royal Air Force and of course, the Royal Air Force Police, celebrated their seventy-fifth anniversary in style, both at home and abroad. At the International Air Tattoo at Fairford, the RAF Police Association operated a hospitality suite where a considerable number of the branch's veterans met up with serving members of the branch and no doubt exchanged various memories of their past service in the Royal Air Force Police and Provost Branch.

In July, an RAF provost officer, Flight Lieutenant Skoyles assumed command of the multinational Military Police section at the NATO War Headquarters located at Ruppertsweiler, having replaced a USAF captain. He was not however, the sole RAF representative at the unit because the section also had a strength of sixteen RAF Police NCOs who had been collectively posted in six months before him. The main task of the multinational police section was to provide security protection for the bunker complex which housed the headquarters situated near Pirmasens in South West Germany. The bunker had originally been built on the instructions of Adolf Hitler and had, towards the end of the Second World War, been used by the SS as a supply depot.

During 1993, in an effort to reduce running costs and to improve liaison with their respective stations, the RAF P&SS regional structure within the UK was once again redefined, using the Scottish region as a model to form six regions instead of the existing three. P&SS Scotland survived unchanged and remained at RAF Turnhouse, near Edinburgh, while the areas previously covered by Northern and Southern were further subdivided. As such, the new UK regions were P&SS Scotland, P&SS Northern Region, P&SS Central Region, P&SS Western Region, P&SS Southern Region and finally, P&SS Northern Ireland. All, with the exception of Northern Ireland, were under the command of a squadron leader, the exception being commanded by a flight lieutenant. Initially, as a temporary measure, both Northern and Central regions were co-located at RAF Newton, while Southern and Western regions were both co-located at RAF Rudloe Manor. When the plans were drawn up, it was intended that Central Region would eventually move to RAF Cranwell and that Northern Region would transfer to RAF Linton-on-Ouse. While in the south, Southern Region was scheduled to move into new accommodation at RAF Halton, while Western Region remained with HQ P&SS(UK) at RAF Rudloe Manor. With the reduction in size of each of the region headquarters, their workload rapidly increased and as a consequence, the Operations Wing at HQ P&SS(UK) was expanded to control and assist with some of the administrative functions previously carried out around the UK by the regions.

On 21st September, following the closure of their base at RAF Gutersloh in Germany, RAF P&SS (Detachment Northern Germany), under the command of Flight Lieutenant R Bishop, disbanded and recovered to their headquarters at RAF Rheindahlen. The move brought to an end the RAF Police presence, which had operated very successfully in the area for many years. During that period, the detachment had earned the respect of not only service personnel and their families but of both the local people and the civilian police, with whom they had worked alongside in close co-operation.

In November 1993, Air Commodore Seymour retired as the Provost Marshal after an extremely busy period in office. During his appointment, the Warsaw Pact had collapsed, the Berlin Wall had been dismantled and the Cold War had ended. With it came the change in defence policy and the government's *Options for Change*. Defence cuts, redundancies and 'value for money studies' followed. Unfortunately, the RAF Police also came under close scrutiny from the Treasury Department. On 1st November, 1991, the establishment of RAF Police and Provost Branch stood at 201 officers and 3,815 NCOs, while on 1st November 1993, that number had been reduced to 178 officers and 3,267 NCOs.

Air Commodore Seymour was succeeded in post on 29th November by Air Commodore J L Uprichard CBE, who had been commissioned into the RAF in 1965 from Queen's University, Belfast. After completing his basic and advanced flying training to qualify as an RAF pilot, he had served with a wide variety of operational squadrons, both at home and abroad as well as filling a number of staff posts at Group, Command and NATO Headquarters and at the Ministry of Defence. Prior to taking up his appointment as the Provost Marshal, the Air Commodore had been the station commander at RAF Waddington in Lincolnshire.

On 7th December, a McDonnell Douglas Delta II rocket was launched from Cape Canaveral, Florida, with the task of placing into orbit the NATO IVB military satellite. The project was an extension of the programme started in 1990 and once again, during the four-month period leading up to the launch, security at the site had been provided by a team of RAF Police NCOs from the P&SS Support Squadron, under the command of Flying Officer A Quinn.

Apart from the white-topped RAF Police service cap, the remainder of the white webbing equipment traditionally worn by the RAF Police NCO had been more or less discontinued some years before. Instead, during the previous two decades, RAF Police NCOs had either been wearing green webbing equipment with their drab camouflage combat clothing or black webbing when dressed in 'blues'. However, with so many armed RAF Police NCOs on duty at the entrances to RAF stations as part of the enhanced counter-terrorist measures, 1994 saw the introduction once again of white webbing belts, holsters and ammunition pouches. The new pattern equipment was manufactured in white leather and as such required only minimum maintenance to keep it tidy and smart. Although the new equipment enhanced the overall appearance of the RAF Police once again, it did suffer initially from one problem in that the holster was so tight that whenever the Browning 9mm pistol was placed into it, the magazine release button was pressed and the magazine was ejected from the weapon. Consequently, the equipment was quickly withdrawn and sent back to the manufacturers where suitable modifications were made to it.

Terrorists, over the years, had always considered aircraft as very viable high-profile targets in the fight to win publicity and public support for their diverse causes. Hijacking and sabotage had certainly been the most effective and commonly used methods adopted by such groups to achieve their objectives. Since the early sixties, a number of very successful and often fatal terrorist incidents had occurred on aircraft, only because of poor security standards at some of the major airports around the world. Unfortunately, airlines and airports are mainly commercial organisations out to make a profit and in the early years most companies considered the introduction of additional security measures as an expensive luxury which rapidly reduced their annual profits. However, the terrorist incidents which had brought down the Pan Am flight over Lockerbie and the Air India flight over the North Atlantic Ocean, both with the loss of all on board, brought about a tightening up of security around the world. The RAF Police had always taken the threat of terrorist action against its aircraft very seriously and had, since the introduction of major air movements on its aircraft, carried out very effective air transport security (AT Sy) measures at their airheads. However, in response to more sophisticated methods being employed by terrorists, the RAF Police School introduced at the start of the year a newly designed and specially produced training course covering all aspects of the subject and using up to date equipment. Training on the subject had always been taught to RAF Police NCOs, either combined with the initial police and further training courses or had simply been given as 'on the job' training at units dealing with large air movements. However, the new eight-day course, had been designed to ensure uniformity and standardisation and as a prerequisite for all NCOs about to be employed on AT Sy duties.

On 1st April, 1994, The Command Headquarters RAF Germany, was quietly demoted in status to a Group Headquarters responsible to the Headquarters Strike Command. In addition, Headquarters RAF Support Command was dissolved and was replaced by two newly formed organisations, Headquarters Personnel and Training Command located at RAF Innsworth and Headquarters Logistics Command located at RAF Wyton and RAF Brampton near Huntingdon. Later in the same month, during the annual conference of provost officers held at RAF North Luffenham, the Provost Marshal announced that the Ministry of Defence were considering a number of radical changes to all aspects of security and policing within the ministry and the three military services. Although he confirmed that no decisions had yet been reached, it was, he said, only a matter of time before the branch would have to face up to these changes as part of the general effort to achieve greater efficiency. Accordingly, he told the conference that he was considering a number of options, aimed at making the branch more cost-effective whilst retaining its identity.

The first option under consideration was the formation of a new tri-service police agency. However, that in itself presented some major constitutional problems involving the Ministry of Defence Police and the other two military services and was therefore extremely unlikely to be successful in the short term.

Option two was the amalgamation of the RAF Police and the RAF Regiment, who were facing an uncertain future, to form a new security branch for the RAF. The principle was based on the system used by the United States Air Force, comprising of two disciplines, a law enforcement and investigation branch, and a security police branch.

The third and final option, involved the recruitment of Locally Employed RAF Police NCOs' at RAF stations. They would be recruited on special short term contracts, serving only at the unit of their choice within the United Kingdom. They would be on a lower rate of pay and would have no promotion or career prospects under that type of engagement.

On 14th July, 1994, as part of the initiative to further reduce the defence budget, the government released another paper entitled *Front Line First*. In doing so, the Defence Secretary, Malcolm Rifkind, announced yet more cuts to the Armed Forces, in an effort to reduce the annual defence budget by a further £750 million. The savings however, signalled the loss of 18,700 jobs within the three military services and the civil service establishment at the Ministry of Defence.

On that occasion, the RAF were hit quite seriously and forced to reduce their manpower by a further 7,500, over a two-year period. In addition to the previously announced unit closures, Mr Rifkind also announced the closure of RAF Petreavie Castle in Scotland, RAF Scampton in Lincolnshire, RAF Finningley in Yorkshire, The RAF Hospital at Wroughton in Wiltshire, RAF North Luffenham in Leicestershire, The RAF Staff College at Bracknell in Berkshire and finally, RAF Laarbruch in Germany.

Shortly after the announcement, the Provost Marshal circulated a bulletin to every provost officer and member of the RAF Police, in which he explained that a number of major surveys were underway, which were examining all aspects of the security, policing and guarding commitment undertaken by the Ministry of Defence and the three military services. It proposed to replace the three single service and the Ministry of Defence Security Directorates by 1st April 1995, with a single security headquarters within the Ministry of Defence. In addition, it was also planned to create a single tri-service Police and Security training establishment and a single Defence Vetting Agency. Although the plans meant the loss of more jobs, they certainly provided for long term efficiency, closer co-operation and an overall reduction in the annual budget.

Closer to home, the use of RAF Police dogs was being closely studied once again and proposals were put forward by the Army to have all RAF Police dogs dual-handled, in a further effort to reduce the overall costs involved. Unfortunately, that was a practice adopted by the Army and it was being fiercely fought off by the RAF, who despite having their limited number of HPCT dogs dual-handled, saw the general concept of dual-handling as unsuited to the work of their dogs. In addition, further proposals were also put forward to dis-establish the RAF Police Dog Demonstration Team and the trade of Kennel Assistant. Again, the branch was facing difficult decisions and the RAF Police Dog Demonstration Team quickly began looking for outside sponsorship. As you can imagine, over that period, with so much uncertainty about and so many studies being conducted, many RAF personnel wondered what the future would hold for them and those serving in the rank and file of the RAF Police, were no exception.

On a glorious afternoon in August, RAF Newton hosted the 37th and final RAF Police (UK) Dog Trials to be held, before the planned division of the school sent basic police training to RAF Halton and dog training to Melton Mowbray. The event was recorded on film by the BBC, who had been invited to the unit to make a presentation for their BBC East *Midlands Today* programme. In addition to over 2000 members of the general public who turned up to watch the event, the principle guests of the Provost Marshal were Air Vice-Marshal Sir Timothy and Lady Garden who were invited to present the prizes to the winning teams. At the end of an extremely competitive event, the 1994 winners of the RAF Police (UK) Dog Trials were declared as Corporal Ian Dormund and Air Dog Gundo from RAF Kinloss, followed up by Corporal Andrew Bednall and Air Dog Tia from RAF Aldergrove, who took second place and Corporal Anna Marie Cameron and Air Dog Bruce from RAF Northolt who took third place.

On 31st August, after twenty-five years of terrorism and bloodshed in Northern Ireland, the Provisional IRA agreed to a permanent cease-fire in order to be accepted into democratic peace talks with the British government on the future of Northern Ireland. Shortly after, as a measure of goodwill, their action was mirrored by the Loyalist terror groups and in the weeks which followed, the province witnessed a calm that had not been known there for a long time.

After maintaining a presence in Berlin for almost fifty years, the American, French and British Forces finally withdrew from the city, on 7th September, a week after the Russian forces had withdrawn and returned home to Russia. Consequently, during an official ceremony, held earlier that day, RAF Gatow was formally handed over to the German *Luftwaffe* who were to become the new tenants. A parade comprising of both RAF and *Luftwaffe* personnel, smartly formed up at the main entrance to the base to await the arrival of the two reviewing officers; Air Vice Marshal R H Goodall, AOC 2 Group and General Major J Hoche, Commander 3rd *Luftwaffe* Division. After a short ceremony, the RAF Station Commander; Group Captain M L Feenan, handed over a symbolic key for the unit and the RAF Ensign was lowered for the last time by Corporal Gardener of the RAF Regiment. Shortly after, the RAF left the base which they had occupied since the end of the Second World War, when it had been handed over to the RAF Regiment by the Russian forces who had captured it. Accordingly, the P&SS detachment there, under the command of Flight Lieutenant S L Mawson, was disbanded and the staff redeployed to other units within Germany and the UK. However, the immaculately maintained Land-Rover used, since 1969, to provide the RAF Police escort for both Royal and VIP visitors to the station, was duly transferred to the RAF Police Museum.

RAF Belize, under the command of the Acting Air Commander, Squadron Leader Adams, officially closed down on 6th September and the last few remaining British military personnel left the garrison a week later. Operational flying in Belize had finally ceased on 31st July, after providing a valuable service within the Central American enclave for sixteen years. The Harrier jump jet aircraft had been returned home during July 1993 and they had been followed by the Puma helicopters of No 1563 Flt (Belize) in August 1994. As a consequence, the RAF Police Flight at Airport Camp had been steadily disbanded, leaving Sergeant P R Baker, who had returned for a second tour of duty, and Corporal P Brand, as the last two remaining RAF Police NCOs serving within the region. Of the four RAF Police dogs serving in Belize, two were transferred to units in Germany and the other two were humanely destroyed after being declared too old and unfit to be transferred. Unfortunately, the withdrawal from Belize highlighted just how quickly the RAF presence around the world was shrinking away.

After receiving a request, through diplomatic channels, from the commander of the Zimbabwe Air Force, Flight Sergeant D Summers, an instructor from the Police School, was promoted to the acting rank of Warrant Officer and detached to Zimbabwe to instruct members of their Air Force Police in the techniques of crime prevention and investigation as used by the RAF Police. After visiting three of their bases and assessing the training requirements, Warrant Officer Summers returned to Manyame Air Base, outside Harare, where he commenced the task of instructing the first members of the force to attend the three week course which he had prepared. In fact, his efforts were so successful that authority was granted for him to conduct a similar course of instruction for the Zimbabwe Military Police. It was quite a challenging detachment for Warrant Officer Summers who conducted a further two courses, one for the Air Force and another for the Army, before returning home. In addition to earning the respect of both the Zimbabwean commanders and his students, his efforts were also rewarded by award of a commendation from the RAF Provost Marshal.

Sadly, after forty-five years, during which millions of people had been thrilled and excited by their spectacular and professional public performances, the RAF Police Dog Demonstration Team, under the final command of Flying Officer Tracy Flett, was finally disbanded on 18th September. Although various attempts had been made to save the team by obtaining private sponsorship, the price set to maintain it (£240,000 per year) proved unattractive and no one was willing to take on the commitment. The melancholy occasion was marked a month later at RAF Newton with a reunion attended by both past and serving members of the team. From that point on, the dog displays given at the major public demonstrations such as the Royal Tournament and the important air displays around the country, were to be provided by an operational team of both RAF Police and Army dog handlers, assembled for the season from the DAC at Melton Mowbray.

On 6th October, some 54,000 Iraqi troops under the command of Saddam Hussein, headed towards the Iraq-Kuwait border sparking off another full-scale alert for the United Nations Security Council. The move was made by Saddam Hussein as a protest against the United Nations sanctions imposed on Iraq. In response to the threatened invasion of Kuwait, America and the UK quickly dispatched major troop reinforcements to the region but Saddam Hussein quickly backed down and withdrew his troops from the border region avoiding further conflict.

Between 17th and 21st October, HM The Queen and HRH The Duke of Edinburgh made their first historic state visit to Russia, the first such visit by a British monarch since the Russian revolution had taken place there.

In November, following an in-depth study, the RAF stations at Lossiemouth in Scotland, Sealand near Chester and Shawbury near Shrewsbury were selected by the Ministry of Defence as suitable units at which to further research the feasibility of an amalgamation between the RAF Police and the RAF Regiment. The on-site study was duly carried out by two wing commanders, one from the Provost Branch and the other from the RAF Regiment, and during their visit they interviewed members of both trades stationed on the units and looked into the tasks being carried out by them. The idea of amalgamation had first been suggested way back in the early Seventies by a number of RAF Regiment officers but the scheme was largely unpopular and had never really gathered much pace.

During January 1995, the DAC at Melton Mowbray announced that for the first time efficiency trials would be held throughout the year for all RAF Police HPCT dogs. It was good news for all HPCT dog handlers who greeted it with considerable enthusiasm because they had previously been excluded from the normal annual RAF Police working dog trials.

On 1st March, the Chief of Air Staff announced that after a very detailed feasibility study, the RAF Police and RAF Regiment were not to be amalgamated and would continue to carry out their unique specialist functions quite separately from each other. However, after forty years of being protected by the RAF Police, the task of providing the security for the nuclear weapons held by the RAF would be taken over completely by the RAF Regiment by the end of the year. In addition, the announcement also indicated that RAF Regiment officers would become a specialist function within a newly formed Operations Support Branch and that provost officers would become a specialisation within the Administrative Branch. The news was certainly welcomed by both branches and certainly helped to lift the cloud of uncertainty which had prevailed for a considerable time. However, it wasn't all good news because it was also announced that the trade of Kennel Assistant was to be disbanded and on top of that, one hundred and fifty members of the branch were invited to take their redundancy. At that point the establishment of the branch stood at 3,076.

The British Army had been conducting their security patrols throughout Northern Ireland for over a quarter of a century in support of law and order but on 24th March, as the cease-fire continued to hold out, it was decided to cease night-time security patrols within Belfast and certain other areas within the province. Daytime patrols inside Belfast had been curtailed on 15th January and there had been no adverse effect on the situation.

On 1st April, in line with further rationalisation of the defence budget, the Directorate of Security (RAF) located within the Main Building at the Ministry of Defence was disestablished and amalgamated into the newly created Ministry of Defence Security Directorate which consolidated the security activities of the Royal Navy, the Army, the Royal Air Force and the MOD Procurement

Executive. As a consequence of the change, the Provost Marshal, retitled The Air Officer Security & Provost Marshal (RAF) (AOSy&PM (RAF)) and his personal staff left London and established themselves at HQ P&SS (UK) Rudloe Manor. The formation of the new security organisation at the MOD had of course allowed for large-scale reductions in the overall staffing levels. Although senior RAF Provost officers were represented within the new organisation, a large number of posts previously held by serving officers were civilianised. From the RAF point of view, the various security disciplines affecting the daily activities of the single service were divided up and delegated down to the Commanders-in-Chief at the three Command Headquarters, who, through their Command Provost & Security Officers, became responsible for the day to day implementation of the security policy in force. Accordingly, HQ Strike Command took on global responsibility for counter terrorism, physical, nuclear and air transport security matters throughout the RAF, while HQ Logistics Command took over global responsibility for computer and document security, the security aspects involved in the various international arms control treaties and the release of official information. Finally, HQ Personnel & Training Command took over global responsibility for vetting and personnel security, security education and training.

On the same day, the Queen's Flight, which had been stationed at RAF Benson, was relocated at RAF Northolt and amalgamated with 32 Squadron which was retitled, No 32 (The Royal) Squadron. During the same month the RAF Police School moved from RAF Newton, which had been earmarked for closure, and after an absence of some fifty-eight years, returned to its very first home at RAF Halton in Buckinghamshire, where it assumed the new title of Provost & Security Training Squadron (P&STS) under the command of Squadron Leader J Whitmell. Their original home however, had long since been demolished and as such, the school moved into Spreckley Hall, a purpose-built instructional block which had been built in 1968 to train RAF apprentices. Unfortunately, for the first time, the general police and the dog training elements of the school were permanently parted. The Newton Wing of the Defence Animal Centre (DAC) had moved from Newton some months before, to the Army unit at Melton Mowbray and became totally integrated into the DAC.

However, an RAF Wing Commander from the Provost Branch had been established to look after the RAF element of training dogs.

After being in existence for twenty-seven years, the four man police element of the Royal Auxiliary Air Force (R Aux AF), attached to No 2 Maritime Headquarters Unit in Edinburgh, was finally disbanded as part of the government's *Options for Change*. The small auxiliary police unit was initially started in 1960 when the then Commanding Officer of No 2 Headquarters Unit, R Aux AF, Wing Commander Grey, received permission to establish a police section to look after security matters which affected his unit. Luckily, a serving member of his unit, Aircraftsman J Kerr, had just completed three years service with the Royal Military Police (Territorial Army) in Edinburgh and was the first to volunteer for the task. After completing a two-week basic police and security course at the Police School he remained the only R Aux AF policeman until 1970 when two further members were recruited. In 1988, a fourth recruit joined the section and that's how it remained until it was finally disbanded.

During October, an announcement was made which effectively disbanded Trade Group 10 (RAF Admin and General Duties), the branch which had since the late 1960s taken over the administration of the guardrooms on RAF stations. The timescale for the total disbandment of the trade group was earmarked for the 1st April, 1997 and although certain parts of their task were still being reviewed, it was announced that the RAF Police would once again move back into and manage the guardrooms after an absence in most cases of some thirty years.

By mid 1996, the five RAF P&SS regions on the UK mainland had settled into their new locations as planned in 1993. In the north of the country, P&SS(NR) was located at RAF Linton-on-Ouse while P&SS(CR) established itself at RAF Cranwell. In the south of the country, P&SS(SR) re-located to RAF Halton while P&SS(WR) remained at RAF Rudloe Manor. The only change to the original plan was the move of P&SS(Scotland) to RAF Buchan near Peterhead, which had been brought about by the closure of RAF Turnhouse in Edinburgh.

Since the end of the Gulf war with Iraq, the RAF as part of the coalition forces deployed to 'police' Saddam Hussein's activities in the region, had been stationed in Saudi Arabia as part of Operation Jural. Accordingly, a large force of RAF Police NCOs under the command of a number of provost officers were deployed at the HQ British Forces in the capital Riyadh, at the Saudi air base in Dhahran and in the neighbouring state of Bahrain to support the RAF forces.

At Dhahran, accommodation in the form of flats located in a number of multi-storey tower blocks, which had originally been intended for the families of Saudi military personnel, had been given over for use by the coalition forces. Two of the blocks were assigned to the British where they established offices and working accommodation on the ground floors and living accommodation on the upper floors. The whole complex had been separated from the Saudi area and secured by the erection of a large wire security fence.

Since the end of the Gulf war, there had been several terrorist attacks, within both Saudi Arabia and Bahrain, which had been directed against the continued presence of the coalition forces and quite understandably, they had been on various levels of security alert for most of 1996. However, during the early part of the evening on the 25th June, 1996, terrorists drove a large truck, containing explosives, up to the accommodation compound at Dhahran and detonated a huge explosion soon after. The result of the attack almost demolished one of the blocks occupied by American service personnel and caused varying degrees of damage to the other blocks. Rescuers, including the RAF Police, quickly scrambled to the scene to assist and some time later it was established that a large number of American service personnel had been killed and more than one hundred others had been injured in the attack.

During its relatively short existence, the Royal Air Force Police and of course the Provost Branch have continually striven hard to take the well-earned position it holds today as a professional part of the Royal Air Force, and remains ready to adapt whenever it is required to support a wide range of operations and commitments at home and abroad. It has achieved an incredible amount during its short life, and has had a colourful and eventful history. However, there is still much to do and as the Royal Air Force prepares to enter into the next century, the future still holds many changes for both the service and of course the policing organisation which supports it, such as the formation of a tri-service police and security training school and the recruitment of locally employed or 'auxiliary' RAF Police personnel throughout the UK. Indeed, as I finish off this book I am informed that the AO (Sy) & PM (RAF) and his staff are getting ready to move once again in March 1997 from RAF Rudloe Manor to new offices within the Headquarters of Strike Command at RAF High Wycombe.

Although I have attempted to collate as much information as possible about the history of the RAF Police and Provost Brank, the story as related within these covers is, I know, certainly nowhere near complete and while many personal anecdotes and memories of events have unfortunately just faded away, there is I'm sure, an absolute abundance of 'yet undiscovered history' still out there and waiting to be recorded. Therefore, I would certainly be most grateful to any reader for any additional information or material which would assist me in my quest to develop the history of the branch even further.